Intended
for Pleasure

Ed Wheat, M.D.
and Gaye Wheat

3rd Edition

Fleming H. Revell
A Division of Baker Book House Co
Grand Rapids, Michigan 49516

Published by Fleming H. Revell
a division of Baker Book House Company
P.O. Box 6287, Grand Rapids, MI 49516-6287

Eleventh printing, July 2004

Printed in the United States of America

Library of Congress Cataloging-in-Publication Data
Wheat, Ed.
    Intended for pleasure / Ed Wheat and Gaye Wheat. — [3rd ed., rev.]
        p.   cm.
    Includes bibliographical references and index.
    ISBN 0-8007-1736-8
    ISBN 0-8007-5856-0 (special edition)
    1. Sex in marriage. 2. Sex instruction. 3. Marriage—Religious aspects—Christianity. 4. Family—Biblical teaching. I. Wheat, Gaye. II. Title.
HQ734.W52   1997
306.8—dc20   96-43365

Scripture quotations not otherwise identified are taken from the King James Version of the Bible.

Scripture quotations identified PHILLIPS are taken from the New Testament in Modern English (Revised Edition), translated by J. B. Phillips. Copyright © 1958, 1960, 1972 by J. B. Phillips and used by permission of Macmillan Publishing Co., Inc.

Scripture quotations identified NIV are taken from the HOLY BIBLE, NEW INTERNATIONAL VERSION®. NIV®. Copyright © 1973, 1978, 1984 by International Bible Society. Used by permission of Zondervan Publishing House. All rights reserved.

Scripture quotations identified NKJV are taken from the New King James Version. Copyright © 1979, 1980, 1982 by Thomas Nelson, Inc. Used by permission. All rights reserved.

Some of the material in chapters 4 and 11 on basic anatomy and contraception comes directly from Dr. Wheat's *Sex Technique and Sex Problems in Marriage* cassettes and appeared by permission in a similar form in *The Act of Marriage* by Tim and Beverly LaHaye, Grand Rapids: Zondervan, 1976.

Material on the P.C. muscles in chapter 6 appears by permission of the Zondervan Publishing House.

Appreciation is expressed to Ortho Pharmaceutical Corporation of Raritan, New Jersey, for their gracious permission to incorporate materials from *Understanding Conception and Contraception* into the text of chapters 4 and 11.

Illustrations by Dale Ellen Beals. Illustrations were adapted from drawings found in a Schering Clinoptikons booklet entitled *Female Pelvic and Obstetrical Anatomy and Male Genitalia*. They are used by permission of the Schering Corporation.

Material from *Love Life for Every Married Couple* by Ed Wheat, M.D. Copyright © 1980 by Ed Wheat, M.D., is used by permission of Zondervan Publishing House.

For current information about all releases from Baker Book House, visit our web site:
http://www.bakerbooks.com

*Intended
for Pleasure*

Other books by Ed Wheat, M.D., with Gloria Okes Perkins
Love Life for Every Married Couple
The First Years of Forever
Secret Choices

To Ed Wheat Sr. and Gladys Gibson Wheat, whose commitment, devotion, warmth, generosity, and integrity stood for fifty years as a beautiful picture of genuine agape love.

Contents

Preface

The first edition of *Intended for Pleasure* came about almost unexpectedly; not because we wanted to write a book, but because we had information to communicate that could dramatically change lives, marriages, homes, and families.

As a Bible-believing, Bible-teaching family doctor I (Ed) found over the years that I was becoming more and more involved in marriage counseling because the need was so great. This led to speaking around the country and finally to producing a set of tapes that could be used by married Christian couples on sex technique and how to deal with sex problems in marriage.

The tapes were widely distributed and it wasn't long before letters arrived daily from Christians who had heard the tapes and wanted to discuss their specific problems with a counselor who was biblically oriented and also had the medical knowledge to help them. There were so many similar questions and problems that I decided to write this book in an attempt to offer both biblical principles and medical solutions to problems of sexual adjustment that appear so frequently in marriage.

Still today a surprising number of couples are simply missing out on what God intended for them in the marriage relationship. Some are aware that the relationship with their marriage partner is not as fulfilling as it should be and they are actively seeking answers. Others don't seem to realize that the physical relationship of a husband and wife should be mutually satisfying and pleasurable.

Today people talk openly about sex but there is little accurate information available for what a married couple can expect from their sexual relationship. Very seldom in the secular media do you hear anything about how to lovingly satisfy the needs of your marriage partner or about how, if sex is to be fulfilling, it must be a part of a complex committed relationship with your spouse. Most Christian couples have never been taught what the Bible actually says about sex, nor, from the medical standpoint, how to fully enjoy what God has designed for man and wife.

So we have realized that the facts and the data in this book are still needed today. This updated edition has information that will benefit every married or soon-to-be-married person who is searching for a medically accurate presentation of sex in marriage within the framework of the Bible's teachings. While the subject matter is discussed quite frankly and with medical precision, it is treated as sacredly and carefully as the Bible itself treats the subject of sex in marriage. The promise of sexual fulfillment is available to any husband and wife who will choose to enter into God's plan for their marriage, and the purpose of this book is to show the way to that fulfillment.

Gaye and I have worked together with our good friend and colleague Dr. Dow Pursley in counseling and presenting seminars. Dr. Pursley has helped update all of the medical information in this new edition of the book and, with Drs. Ball, Valvo, and Hartzheim, has written the chapter on sexually transmitted diseases, a subject about which accurate information is needed today.

Through these pages we have tried to communicate to every reader our own sense of wonder and joy at what God can do in a marriage when it is committed to Him, with husband and wife possessing both the attitudes and the information necessary for a joyous relationship

As you read this book, keep this one tremendous fact in mind: God Himself invented sex for our delight. It was His gift to us—*intended for pleasure.*

Acknowledgments

Our deepest appreciation goes to Gloria Okes Perkins and we gratefully acknowledge her diligent, loving, and skillful work. The original book and subsequent revision could not have been produced without Gloria's disciplined efforts and invaluable skills. She is a gifted professional writer with a thorough knowledge of the Bible and has worked closely with us for many years.

We are grateful to Richard and Linda Nilsen; Jerry and Sandi Knode; Henry Taylor; our daughter, Merry Ann; Susan Vanderwater; Kayda Grace, M.D.; Joan McDonald; Alma Beard; Martin Bak; Dale Ellen and Benny Beals; Michael Cocoris; LeMon Clark, M.D.; Jody Dillow; and Don Meredith.

We appreciate you dear ones who have helped make this latest revision possible. Thanks are due Marcia Ball, Ed.D.; John Valvo, M.D.; and Paul Hartzheim, M.D., whose knowledge assures the reader of the very latest medical findings. Our thanks go to Rev. Paul Sagan for his expertise in the English language and to Joanne Pursley for her sensitivity to the feminine viewpoint.

Last, but assuredly not least, our grateful thanks to Dr. Dow Pursley. Without his impetus, this revision would never have been started and without his hours of untiring effort, it definitely would not have been completed. Dr. Pursley continues the counseling and teaching ministry of Dr. Wheat, who is now retired and disabled.

It was Dr. Wheat's love for his patients that prompted the writing of this book.

May the Lord richly bless each of you.

Ed and Gaye Wheat

11

1

Intended for Pleasure

Scores of people—many of them Christians—come to my office looking for a medical solution to their particular marriage problem. While as an M.D. I can do a great deal to help medically, often there is a greater need for me to first communicate biblical information that can heal wounds, restore relationships, and establish the right foundation for healthy attitudes toward sex in marriage.

Knowing and understanding what God says about any phase of life leads to wholeness in that area; nowhere is this more necessary than in the sexual realm, where negative attitudes have virtually destroyed marriage relationships.

I think of the man who was deeply disturbed when God and sex were mentioned in the same discussion. To him, sex was altogether separate from his Christian life. The sexual relationship was an unholy activity in his opinion and yet he continued it with deep guilt feelings, which tarnished the experience for both him and his wife. His misconceptions of God's view of sex resulted in a hurried physical act without tenderness or pleasure.

Then I think of the woman who has been married twenty-five years and is still not sure what an orgasm is or whether she has ever experienced one . . . the husband and wife whose egos have been so wounded in the bedroom that they barely speak to each other . . . the earnest Christian couple who have no serious problems but little joy in their sex relationship . . . and many other

13

troubled people whose marriages are filled with misery rather than pleasure.

God has so much to say to all these through His Word! As a Christian physician, it is my privilege to communicate an important message to unhappy couples with wrong attitudes and faulty approaches to sex. The message, in brief, is this: You have God's permission to enjoy sex within your marriage. He invented sex; He thought it up to begin with. You can learn to enjoy it, and, husbands, you can develop a thrilling, happy marriage with "the wife of your youth." If your marriage has been a civil-war battlefield or a dreary wasteland, instead of a lovers' trysting place, all that can change. You see, God has a perfect plan for marriage, which we may choose to step into at any time, and the mistakes of the past can be dealt with and left behind.

The ancient counsel given by father to son, based on the wisdom of God in Proverbs 5:18–19, comes across just as clearly to the reader of today: "Let your fountain [your body parts that produce life] be blessed, And rejoice [or ecstatically delight] with the wife of your youth. . . . Let her breasts satisfy you at all times; And always be enraptured [or filled] with her love" (NKJV).

It may surprise some of you to learn that the Bible speaks so openly, so joyously of sex in marriage. Almost every book of the Bible has something to say about sex, and Song of Solomon exquisitely depicts the love relationship in marriage. But Genesis, the book of beginnings, shows us most unforgettably what God has always thought about married love.

If we read the first three chapters of Genesis, where it is recorded that God created *male* and *female,* we find that "God saw everything that he had made, and, behold, it was very good" (Gen. 1:31). Interestingly, the creation of light was "good," the creation of land and sea was "good," and, likewise, the creation of vegetation, of fish and birds and animals was also "good." But not until he had created man and woman did God call for our attention with "Behold, it was *very* good."

With so many "good" things in the Garden and on earth, only one thing was *not good:* "And the LORD God said, It is not good that the man should be alone; I will make him an help meet for him" (Gen. 2:18). In those few words God taught us that for man there is no substitute, no alternative plan, no better companion than his wife. The void that was originally caused by taking "bone of my bone, flesh of my flesh" can be filled only by the presence of woman. Since a part of Adam went to make Eve, a man remains incomplete without his Eve.

God placed almost top priority on sexual union in marriage. We can see in the Genesis account that after God told man not to learn evil by experience (Gen. 2:17), His *second* teaching told man and woman how to relate in marriage: "Therefore shall a man leave his father and his mother, and shall cleave unto his wife: and they shall be one flesh" (Gen. 2:24). God had first divided the woman from the man when he made Eve. But now He commands them to be joined together again as one flesh. In this brief counseling session, even before any sin and its resulting selfishness had entered the human race, we find three basic commands:

First, when we marry, we should stop being dependent on our parents or our in-laws. We are to become completely dependent on our mates to satisfy *all* our needs.

Second, the man is the one who is responsible for holding the marriage together by "cleaving" to his wife. *Cleaving* in this sense means to be welded inseparably, so that each becomes a part of the other. Therefore, the man is to be totally committed to his one wife.

Third, we are commanded to be joined together in sexual union, to be *one flesh.*

The ideal situation God intended for us is shown by the blissful words "they were both naked, the man and his wife, and were not ashamed" (Gen. 2:25). Adam and Eve could see each other as they really were, without shame, disappointment, or frustration. The sex relationship God had designed for them brought the blessings of companionship, unity, and delight—and note that this was some time *before* the command to bear children was given (Gen. 3:16).

God's plan for our pleasure has never changed, and we realize this even more as we consider how we are "fearfully and wonderfully made" (Ps. 139:14). When we discover the many intricate details of our bodies that provide so many intense, wonderful physical sensations for husbands and wives to enjoy together, we can be sure that He intended us to experience full satisfaction in the marriage relationship.

Some have assumed that the sex act became an unholy practice when sin entered into the world. However, this is ruled out when we see that God's basic counsel on sex in the first chapters of Genesis was repeated by Jesus Christ to the religious leaders of His day: "But from the beginning of the creation God made them male and female. For this cause shall a man leave his father and mother, and cleave to his wife; and [the two] shall be one flesh. . . . What therefore God hath joined together, let not man put asunder" (Mark 10:6–9; Matt. 19:5–6). Jesus reemphasized this to His disciples in Mark 10:10–11, and again we find these commands reinforced in Ephesians 5:31.

As a matter of fact, the sex relationship in marriage receives such emphasis in the Scriptures that we begin to see it was meant not only to be a wonderful, continuing experience for the husband and wife, but it was also intended to show us something even more wonderful about God and His relationship with us. Ephesians 5:31–32 spells it out: "For this cause shall a man leave his father and mother, and shall be joined unto his wife, and they two shall be one flesh. This is a great mystery: but I speak concerning Christ and the church." *Thus the properly and lovingly executed and mutually satisfying sexual union is God's way of demonstrating to us a great spiritual truth.* It speaks to us of the greatest love story ever told—of how Jesus Christ gave Himself for us and is intimately involved with and loves the Church (those who believe in Him). In this framework, the sexual relationship between two growing Christians can be intimate fellowship as well as delight.

This, of course, explains why the marriage union is the only way man and woman can truly enjoy the riches God has planned for them. Because the relationship is specifically designed to illustrate God's unending love for His people, sexual intercourse must be experienced in the context of a permanent, giving commitment. Anything less shortchanges those involved.

Some people have felt uncomfortable about sex because they somehow equate the sexual desire of men with the sexual drive of animals. They should remember that animals breed according to instinct, with biological motivation. But man uses reason in choosing to have sexual relations. He is the only creature that has intercourse as a whole person. Husband and wife are the only creatures capable of gaining spiritual unity and a deeper knowledge of each other through the sexual relationship. Let us realize how the bodies of men and women are designed. Even in the sex act itself we are reminded that this is a relationship of persons, not just bodies, for it is no coincidence that man is the *only* creature of God's creation who relates sexually face-to-face.

Scripture suggests that just as we can know God, so we can know our husband or wife in a deeper, higher, more intimate way through the physical act of marriage. *Know* is the term used in the Bible to define our relationship to God; it also is the term used to designate the intimate union of husband and wife. "Adam knew Eve" (Gen. 4:1). Mary, speaking of her pregnancy in light of her virginity, said, "How shall this be, seeing I know not a man?" (Luke 1:34). Matthew 1:25 says that Joseph "knew her not" until after the birth of Christ. The sex relationship offers no more cherished pleasure than this *knowing* of the one you love. With the understanding that our marriage relationship portrays the truths of our relationship with God, we can become free as never before to fully express our love for our husband or wife through the dynamic opportunity of the sex act.

God's viewpoint comes forth vigorously in 1 Corinthians 7:3–5 where the husband and wife are told they actually *defraud* one another when they refuse to give physical pleasure and satisfaction to their mate. The only activity that is to break regular sexual relations is prayer and fasting for some specific cause, and this is to be only by mutual consent for a very limited time.

Although sin did enter the human race in the Garden and brought with it the possibility of perversion of every good thing (including sex), God's plan for His beloved creation has continued to operate through the provision of the Redeemer, Jesus Christ. By faith, people can choose God's way! It is true that our culture is saturated with sex distorted into lust, and desire has been twisted and deformed, until it appears as a beast running loose in the streets, destroying God-given boundaries. *Nevertheless, our marriage bed is a holy place in the sight of God.* We must be careful to maintain this viewpoint concerning sex in marriage, for it is God's. Hebrews 13:4 says, "Marriage is honourable in all, and the bed undefiled." We need to treasure and share with our children these positive values God Himself teaches in Scripture concerning the love/sex relationship, always placing sex in marriage in an entirely different light from sex outside of marriage. Sex apart from marriage is spelled out as obviously wrong. Sex in marriage is wonderfully right. Let us never forget it!

I cannot begin to describe the dimensions of the marriage relationship as experienced by the Christian couple who have a total commitment to Jesus Christ and, flowing from that, a realization of their own security in spiritual and physical oneness; who have an excitement found only in each other, knowing this is for as long as they live. This genuine, total oneness and completeness somehow cannot be explained to the one who has not yet experienced it. When this kind of relationship exists, you will both want to praise our Lord many times and have communion with Him in prayer, each thanking Him for the other and the complete love you share.

Intended for pleasure—yes, in the fullest meaning of the word. And even then, language does not convey what God has prepared for us! When Sarah heard that she was going to become pregnant at ninety years of age, she laughed and then made this statement to herself: "After I have grown old, shall I have pleasure, my lord being old also?" (Gen. 18:12 NKJV). Sarah was given to us as an example of one of the most godly women (1 Peter 3:6), and one of her secret concerns was whether the sexual union between her and Abraham in their golden years would produce pleasurable feelings. It is God's will and design, both then and now, that the sexual experience for a man and woman in marriage produce wonderful feelings, for God intended sexual relations for our great pleasure.

2

Finding God's Design

Many of you who are seeking sexual fulfillment in your marriage realize that mastery of physical techniques is only part of the answer. Despite the claims of some sex manuals, a couple cannot separate sex from the rest of the marriage, perfecting it and then isolating it, as it were, in an airtight compartment to be used when desired. Everything that happens in a marriage has its effect on the lovemaking experience.

Because all phases of the biblical plan for marriage must be in operation before we can fully enjoy the sexual union as God designed it, we need to have a clear understanding of His plan. Unfortunately most of us were not counseled in these matters before we married and so we stumbled through the first few years, at least, trying to find our way to happiness. As a family physician for almost four decades, I have observed that marriage with its tremendous significance often turns out to be the least-prepared-for event of life. Even as divorce takes on epidemic proportions, young couples continue to venture into marriage remarkably unprepared. Sometimes a brief meeting with the minister before the wedding, then an often elaborate ceremony, and the newlyweds are on their own, to hit or miss in their quest for happiness, while family and friends hope for the best.

I consider premarriage counseling an essential part of my responsibility as a family doctor. It is not only a preventive measure,

protecting against family breakups, but it also can trigger a positive course of action that will bring pleasure and joy as the young
couple learn to love in an enduring relationship.

The same basic principles that I discuss in premarriage counseling need to be underscored for every reader before we go on
to the physical aspects of lovemaking. Although I usually share
these with engaged couples, they will undoubtedly be of help to
you whether you are a newlywed or celebrating your twenty-eighth
wedding anniversary. Actually, very few couples are so advanced
in wisdom and years that they could not profit from the following biblical principles.

Since this is almost the equivalent of listening in on a premarriage counseling session in my office, perhaps you would like to
know how it takes place. When a couple call for an appointment
for the blood tests, which are required by state law, I ask them to
read my books, *Intended for Pleasure, Love Life for Every Married
Couple, Secret Choices,* and *The First Years of Forever.* The premarriage counsel in these books provides a couple with an opportunity to plan their marriage in the vital areas where planning is
essential for success.

I then ask the couple to listen to my teaching tapes *Sex Technique and Sex Problems in Marriage* and *Before the Wedding Night*
before they come in for their appointment. The tapes clearly present the information every married couple needs for good sexual
adjustment, including specific advice for the first few weeks of
intercourse. This information can be found in chapter 4 of this
book. As the couple listen to the tapes together, the man knows
what the woman should do, she knows what he should do, and
they both know that they know. Many uncertainties and fears are
dispelled, and the couple begin their marriage with an openness
of communication in this most intimate part of their life.

When they come to my office, they both receive physical examinations, and at that time they ask specific questions based on the
information they have received from the tapes. This procedure
assures me that they have been told what they need to know and
it affords me the time to go over these basic principles of the God-
planned marriage with them during the office call. I generally find

that this is the only specific counseling they have received at this turning point in their lives.

At the premarriage counseling session I give to the couple a brief outline of eleven biblical principles that help to ensure a happy marriage. Applying these vital principles will improve anyone's marriage, whether that person is a believer in Christ or not. God has set up certain principles by which men and women are to operate, and these are effective in anyone's life. The only problem is that the non-Christian is unable to implement these principles consistently on a lifelong basis. Only Christians have within them the person of the Lord Jesus Christ and the Holy Spirit to empower them to carry out what is so clearly specified in the Bible.

Here is the way I discuss these principles point by point with the engaged couple:

1. Reserve funds to allow for a few weeks of uninterrupted time for a honeymoon. "When a man hath taken a new wife, he shall not go out to war, neither shall he be charged with any business: but he shall be free at home one year, and shall cheer up his wife which he hath taken" (Deut. 24:5).

In our day of poor marriage planning we could hardly expect a man to take off from work for one year. However, there is a definite scriptural principle here. It is that the first few weeks of the marriage are a crucial time for the young couple. To "cheer up" the wife means literally in the Hebrew "to know sexually and understand what is exquisitely pleasing to her" in the physical relationship.

If, like other young people, you are considering spending several thousand dollars for the wedding and a few leftover dollars for an overnight honeymoon, I certainly advise balancing your funds so that you can be free of responsibility for a few weeks, while you have time to get to know each other. During that period you will have clearer communication lines than you may ever have again, and if each of you does not come to know the other at the first of your marriage, you will find those communication lines becoming progressively blocked as time goes on.

Never plan on getting married just before entering college or graduate school or starting a new business, when the demand on your time and efforts will be so great. Seminary or medical school, for instance, will require intense concentrated study. So schedule your marriage at the beginning of a vacation time or during a break in employment. Concentrate on each other to establish the right pattern of caring in your marriage.

2. *Borrow no money.* "Owe no man any thing, but to love one another" (Rom. 13:8). Borrowing money before marriage or soon after is like adding another phrase to the marriage vows: "Till debt do us part." In other words, let not money put asunder what God has put together. A psychology textbook's listing of the most common problems in marriage puts the handling of money at the head of the list. The key factor that creates problems is not how much money but the attitude toward money or the use of money. In fact in my counseling experience I have found much more conflict among people with a surplus of money than those with limited funds.

This advice could be rephrased "Borrow no money to buy depreciating items." Many young couples go deeply into debt to purchase an expensive automobile or a house full of fine furniture. You will be much happier if you buy only what you can afford, and then spend your weekends together, fixing up your car or building furniture or searching for "treasures" at used furniture sales.

I know one young couple who make a car payment to their savings account each month. When they have enough cash, they buy a car, and go on making payments to themselves for the next car. They collect interest instead of paying it out to someone else and enjoy freedom from debt at the same time. Financial freedom gives you power to utilize your money as *you* choose, not as the moneylenders choose for you. If you want to enjoy each other and find pleasure in your marriage, do not commit your funds to such an extent that you do not have available cash for the little things that are so much fun to do together.

3. *Be independent of in-laws. Leave father and mother.* "For this cause shall a man leave his father and mother, and shall be joined unto his wife, and they two shall be one flesh" (Eph. 5:31). However, *you should not marry without their approval.* "Children, obey your parents in the Lord: for this is right" (Eph. 6:1).

Before sin entered into the human race, two commands were given to Adam. One was not to eat of the tree of the knowledge of good and evil (in other words, not to learn evil by experience). The other command was to get in-laws out of marriage! Looking down the corridors of time at future causes of marriage problems, God said in-laws should not be involved in your marriage (Gen. 2:24). Separating from parents physically, emotionally, and financially is the best possible way to begin a new social unit.

The *man,* by the way, is told to leave his father and his mother and to cleave (to be united totally and inseparably) to his wife—a welding together so that there can be no taking apart. He is commanded to cleave to his wife, even before he is told to love her. The Bible does not specify the best age for marriage but it does establish the principle that the man must be able to be totally independent of his parents and to establish his own home. In our culture, age twenty-six is statistically the best time for a woman to get married, and age twenty-seven to thirty-one for a man. That is, fewer divorces result when people marry at these ages. Three out of five teenage marriages now end in divorce. Regardless of age, any Christian couple working hard to apply God's principles to a good marriage plan will enjoy God's blessings in marriage.

I encourage you to listen to your parents if they do not want you to marry or if they disapprove of your choice of mate. Not only is this biblical, but remember that your parents know you better than anyone else does. They have the knowledge to discern the qualities you need in a marriage partner, far better perhaps than you do. I suspect that many marital problems could be avoided if children would listen to their parents' careful evaluation before they marry.

4. *Do not get a T.V. set for at least one year.* "Ye husbands, dwell with them according to knowledge, giving honour unto the wife. . . . Be ye all of one mind" (1 Peter 3:7, 8). This is one of the most surprising things that young people hear from me. It may sound absurd. But did you know that television can be the greatest, most subtle thief of your time? It will steal away those moments that you should be devoting to your mate and, later, to your family. It will take away the most wonderful hours of your day—hours that

could be spent in personal communication and sharing, moments when you can best learn to relate to each other. There is no giving, no receiving, when you spend your time watching television. Television doesn't produce "prime time"; it steals your prime time as a couple.

Husband, you are urged to do two things in Scripture: First, study the Scripture, then study your wife. Dwell with her. Be totally at ease together, with full knowledge of each other. This is what marriage is all about.

5. *Never go to bed with an unreconciled relationship.* "Let not the sun go down upon your wrath" (Eph. 4:26). "Forgive as the Lord forgave you" (Col. 3:13 NIV).

The Bible warns us not to harbor anger so that it corrodes, causing resentment or bitterness. Some people simmer and fume under the surface for days or weeks at a time, but this is not God's way and it will damage any marriage. Resolve negative attitudes toward each other by the end of the day or do not go to bed until you do. Conflicts arise because two people have come together from different backgrounds, with different educational levels, emotional makeups, desires, and objectives. Conflicts are inevitable. But a conflict becomes a problem only when it is not quickly resolved.

6. *Seek outside spiritual counsel if unable to resolve a major conflict within one week.* The one week is a time limit I have suggested. The Bible does not say how soon spiritual counsel is to be sought. But it is important not to let a seed of bitterness take root and grow up to smother your marriage. "Brethren, if a man be overtaken in a fault, ye which are spiritual, restore such an one in the spirit of meekness" (Gal. 6:1). "Follow peace with all men, and holiness, without which no man shall see the Lord: Looking diligently lest any man fail of the grace of God; lest any root of bitterness springing up trouble you, and thereby many be defiled" (Heb. 12:14–15). ". . . forgetting those things which are behind . . ." (Phil. 3:13). All of these Scriptures encourage forgiveness, reconciliation, and restoration.

7. *Seek counsel if the wife is consistently unable to attain good sexual release.* "Let the husband render unto the wife due benevolence: and likewise also the wife unto the husband. The wife hath

not power of her own body, but the husband: and likewise also the husband hath not power of his own body, but the wife. Defraud ye not one the other" (1 Cor. 7:3–5).

We are told in this passage that the husband and wife are actually robbing each other if there is not mutual pleasure in the sexual relationship. The Bible implies that husbands and wives are entitled to certain rights, and sexual fulfillment is the clearest, most specifically spelled out. God says a husband and wife have the right to be sexually satisfied.

If, early in your marriage, each of you comes to realize how great your responsibility is to fulfill your mate sexually, most problems will be eliminated even before they begin. In almost every case sexual satisfaction can be reached with good counsel, proper information, and an application and practice of the right techniques.

8. Have Bible study together every day. "Man shall not live by bread alone" (Matt. 4:4). "Let the word of Christ dwell in you richly" (Col. 3:16). "Cleanse it with the washing of water by the word" (Eph. 5:26). *Accompany this with prayer:* "If any of you lack wisdom, let him ask of God" (James 1:5).

In Ephesians 5:25–28 we read something that is highly applicable to this principle of marriage: "Husbands, love your wives, even as Christ also loved the church, and gave himself for it; that he might sanctify and cleanse it with the washing of water by the word, that he might present it to himself a glorious church, not having spot, or wrinkle, or any such thing; but that it should be holy and without blemish. So ought men to love their wives as their own bodies."

Christ meets the needs of the Church by washing it and cleansing it with the water of the Word. So ought we to love our wives. It is our responsibility to place before our wives and our families the Word of God.

Husband, as the Word of God is allowed to course through your wife's mind, personality, and very being, she will become the beautiful person God designed her to be. All that would make her less than pure, all that would limit her from becoming a wonderful wife will gradually be removed as the two of you share in daily Bible study. It is the responsibility of the husband to initiate this.

If you don't know how to begin, one way is to listen together to Bible teaching on cassette. Bible Believers Cassettes, Inc., a free-loan library, offers more than a thousand different messages on the subjects of dating, marriage, and the Christian home. (Send for your catalog to: 130 N. Spring St., Springdale, AR 72764.) You may obtain Bible study that is specifically applicable to your personal situation. Build your home life around Bible study and prayer; this can lead to more happiness and harmony in your home than you could ever imagine.

9. *The husband must be 100 percent committed to loving his wife. The wife must be 100 percent committed to being submissive* (Eph. 5). As the husband loves his wife, she is willing to be submissive to him. As the wife submits to her husband, his love for her will surely grow. Do not marry someone who is not a Christian (2 Cor. 6:14). Only when a person trusts in our Lord Jesus Christ alone for salvation can that person be considered a Christian (Acts 4:12). Only when submitting to Christ can anyone live the lifestyle of submission (1 Cor. 11:3; Eph. 5:21).

What kind of love is a husband to bring to his wife? It is a strong, stable, mental attitude, always seeking nothing but the highest good for the one he loves. It is a love expressed in word and action that motivates the one being loved to give of herself in return.

What does it mean for a wife to be in submission to her husband? The word *submit* comes from a military term that actually means to move in an organized manner, to do an assigned job in an assigned way. But in the marriage relationship, the term for submission in the Bible is always used in the middle or passive voice in the original Greek. The voice in Greek is significant because it indicates whether someone is imposing the submission or whether submission comes from within. Submission that a wife gives her husband is a free gift that springs up from within the wife like life-giving water bubbling up from a fresh well, not something imposed through intimidation or other outside force. Submission is the most important gift a wife can give her husband. A responsive and receptive wife willingly demonstrates that she surrenders her freedom for his love, adoration, protection, and provision.

Marriage must be a giving relationship. While the husband is giving love, giving every bit of energy, every bit of knowledge that he possesses to do that which is best for his wife and family, the wife is to respond to that love, adoration, and provision. This response will lead to an eagerness to meet her husband's needs, even before he asks. It is an attitude of willing adaptation to that which God is leading her husband to do. We know submission has to be a gift from her to him, because it is contrary to all natural tendencies. As it is given, it releases a supernatural flow of love between the husband and the wife.

If these two attitudes of love and submission are ignored, difficulty, possibly disaster, looms ahead. If love and submission are put into action, a wonderful marriage will result, because God says very simply that this is the way He designed it.

10. The husband is to be head of his wife. "But I would have you know, that the head of every man is Christ; and the head of the woman is the man; and the head of Christ is God" (1 Cor. 11:3). "For the husband is the head of the wife, even as Christ is the head of the church" (Eph. 5:23). "One that ruleth well his own house . . ." (1 Tim. 3:4).

The husband's authority over the wife is rooted in Christ's authority over the church. In fact all authority we have is delegated authority, and the husband who keeps this in mind will never abuse that authority. On the other hand, the man who relinquishes his leadership position is sowing seeds that will yield trouble in due season.

The husband *is* the spiritual leader of the home and the head of his wife whether he functions in that capacity or not. Any break in the marriage relationship is the man's responsibility. Now I did not say it was his fault. I said that God holds the man accountable for any break in the marriage, because he is the one commanded to cleave inseparably to his wife. This principle of responsibility applies in every area of the relationship, whether spiritual, emotional, or physical.

The bride-to-be should realize before the wedding how important it is to marry a man she can gladly respond to and submit to as her spiritual leader and protective head. I have told many young women, "If you cannot look up to a man, do not look at him."

11. "And the wife see that she reverence her husband" (Eph. 5:33). What does it mean to reverence the husband? It means to give him respect. Men, it is difficult for your wife to respect you, if you are not respectable. It is impossible for a woman to revere her husband, if he is not worthy of reverence. The husband needs to live his life before his wife so that she can see that he is worthy of the respect God asks her to have. In the full meaning of the language of the Greek New Testament, the wife is told to respect, admire, enjoy, fear or be in awe of, defer to, revere, adore, be devoted to, esteem, praise, and deeply love her husband. This is her full-time job, and the original language of the Bible implies that she will be personally benefited as she does it.

If the wife does not trust and respect her husband, it is devastating to him and finally to the marriage. The greatest desire of love is to find an answering love. The greatest grief of love is not to be believed. But if a wife is able to look at her husband with eyes of reverence, he becomes a king among men!

In turn, he should give his wife the place of honor, a place of special privilege and preciousness. Many men have second-rate wives because they treat them in a second-rate manner. They never gain the real queen they would like to be married to; they just do not realize that the wife in many ways is a reflection of her husband. The wife is elevated to a queenly position by the wise and loving husband who puts into operation the great principles of the God-planned marriage.

Some of you reading this chapter have children who will be entering marriage in a few years and you want to do all you can to prepare them for a good marriage. Let me make the following suggestions.

The most important thing a father can do for his children is to love their mother. The home should be the most attractive place in the world to the children, and the mother should be the greatest attraction.

Without a warm atmosphere in your home and marriage—an atmosphere of love, generosity, and forgiveness—your children will not know how to love. The only person who knows how to love is the person who has been loved, who has seen love, who has experienced love. The Christian home is a laboratory in which the love of God is demonstrated.

If you do not have this kind of love in your home, your children are likely to grow up with a feeling of inferiority, emptiness, and lack of worth. But it is not too late for you to develop a home of love. It is never too late for two people who want a transformed marriage. Remember that the only course on marriage most children will ever take is the one in their home! As fathers and mothers in a Christian home, we can provide the best in marriage preparation for our children by having a genuine love for each other and by learning all we can about how to express that love so our children will have a visible, ongoing demonstration of real love.

I have had the opportunity as a family doctor to see results in the marriages of the couples who received this kind of premarriage counseling, based on the absolutes of the Word of God. Over a period of years I have watched the couples who have applied these principles develop stable, loving, satisfying relationships. *These basic instructions from the Bible, if followed, will ensure happy marriages.*

Applying heavenly principles to a marriage can produce a heaven on earth. This is my desire for every young couple and for every home.

3

Choosing to Love

Sex within the marriage of a man and woman who *love* each other can be like a precious stone shining and sparkling in the perfect setting.

But what if you're married and feel that you no longer love your partner? Is it possible to change your feelings? Is there any hope of finding sexual fulfillment together?

This question has been asked of me many times. My answer is a simple yes. Yes, you can change your feelings. Yes, there is still hope of finding sexual fulfillment with your mate. This chapter tells you how. But we have to begin by defining what love is.

This becomes a difficult task, when we find that the *Oxford English Dictionary* takes five pages to define *love* without much success, even after all that. Ask a hundred people for a definition of love, and the chances are good that you will get at least ninety different answers.

Obviously the world has no clear-cut definition of love. Meanings of the word vary according to individual experiences and viewpoints. Love can be passion, affection, romantic feelings, friendship, fondness, infatuation, or innumerable combinations of those qualities. But almost always, *love,* as the world uses it, includes an expectation of getting something in return.

The Bible reveals another kind of love, which the world does not understand, and it is this kind of love that provides the perfect setting for the "one flesh" experience of sex in marriage. The New Testament calls it *agape* love and so fully pictures it in word and action that, as Christians, we can begin to comprehend it, though we cannot plumb its depths.

Agape love is unconditional and irrevocable. God chose to love us first, before we gave Him our love in return, or even knew who He is. Agape love gives without measuring the cost or seeking personal advantage. "For God so loved the world, that he gave his only begotten Son, that whosoever believeth in him should not perish, but have everlasting life" (John 3:16). Agape love is not natural; it is supernatural! It is a love poured out on us in a beautiful abundance, seeking nothing but our highest good. It does not depend on our actions. While God deeply desires our response, our reaction to Him has no bearing on *whether* He will love us. That is already decided. He *does* love us; He has made the irrevocable choice to love us; and He has proved it by giving His best to us—His Son.

Agape love has something both glorious and practical to say to the married couple, for it is this amazing way of loving, *God's way,* that can become *our* way of loving by God's power. The principles of agape love, operating in the marriage relationship, can answer every need, solve every problem, and show us the way to regions of joy unending.

The New Testament writings show us that agape love in the marriage must involve total commitment, just as God is totally committed to us. God's command is for Adam to "cleave" to Eve. "Therefore shall a man leave his father and his mother, and shall cleave unto his wife: and they shall be one flesh" (Gen. 2:24). This means that even before God expects man to love his mate, He expects him to be totally committed to her. Deep in our minds and hearts as man and wife, there needs to be an irrevocable commitment to the marriage.

With today's no-fault divorce laws, marriages seem almost disposable. Total commitment seems almost out of date. But perhaps we have allowed the world to set our expectations for us, making divorce the norm instead of the exception. There are still plenty of people who get married, intending their relationship to be permanent, but the divorce rate in many regions of our nation continues to climb. Some of those people failed somewhere. Perhaps part of the problem is a lack of commitment to commitment.

"To cherish for better or for worse, in sickness and in health, till death do us part" should remind a couple that in marriage, storms may blow up and they have to be ridden out. If we think in terms of a foreseeable time when things will be tough enough to quit, quitting becomes an alternative. Often it is all too short a step from possibility to probability. Jesus' statement, "What therefore God hath joined together, let not man put asunder" (Mark 10:9), needs to become such a part of our thinking that full commitment to marriage, no matter what, will be our only option. In other words, when we go into marriage, it should be with the conviction that *there is no way out*. Then both partners will be committed to making the marriage a success.

But far too many couples come to the painful point of admitting, "We don't love each other anymore." When they say it, they assume, of course, that the marriage must be over. This attitude indicates that the couple had a misplaced confidence in the world's vague idea of love and suggests that God's way of loving never existed in their marriage in the first place.

The fact is, the Bible gives no indication that the feeling the world calls *love* is to be the foundation for marriage. A marriage built entirely on this feeling will be characterized by fluctuating feelings as the circumstances change. Result: shaky emotions, shaky marriage!

Emotions do not and never will sustain a marriage. There are those cold, gray mornings of life when one awakens emotionally weary; obviously, emotions cannot be depended on for stability in marriage. And we do not have to be helpless slaves to love or any other emotion that we slip into or fall out of. But as commitment binds husband and wife together through shared happiness and trouble, all the wonderful, pleasurable emotions they could wish for will spring forth from agape love in action. Commitment is the bond; the feeling of love is the result. The *feeling* comes because of the *fact* of commitment through every changing circumstance.

Marriage does not necessarily make people happy. But people can make their marriage a happy one by giving to each other, working together, serving together, and growing together. Or they can allow the marriage to disintegrate by not doing these things.

We have all experienced times when we actively pursued happiness for ourselves. We found that it seemed to run away from us, like a startled deer in the woods, as soon as it was almost within our grasp. Most of us know by now that happiness can never be caught when we chase it. Instead, it comes to us freely, surprisingly, when we are concentrating on something else and least expect it. If we grab for emotional happiness without committing and giving first, our selfishness will reap only misery and coldness. But an honest desire for the happiness of our partner will bring a surprising degree of happiness into our own lives—a fringe benefit based on the principles of God's Word: "Give, and it shall be given unto you; good measure, pressed down, and shaken together, and running over" (Luke 6:38).

Love, in essence, is that deliberate act of giving one's self to another, so that the other person constantly receives enjoyment. Love gives, and love's richest reward comes when the object of love responds to the gift of one's self. If a man and wife so give themselves for each other, each will have a sense of completeness and contentment. Not only that! The conditions have then become right for building a love relationship that will bring to the marriage all the richly delightful feelings of being in love. Agape love is always the fertile soil for God-planned pleasure in the physical marriage relationship.

God so designed us that we cannot be truly satisfied with mere physical and physiological relief in sex. The world, which often tries to view love and sex in marriage as two separate entities, has missed the point. In God's perfect design, it is in a marriage characterized by agape love that all the emotions of loving increase and multiply. We find our greatest satisfaction in becoming one with our beloved, in both possessing and serving the beloved. Yet love is not a fixed thing, although the context of commitment never changes. From day to day, even from hour to hour, within the framework of commitment, our emotions of loving may change. At one time physical desire may be paramount. At other times, desire for affection and close companionship may be the only ele-

ment present. Sexual desire as a conscious need will arise sometimes only after intimate time has been spent together. But if we
have entered into God's way of loving and cultivated this love in
our marriage, we will know a blessed security together in the midst
of life with all its perplexing changes and unexpected demands on
us. Love—God's kind of love—is the answer!

Love Renewal in the Marriage

The couple who assume their marriage is over, because they no
longer love each other, need to know that no matter what has
occurred in the past, agape love, which God makes available to
the believer, can renew and transform their marriage in every area,
touching the smallest practical details of daily life and improving
the physical relationship to an amazing degree.

Renewal of love takes place in three areas: choice of the will,
action, and feeling. Note that feeling comes last, because the *feeling* of love is not the most crucial ingredient of the marriage. The
fact of love, based on an unchanging commitment to the other
person, is the most crucial.

Renewal of love begins in your mind, where your will exercises
the choice and makes the decision to love no matter what—and
never to stop loving. Here the wounds you and your partner have
suffered must be dealt with first. Where the feelings of love have
departed, all the unhappy emotions—anger, guilt, hurt, resentment, or bitterness—are sure to be lurking in the shadows. Find
them and send them packing! They deserve nothing but dismissal,
for they will give you nothing but grief. You and your partner
need to realize that there must be open communication, which is
healing in nature when it springs from total forgiveness. Let it
begin with you. Start by admitting that your loss of love is a result
of wanting to receive rather than wanting to give. Recognize that
you can be the instrument through whom God will communicate
His love to your partner. Pray and commit yourself to this. Thank
God in advance for the supernatural agape love that will flow
through you as He promised.

This love, which must be learned, which starts in the mind,
which is subject to the will, not the emotions, always results in

action. Love becomes something we *do,* before it is something we *feel.* Thus we choose to demonstrate and initiate love.

How we show our love is vitally important. God has given certain specific guidelines on the parts the husband and wife each are to have in the marriage relationship. The husband, according to Scripture, is the leader and the lover, while the wife is the helper and the responder. This intertwining nature of love and response or submission, which is so crucial, may become obscured during times of culturally mandated change. God has designed the relationship of husband and wife with an understanding of their unique strengths and differences, so that the husband delights in loving a wife who is submissive and responsive; a wife gladly submits to a husband who loves in God's way. But neither can *demand* the appropriate response from the other. It must be a gift. The wonderful thing is, it can start with either partner. The wife wants to obey a truly loving, caring, protective husband. Her resulting submission makes him love her all the more, and he will want to reciprocate with whatever will make her happy. Her quick response causes him to love her more, and the cycle goes on and on—gloriously.

The husband must be 100 percent committed to loving his wife. "Husbands, love your wives, even as Christ also loved the church, and gave himself for it" (Eph. 5:25). The wife must be 100 percent committed to being submissive to her husband. "Therefore as the church is subject unto Christ, so let the wives be to their own husbands in every thing" (Eph. 5:24).

Some people talk of marriage as ideally a fifty-fifty proposition. The problem with this idea is that each partner is always waiting for the other to do something first. With a one hundred–one hundred partnership, either partner acting with a 100 percent giving attitude will contribute to the total marriage, so that there will be a reciprocating love from the other partner.

The submissive role of the wife implies that whether the husband acts like it or not, he is responsible for the important decisions in the home. "For the husband is the head of the wife, even as Christ is the head of the church" (Eph. 5:23). This is not to demote or put down the wife. Rather, it takes an unnecessary load from her. If the wife assumes the responsibilities the husband has neglected, she takes on pressures she was never created to handle. The husband is allowed to escape his responsibilities, and the family structure deteriorates. This has occurred in many American homes today.

Love is the preeminent characteristic of the emotionally mature person, because as 1 Corinthians 13 says, love seeketh not its own. Therefore the wise husband who truly loves his wife will maturely shoulder his responsibilities. The wise wife who truly loves her husband will not demand her rights when he asks something of her. If she maturely loves her husband, she will not need to try to defend her self-image. She will seek to please. In fact she will try to please her husband creatively and do his will, even before he asks—just as the husband will look for creative ways to express his love to her, even before she shows any obvious need for reassurance.

If you choose to love according to God's way of loving, you will find yourself watching for needs you can meet in your mate. God will show you specific needs, actual needs, which you can rejoice in meeting. And what you sow you will reap. (See Galatians 6:7–10.) What you give will be returned to you. These divine principles will prove themselves again and again in the realm of your marriage.

Although this can begin with either partner, I want to address the husbands with some specific applications of these principles.

Husband, if you want to learn *how* to love your wife all over again, start by giving to her, knowing that the agape love of God is energizing you. As you give yourself (your time, your attention, your caring), your feelings of love for her will grow. You have been instructed in Ephesians 5 to give yourself sacrificially to your wife, in the same way that Christ gave Himself to the Church. In other words, He loved the Church enough to die for her. How often does a husband affirm that he would give his life to save the life of his wife in a moment of danger and yet he does not have time to give himself daily to her emotional, physical, and spiritual needs! You must give—give first, give generously, and continue to give— if you hope to experience the expanding joys of love. If you are not giving, you are merely taking. There is no natural momentum to keep a marriage going, apart from the powerful force of giving to one another. Keep in mind that the opposite of love is not hate but *indifference*.

Now, husband, how do you initiate love? Coming home from work you can either be grumpy from the day's pressures or you can come into the house cheerfully and with an attitude of concern and respect for what your wife has experienced during the day. A wise friend says he has picked a certain stoplight between his office and home where he dumps his office problems and tensions and refuses to pick them up again until the next day. To bring problems home with you and try to escape behind a newspaper or the television set does not demonstrate love for your wife.

Conveying the attitude of concern for her builds the right atmosphere for satisfaction in sex. After all, most men can begin sexual intercourse after a bad day, a family argument, with worries galore, or with supper burning on the stove! But your wife will respond much more readily when motivated by respect and consideration on your part. She needs an introductory period of sensitive consideration and without that, she cannot fully respond in a satisfying physical relationship. Building an atmosphere of caring and romance is a sign of true love on the part of the husband.

A woman's emotional makeup requires verbal expression from her husband to assure her of continuing love and security. You should be wise enough to know this about your wife and loving enough to do it. You can build up her self-esteem just through your words to her. Words have power! There are so many ways a man can show his love and regard for his wife. Say it with a card or candy or flowers. But by all means say it with *words*. There is the tired joke about the husband who said, "In ten years of married life the reason I never told my wife I loved her is because I told her in our marriage vows, and I haven't taken it back yet." This is not only a bad joke; it is unfortunately a living reality to all too many couples.

Another aspect of loving your partner involves thanking God for every good quality in her. People often complain about the undesirable qualities in their mate, while overlooking those qualities that originally attracted them. Agape love in marriage expresses by word and action, thought and prayer, the deepest appreciation for your partner, with the intense awareness of her needs and longings, past, present, and future.

Love in action on the part of both marriage partners involves physical touching. In fact because the greatest desire of love is to find an answering love, there is nothing that can so quickly build the intense feeling of love in marriage than repeatedly reaching out to a responding partner, and having that one lovingly reach back to you with tender touching—both of you gently drawing closer and closer, cuddling and snuggling and fondling.

This is vividly illustrated by teenagers, who spend too much time in close physical contact, causing their relationship to become a helpless enslavement to an overwhelming emotion, unable to see any defects, attributing all that is desirable and admirable to each other, and generating a blind compulsion to possess each other.

Oh, that more Christian married couples could learn the importance of loving physical communication to attain greater oneness within their marriage by giving to each other more and more intimate physical attention. The sexual relationship is perhaps the most logical place for both husband and wife to begin giving to each other.

As you read this book and gain new understanding and knowledge of the sexual relationship, you will find that obstacles in the physical area are being removed, and your love, which was previously hindered, is now being freed. The more freely you express your affection in physical terms by touching and giving pleasure to the other, the more love you will "feel" for your marriage partner. The physical expressions of affection will allow the love emotion, which was previously blocked, to be liberated. The feeling of love, which had been hopelessly buried under defenses and weapons, can emerge from its protective shell to bless the marriage in a most wonderful way.

The renewal of love starts with a choice of the will, a commitment to love, followed by actions that demonstrate loving concern, and the feeling of love naturally follows. Feeling is the third stage in the process. Remember that it is easier to change actions than it is to change feelings. As your actions become markedly different, you will discover that the desired feelings are following closely behind.

Renewal of love in marriage can be the springboard to experiencing the joys of the "one flesh" relationship as God planned it in the beginning.

4

Understanding the Basics

Any helpful counsel concerning the physical relationship between husband and wife must include an explanation of the basic facts of human anatomy. This information may seem elementary to you (if you have already studied the subject), but a clear understanding of the sex organs with their intricate functions should inspire a sense of wonder at the perfect design God has built into our bodies, so that we might experience the deepest pleasure in love-making and so that we might successfully reproduce children in our marriage. Please go over the material carefully. Even one bit of misinformation or misunderstanding in this area can lead to a less-than-satisfactory relationship in your marriage. These "basics" include an explanation of medical problems that directly affect sexual activity. Couples who will soon marry will be particularly interested in the instructions for the wedding night.

We are presenting this specialized knowledge in words and illustrations that can be easily understood. Parents, you will find this section helpful in preparing for the time when your children begin to seek information. The truth given here is expressed in language as specific—but as simple and discreet—as the complex nature of this subject will permit.

To begin at the beginning, we must start with names, the proper vocabulary for discussion of sexual functions.

The mystery connected with the giving of names traces back to Adam's job of naming the animals in the Garden (Gen. 2:20). That naming was somehow the first step toward having "dominion" over the earth. You will find that knowing the correct names of the sex organs and functions is the first step to real understanding of the sex relationship. Many people have been handicapped by the wrong vocabulary, by words that are embarrassing to think of, let alone use. The right names will give you and your children a proper appreciation of the sanctity and dignity of God's provision for pleasure in marriage.

We need to know not only the names of the sex organs, but also their locations, specific functions, and relationships to each other. Remember as you read that our goal is to give you the information that will lead you into a more wonderful experience of all that marriage offers.

The Female Reproductive System

The organs that can give genesis to life are called the *genitalia,* a Latin word that means "to give birth." The female birth-giving organs are in two groups. One group is outside the body and easily visible; it is called the external genitalia. The *vulva* (Latin for *covering*) is the collective name for the entire group of female external genital organs. This group is the gateway to the second group of reproductive organs inside the body, called the internal genitalia. These are made up of two ovaries, two oviducts (tubes), the uterus, and the vagina (see figures 1 and 2).

The reproductive organs are formed several months before one's own birth but remain inactive until puberty (usually ages twelve to fifteen), when they receive the signal to come to sexual maturity. This important signal is given by the pituitary, a small gland situated at the base of the brain.

Pituitary gland. The pituitary gland lies in a bony saddle of the skull, under the brain and near the middle of the head. It is no larger than a small lima bean, yet it is a major control gland that sends chemical signals through the bloodstream to other parts of the body. These signals are in the form of chemical substances called hormones. Through a complex relay system, these pituitary

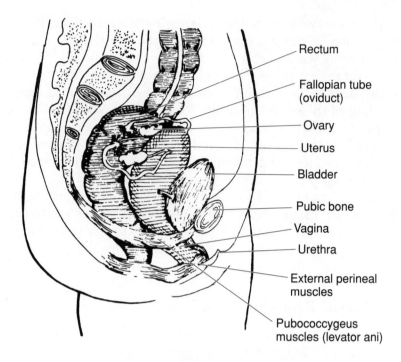

Rectum

Fallopian tube
(oviduct)

Ovary

Uterus

Bladder

Pubic bone

Vagina

Urethra

External perineal
muscles

Pubococcygeus
muscles (levator ani)

Figure 1
Side view of female reproductive system

Especially note the location of P.C. muscles, which provide an
important part of the support for the reproductive organs.
Controlled contraction of these muscles gives added sexual
pleasure for both husband and wife.

hormones control many functions, including growth of bone and
body.

Medical research indicates that the pituitary gland responds to
signals from a part of the brain called the hypothalamus. This means
that the amount of some of our hormones can be indirectly, but
partially, governed by what we think or by our attitudes.

At puberty a girl's pituitary gland actively secretes two main
female hormones that arouse the reproductive organs to maturity. The internal organs, which lie inside the protective pelvic
bones, begin their response just before the external organs of sex
give evidence of beginning maturity.

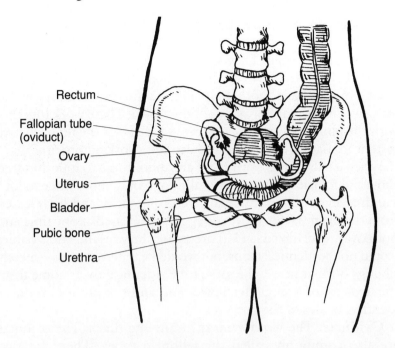

Figure 2
Front view of female reproductive system

This shows the relationship between the various organs of
reproduction. Notice here and in figure 1 that the urethra lies
between the vagina and the pubic bone. Thus it can be easily
bruised during coitus.

Ovaries. The word *ovary* comes from the Latin word *ova*, which
means eggs. The ovaries are the main target organs for the pituitary hormones. At puberty the pituitary secretions carried by the
bloodstream signal the ovaries to begin to develop eggs. Soon the
ovaries will be in full production to continue for thirty or more
years.

There are two ovaries, each suspended near the internal center
of the lower body about four to five inches below the waist, halfway
between the back of the pelvis and the groin. Each ovary is about
the size of a robin's egg. At the time of puberty, the surface of the
ovary is smooth. Shimmering through the surface there are many
tiny glistening droplets called follicles. Each of these ovarian fol-

licles holds an immature egg, or ovum, that is the female cell of reproduction. The eggs in the droplets are so small they would be only barely visible. They are smaller than the dot on an *i*, and it would take at least two million of them to fill a sewing thimble.

The ovaries have another equally vital function: to produce at least two important hormones of their own. These work together with the pituitary hormones to bring the rest of the reproductive system to maturity and then to keep it in working order.

When a baby girl is born there are about three to four hundred thousand follicles in the ovaries, although only about three to four hundred eggs will ever actually reach maturity and be released from the ovaries. If two ova, or eggs, are released at one time and both ova are fertilized, a twin pregnancy may result. These babies would not be identical twins, but would be fraternal twins—merely siblings born at nearly the same time. Identical twins come from the division of a single fertilized egg, and this always produces identical babies of the same sex.

Oviducts. The word *oviduct* means egg ducts. The oviducts are also commonly called the fallopian tubes. There are two oviducts, or tubes—one for each ovary. Primarily made of muscle, each of these tubes is about four inches long and about the same diameter as a small telephone cord.

These muscular oviducts are essential to the transport of the tiny immobile eggs from the ovaries. At the same time, the oviducts provide the meeting ground for the female egg and male sperm, which are coming to each other from opposite directions.

An egg coming from the ovary must first of all be caught by the oviduct. Neither oviduct is directly attached to its ovary. Instead, each oviduct has a trumpet-shaped widened opening near the ovary. This opening is rimmed with fingerlike fringes (fimbriae) that conduct a sweeping motion, which carries all before it into the oviduct. After the egg is taken into the opening of the oviduct by the sweeping fringe, waves of muscular contractions continue to aid its transport downstream toward the womb.

The trumpet-shaped opening of the oviduct leads to a passage that is no wider than this hyphen (-). This internal passage, about the size of the point of a pencil, is lined with minute clumps of brushlike hairs called *cilia*. The size of the cilia, in proportion to the egg, is like that of eyelashes in comparison to an orange. The cilia are the sweepers that help to keep the egg gently flowing toward the womb.

An infection, particularly a venereal infection, may block these fallopian tubes by scarring them on the inside. This may cause a woman to be unable to have children. Sometimes these obstructions can be removed by careful surgery. Tubal obstructions are seen by injecting a liquid that shows clearly on X rays as it flows through the *os,* or mouth, of the cervix, into the uterus, and through the tubes. This is called a salpingogram and can be done in a doctor's office or in any hospital X-ray department on an outpatient basis. This procedure may cause some pain and discomfort, but nothing that is unbearable. It requires no anesthesia.

In performing sterilization for birth control, the surgeon usually double-ties each tube with silk thread and then removes a section of each of these oviducts or tubes. This requires the opening of the abdomen and is thus a major operation requiring a stay in the hospital. However, there is another method that does not require a woman to be hospitalized. Some physicians are able to do laparoscopic surgery in which a laparoscope—a small, lighted tube instrument—is passed through an incision in the area just below the navel.

Through another small incision in the lower abdomen, another instrument is inserted with which the surgeon is able to grasp and manipulate each oviduct. While he watches through the laparoscope, a loop of the oviduct is grasped and an electrocautery tip is used to burn and do away with about one or two inches of the mid portion of each oviduct. There are some other techniques used to close these oviducts. One of the simplest ones is to insert through the small lower abdominal incision an instrument with which the oviduct can be manipulated, grasped, and pulled up into a loop. A small circular elastic ring (similar to a small rubber band) is then slipped over the loop. The ring very tightly squeezes the oviduct closed in two places. At present the elastic-ring method probably offers the best possibility for success of surgery to reconstruct the tubes at a later time, if the woman decides she wants to have another baby. I would not, however, want to convey the idea that any operative sterilization method is reversible. An operation for sterilization should be considered permanent sterilization. Reconstruction surgery would be a very tedious and delicate major operation and would certainly cause some discomfort.

By describing these methods, I am merely explaining for you how and why certain techniques of birth control work. Whether or not you practice family planning is your decision and yours alone. However, every married couple is entitled to have information about each method of birth control, when making this decision. (For more information on family planning, see chapter 11.)

Uterus. The Latin word *uterus* means womb or belly. The uterus, usually the size and shape of a small pear, is firm and muscular. It is about four inches long. When the woman is standing, it is suspended in a nearly horizontal position in the body, so that the small end of the pear points toward the tip of the spine, while the bulbous upper end points forward.

During pregnancy, the uterus can expand greatly to accommodate, as we know, up to six babies. This is possible because the uterus has many elastic fibers meshed in with the powerful muscle fibers. These muscles later play an important part in labor by contracting forcefully to deliver the baby.

The outside of the uterus is flesh pink in color. Inside there is a red velvety lining called endometrium, from the Greek for "within the womb." The interior of the uterus is a narrow, triangle-shaped cavity surrounded by thick muscular walls.

The two incoming oviduct canals enter at the top of the uterine cavity. The lower part of the uterine cavity that forms the narrow base is called the cervical canal.

Cervix. The word *cervix* means neck in Latin. Here it refers to the neck of the uterus. Surrounding the cervical canal, the cervix forms the narrow lower end of the uterus. It can be easily examined by the physician, since about half the cervix projects into the vagina.

Like the rest of the uterus, the cervix is firm and muscular. Medical students are sometimes taught that before the first pregnancy the cervix feels like the tip of the nose, and after childbirth it feels like the point of the chin.

The *cervical os* is the opening of the cervix into the vagina. This passageway is as narrow as the lead in a pencil and is framed by strong muscles. Only under strong pressure, as in childbirth, does the fibroelastic tissue of the cervix dilate to increase the size of the opening. The normally tight passage helps to keep the interior of the uterus virtually germfree, especially since a constant slight current of cleansing moisture flows outward.

This moisture, along with a light scraping of cervical cells, is examined for cancer cells in the Papanicolaou, or Pap, smear. It is recommended that women have a Pap smear about once each year, as the cervix is the site of most of the cancer of the female organs. It takes two to six days to get a final report on the Pap smear. When cervical cancer is found early, more than 90 percent is curable with correct treatment (see figure 3).

Vagina. The word *vagina* means sheath in Latin. The vagina is a very elastic, sheathlike canal that serves as a passage to and from the sheltered genital organs inside the body. At its upper end, the vagina forms a curving vault that encloses the tip of the cervix. The inner walls of the vagina consist of folds of tissue, which tend to lie in contact. The vagina, normally three to five inches long, can expand easily to receive the penis. Its greatest expansion, of course, occurs during childbirth. The folds contain many tiny glands, which continuously produce a cleansing film of moisture so that the vagina is self-cleansing. For this reason douches are seldom necessary.

Near the external opening of the vagina, there is a concentration of sensory nerves that play a significant role in sexual arousal when stimulated by touch. The opening is encircled by a constrictor muscle that responds to communications from the sensory nerves. This muscle can be tightened and relaxed at will.

The first response to sexual stimulation in a woman is the lubrication of the vagina, which occurs within ten to thirty seconds in

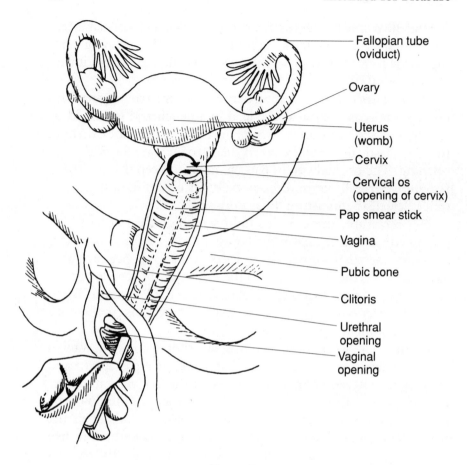

Fallopian tube
(oviduct)

Ovary

Uterus
(womb)

Cervix

Cervical os
(opening of cervix)

Pap smear stick

Vagina

Pubic bone

Clitoris

Urethral
opening

Vaginal
opening

Figure 3
Obtaining a Pap smear from the cervix

This simple and painless procedure helps to save many lives
annually, as it detects cervical cancer before it can be seen
with the eye.

the younger woman and within one to three minutes in the older
woman. Sexual excitement causes the walls of the upper vagina to
be covered with beads of lubricant, like moisture on a cold glass.
This prepares the vagina for an easier insertion of the penis.

Knowing the precise location of this natural lubrication can
enhance sexual pleasure during the excitement phase. The knowl-

edgeable husband will gently reach up into the vagina and bring lubricant down to the clitoral area for more enjoyable stimulation. Remember, if the wife is lying on her back, all the lubricant will remain in the upper vagina, unless it is brought down.

Adequate vaginal lubrication is absolutely essential for pleasure during intercourse. If it is not present, the husband will need to apply some form of artificial lubricant, obtainable at any drugstore or supermarket. Be sure to apply the lubricant to the head of the penis and to the outside of the vagina before penetration.

The nursing mother should be aware that her capacity to lubricate may be restricted because of low estrogen levels. This vaginal dryness usually persists as long as she continues to nurse. It may be relieved by her obstetrician's prescription for an estrogen cream to apply up into the vagina. While the capacity for vaginal lubrication does continue throughout the female life cycle, low estrogen levels in the menopausal woman will almost always result in vaginal dryness, requiring the use of an artificial lubricant with every intercourse.

Never think of the vagina as a passive organ, but a very active one. When sexually stimulated, it increases in length and widens to twice its diameter. At the beginning of arousal, the upper vagina expands, and the uterus lifts up toward the abdomen. In the second phase, the vagina constricts to conform to the penis. After orgasm the uterus moves downward, so that the cervix rests in the pool of semen deposited in the upper vagina.

Hymen. The *hymen,* which has been given the name of the mythical god of marriage, is a shelflike membrane that surrounds but does not cover the lower opening to the vagina. The hymen has no physiologic function and never grows back after it has been dilated. In some females, the hymen is extremely tough and resistant. There are baby girls who are born without a hymen, so its absence is not necessarily an indication of loss of virginity.

The opening in the hymen of a virgin is usually about one inch in diameter (large enough for tampon use). However, for comfortable intercourse, a diameter of about one and one-half inches is needed. Thus, statistically, at the time of their first intercourse,

50 percent of brides experience some pain, but not enough to complain about; 20 percent say they have no pain at all; and 30 percent experience rather severe pain.

About six weeks before marriage, every woman should have a pelvic examination. A thoughtful, interested physician can give her specific instructions that will help remove much of her fear of physical pain due to intercourse.

If the pelvic examination reveals a thick or tight hymen, the prospective bride may wish to have this tissue stretched, so there will be less difficulty and discomfort during the first intercourse. The physician can do this; or she may use her own fingers to stretch the hymen, according to the physician's instructions; or she may ask for exact instructions and a demonstration of how her husband can carefully stretch the hymen on their wedding night before intercourse (see figure 4).

I believe it is best for the prospective bride to devote a few moments each day for two to four weeks before the wedding in stretching the vaginal opening, so that her initial sexual experience with her husband will be as pleasant and painless as possible.

Here are the directions I give for the vaginal stretching. The woman should slowly insert one finger, well lubricated with artificial lubricant, all the way to the base of the finger, then gently, very slowly, yet forcibly, press downward and backward against this most resistant part of the hymen. When you finally are able to insert one finger all the way to the base, then try to place two well-lubricated fingers into the vagina, again pressing slowly downward and backward with a quite firm pressure.

If the husband is attempting to stretch the vaginal opening on the wedding night, he should make sure his fingernails are filed very smooth and short and then follow these instructions: Insert the tips of three fingers, held in a wedge shape and well lubricated with artificial lubricant, into the vaginal opening. Press down toward the back, very firmly but *very* slowly. It should take from fifteen to thirty minutes to fully stretch the hymen. Move your fingers only about one-eighth inch at a time, until finally you can insert all three fingers to the base.

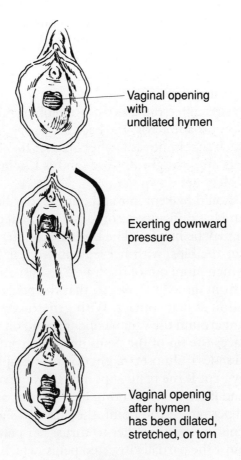

Vaginal opening
with
undilated hymen

Exerting downward
pressure

Vaginal opening
after hymen
has been dilated,
stretched, or torn

Figure 4
Stretching the hymen

This procedure can be done by the physician or by the bride-
groom to avoid discomfort during the first intercourse. Observe
that finger pressure should be downward and toward the back.

This procedure will result in the stretching of the vaginal opening. Small tears may occur as well. If there happens to be a small
area of bleeding, do not be afraid. Simply look for the exact spot
that is bleeding, take a piece of tissue, put it on the spot, and hold
it there with a firm pressure. You will be able to stop whatever
bleeding occurs in this manner. If another tear and more bleed-

ing occur when you have intercourse, you can stop it the same way by holding tissue on the exact spot with a firm pressure. The tissue may be left in place about twelve hours and then soaked loose in warm water to avoid new bleeding. Intercourse can begin again the next day.

After such stretching, the major portion of the remaining hymen lies in a crescent shape across the back of the vaginal opening. Its position is such that it moves farther up over the vaginal opening when the legs are brought upward, and is less in the way when the woman's legs are down flat.

This fact should be kept in mind during your first intercourse. If the husband has difficulty accomplishing initial entrance, a special position may be helpful. The bride lies on her back with two pillows under the hips, with her legs down as flat as possible to move the hymen more out of the way. The husband faces her and approaches from directly above, so that the penis is in an almost vertical position at first contact. With generous amounts of artificial lubricant around the vaginal opening and on the head of the penis, he places the tip of the penis near the front of the vaginal opening and slides it almost straight down, attempting to slip past the elastic hymen. If the penis slips into the vagina, then the wife can slowly and intermittently bring her knees up as far as her discomfort will permit. At this point, the husband should no longer force the penis in, but allow her to thrust her pelvis upward and forward against the partially inserted penis, which should still be in an almost vertically straight-down position.

As a last resort only, if there is a great deal of pain, Nupercainal Ointment may be applied around the vaginal opening, especially toward the back, and left for a period of five minutes. This is a local anesthetic ointment, available without a prescription. If your physician has warned of a vaginal opening that seems to be unusually tight, you may wish to have the ointment on hand.

Following the procedures I have described, however, should ensure a pleasant first-time experience for the newlyweds in almost every case.

The husband should keep in mind that most pain occurs from entering too quickly, not allowing enough time for the muscles around the vagina to relax. At the time of first intercourse, the husband should not persist in striving to bring his wife to orgasm with his penis in the vagina. If she has some soreness, there is no reason to make this worse. After the penis is inserted, the husband should have his orgasm quickly, withdraw the penis, and stimulate his wife's clitoral area gently with his fingers to bring her to orgasm.

The husband's tender care of his wife at this crucial time will do much to help her develop trust in him, so that in the weeks to come, she will be able to totally relax and let herself go in the enjoyment of his lovemaking.

The objective of your first few weeks of sexual encounters should be the development of loving intimacy, as the wife experiences maximum comfort and the husband demonstrates maximum self-control. The honeymoon can be a disappointing time for couples who have gone into it unprepared or misinformed. But by applying the right information, you can have a wonderful time together on your wedding night, establishing the right patterns from the beginning.

I must encourage the husband not to be goal oriented in his lovemaking, especially on the wedding night. Men are sometimes prone to judge themselves as lovers on the basis of whether they can bring their brides to sexual climax during intercourse, but do not make this the supreme goal. Your striving to reach that goal would put strong pressure on your bride to respond and perform properly, when she really cannot force her body to climax. Orgasm only happens in a relaxed atmosphere, after emotional and physical arousal have occurred and enough skilled physical stimulation has taken place. The feeling of pressure that comes from the husband's expectation and her fear of failure can completely hinder the physical response she otherwise would have.

The husband's purpose on the wedding night should be to develop emotional intimacy through physical closeness. You need to concentrate simply on pleasing your wife with tenderness—romantic words, warmth and cuddling, total body caressing—done in a meaningful way that shows your appreciation of her as a desirable woman. She must be aroused emotionally, and this seldom happens quickly. So take plenty of time and savor every moment of it.

Don't be alarmed if you ejaculate before you want to on your wedding night. This may happen because of your intense feelings. But this is by no means the end of the lovemaking experience. No matter when the lover ejaculates, he continues to bring his wife to orgasm, if she desires it, and finds added pleasure in her response.

On your honeymoon, another erection will probably come in a few minutes, even if you ejaculate early, but do not wait for that. Continue providing the caresses and manual stimulation that give your wife sexual satisfaction. Actually, at this time, the manual stimulation will be more pleasing to her and much more effective than the sensations of intercourse, because the vaginal muscles are extra tense at first, and there is always some discomfort for the bride.

By the way, the counsel I am giving will apply to you even if you have been married before, with previous sexual experiences. This should be a fresh start, and the husband needs to show tender care and concern for his bride, as though it were the first experience for both.

Urethra. The *urethra* is the outlet for the urine from the bladder. The urethral opening is about one-half inch above the vaginal opening and entirely separate from it. It resembles a rounded dimple containing a tiny slit. The urethra is actually a tube that runs beneath the pubic bone and can be easily bruised in the first few days after marriage, unless plenty of lubrication is provided for the penis in the vagina.

This bruising produces what is commonly called "newlywed cystitis" or "honeymoon cystitis" and is characterized by pain in the bladder area, blood in the urine, and rather severe burning when the urine passes. It is an indication that injury to the urethra has allowed bacteria to grow. These bacteria may ascend to produce a severe bladder infection called cystitis. The infection and resulting pain will clear up quickly, if the bride increases her intake of fluids and uses medication as prescribed by her physician. Use of a lubricant such as Astroglide is absolutely essential the first few weeks to help prevent this painful condition caused by bruising.

Some women are especially susceptible to intercourse cystitis, just as others are prone to develop sore throats and colds. A woman's anatomy sets up the conditions under which urinary tract infections easily occur. The urethra can be the recipient of contamination from both the vagina and rectum. The anus provides a hospitable site for bacteria, and from there it is only a short ascent to the bladder and beyond. Women should wash after bowel movements whenever feasible and always wipe from front to back.

Most urinary tract infections in women occur within forty-eight hours after sexual relations. Voiding within a few minutes after intercourse is important, since this helps rid the urethra of bacteria. Bladder urine is usually sterile and the voiding of urine cleanses the urethral mechanism. When bladder emptying is normal and complete, the ascent of bacteria is avoided. Of course, extra intake of fluid helps this urethral flushing. If frequent episodes of cystitis continue, you will need to see your physician for prescription antibiotics to take after each intercourse. This allows the elimination of bacteria before they have time to multiply enough to produce infection.

Clitoris. This is the Latin word for "that which is closed in." Closed in by the peak of the labia, the shaft of the clitoris, which is about one inch long, is located about one inch above the entrance to the vagina. At its outer end is a small, rounded body about the size of a pea, which is called the *glans,* from a Latin word meaning acorn. A fold of skin called the *prepuce*, or the clitoral hood, partly covers the glans (see figure 5).

The clitoris has been called the trigger of female desire. It is the most keenly sensitive point a woman has for sexual arousal and has, as far as we know, no other function. Sufficient physical stimulation of the clitoris alone will produce orgasm in nearly all women. For this reason, many have thought that contact between the penis and clitoris is the only important factor in achieving orgasm. Operations have been performed to provide greater exposure of the clitoris. Yet such surgery does not help to attain orgasm and it is apt to cause other problems—for instance, the development of scar tissue, which occurs in any operative procedure. Removal of the

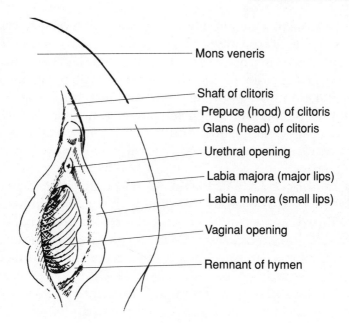

Mons veneris

Shaft of clitoris
Prepuce (hood) of clitoris
Glans (head) of clitoris

Urethral opening

Labia majora (major lips)

Labia minora (small lips)

Vaginal opening

Remnant of hymen

Figure 5
Vulva or external female organs (external genitalia)

The area between the urethral opening and the upper shaft of
the clitoris is the most sexually sensitive region of a woman's
body. During arousal, the labia minora swell and the size of
the vaginal opening decreases.

clitoral hood exposes the clitoris to trauma, and direct contact with
it is likely to bring more discomfort than pleasure.

If sexual stimulation causes pain in the clitoris, there may be
some rock-hard particles of dried secretion (smegma) beneath
some adhesions of the prepuce. These particles can be easily
removed, using a small metal probe, and the adhesions will be released. This is a simple procedure done in the doctor's office, not
usually requiring even a local anesthetic. Minor clitoral adhesions
can be freed at home using a cotton swab, preferably following a
hot bath.

The clitoris sometimes enlarges when caressed, but there is no
need for anxiety if it does not. In a study of hundreds of women
able to reach orgasm, more than half showed no visible enlarge-

ment of the clitoris. Enlargement was only barely noticeable by either sight or touch in others. Most of the enlargement is in diameter, not in length. The size of the clitoris, or its enlargement, has nothing to do with sexual satisfaction or sexual capacity. During the latter stages of sexual arousal, the clitoris is submerged in the engorged surrounding tissues. Therefore, size is never a significant factor in reaching orgasm.

The important points to remember are:

1. The clitoris must be stimulated either directly or indirectly for the wife to achieve orgasm.
2. The basic physiologic response of orgasm is the same, no matter what the method of stimulation.
3. Women often report a subjective difference in feelings produced by the clitoral orgasm and feelings produced by the orgasm achieved during vaginal stimulation.

The essential anatomical fact a couple must learn is the exact location of the clitoris. This can be most precisely determined during the time of sexual arousal by sensitively placing well-lubricated fingertips alongside the shaft of the clitoris, as it extends upward onto the pelvic bone. You will be able to feel it as you move your fingers back and forth the length of the shaft. Also move your fingers across the shaft from side to side. It is similar to rolling your fingers across a very small telephone cord. Persistent, loving, gentle, sensitive, well-lubricated stimulation along this clitoral shaft will bring almost any wife to orgasm within three to twenty minutes. As orgasm is approached, the tempo of the stimulation needs to increase.

When the clitoris is first stimulated in foreplay, very light, gentle, slow caressing usually gives the most satisfaction. In a few seconds, the glans may become overly sensitive or even irritated, and stroking farther up on the shaft, or at the side of the shaft, will give a more pleasurable sensation. When the glans of the clitoris is feeling overly sensitive, the wife may prefer to be stimulated in an entirely different area, such as the breast or the inner thighs, before returning to stimulation of the clitoral area.

Labia minora. *Labia minora* are the Latin words for "small lips." They are two parallel folds of smooth, hairless, soft tissue that connect to the hood over the clitoris and can be most easily identified just above and beside the entrance to the vagina. At times the gentle stroking of these small lips gives a very pleasant sensation. Since these lips are connected directly above the clitoris, when the penis moves in the vagina and against these delicate lips, there is friction, tugging, and pulling, which carries sensation to the clitoris. Thus, *direct* stimulation of the clitoris is not always desired or necessary for sexual pleasure. The most consistent and easily detected physical sign of the wife's sexual arousal and readiness for intercourse is the expansion of the labia minora to two or three times their normal thickness. Expansion is detected by gentle touching with the fingers.

Labia majora. These "major lips" appear as a mound of flesh, lying outside and parallel to the labia minora. They are normally over the vaginal opening, providing protection against entrance of the penis or other objects into the unstimulated vagina. With sexual arousal, the major lips lie back and flatten, but you probably will not be able to detect this small change. They are not nearly so sensitive to stimulation as the small lips and the clitoral area.

Mons veneris. *Mons veneris* is Latin for "Mount of Venus." It is a small cushion of fat to serve as a shock absorber over the pubic symphysis (the bony prominence above the peak of the labia majora). Caresses in this area are quite pleasing.

The Menstrual Cycle

The menstrual cycle prepares, renews, and refreshes the reproductive system for thirty to forty years of a woman's life. Continuous daily activity, mostly unseen and unfelt, occurs in these organs as a result of the stimulation of the female hormones. Until recently this activity was not well understood. Today it is, and this has made possible many advances in the control of conception and in the treatment of menstrual irregularities and infertility.

Only one step of the whole cycle has always made itself plainly known: menstruation. Coming from the Latin word *mensis*, meaning month, menstruation occurs approximately monthly in most women and is the shedding of the lining of the uterus. Menstruation makes way for a new lining and is the only instance in nature where a loss of blood does not signify injury but is, instead, a sign of good health. (We might mention here that the word *menopause* has the obvious meaning of a pause in menstruation.)

Beginning the Cycle

The first day of the menstrual flow is counted as day one of the menstrual cycle. On the day that the menstrual flow starts, the inner lining of the uterine cavity has grown to be nearly twice as deep as it was after the last menstruation. The menstrual flow is caused by the shedding of this thickened lining. The shedding takes place because the body stops the supply of certain hormones. These hormones are called estrogen and progesterone.

The fully developed lining is composed of thousands of microscopically small blood vessels, with millions of cells of a soft, spongy tissue packed around them. The blood vessels act as a support and at the same time carry nourishment to the tissues. These soft tissues, rich in blood supply, have stood in readiness for the possible arrival of a fertilized egg. Had there been a fertilized egg, the supply of the one hormone, progesterone (meaning "for gestation or pregnancy"), would have continued to maintain the lining and prevent menstruation.

When the supply of hormones stops, growth of the lining stops, and within two or three days the network of tiny blood vessels begins to shrink in size. This deprives the surrounding tissues of both support and nourishment. The whole structure gradually becomes detached and small pieces of the lining start to shed. Within a few hours some of the weakened blood vessels open, first only a few at a time, then steadily increasing in number. Each tiny vessel empties its droplets. This is how the flow begins and soon increases.

The total amount of the average menstrual flow is about two to three ounces, which is only about four to six tablespoonsful of liquid. The amount may vary. For some women it may be less than an ounce; for others it may be much more.

There is no medical reason for avoiding intercourse during any part of the menstrual period. No ill effects occur from penetration by the penis, nor is menstrual blood harmful. However, if either husband or wife considers intercourse distasteful at this time, it should be avoided.

Very effective and harmless medications are now available for the mild to severe menstrual cramps that some women experience. The cramps are caused by the formation of prostaglandins, chemicals that stimulate the uterus to abnormally contract. Ask your physician for a prescription for antiprostaglandins, which prevent the development of these chemicals and thus actually prevent pain rather than simply relieving it. There is little reason to suffer from menstrual cramps today.

Mothers are sometimes concerned that the use of a tampon for menstrual hygiene will destroy a girl's virginity. Only penetration by the penis does this. Tampons are so slender that they can be inserted by most virgins without breaking or stretching the hymen. In answer to questions from mothers, no, there is no sexual stimulation from a tampon as almost all of a girl's sexually sensitive areas are well in front of and above the vaginal opening.

A more serious consideration is the occurrence of toxic shock syndrome in a few teenage girls and young married women. The United States Centers for Disease Control has connected the use of tampons with this rare but sometimes deadly infection, particularly tampons made of synthetic materials rather than cotton. This infection is caused by a staphylococcus bacteria that can grow rapidly in the blood accumulated in a tampon. In almost every case studied the tampons were not changed often enough throughout the menstrual period.

Research has indicated that the type of fibers used in Rely tampons encouraged the growth of the staphylococcus bacteria. Rely tampons were removed from the market, and no tampons are now made with that fiber. All types of tampons, however, have been associated to some extent with the development of toxic shock syndrome. It is recommended that tampons be changed at least every six to eight hours or that a pad be alternated with a tampon during menstruation and a pad used at night.

A menstruating girl or woman should be free to engage in any activity she would pursue if she were not menstruating, such as riding horseback, swimming, engaging in strenuous games, washing her hair, or bathing. A study done at the University of Illinois proved conclusively that a significant amount of water does not enter the vagina when a woman sits in a bathtub, or when she swims.

How Menstruation Stops

As soon as each area of old lining has been shed and washed away, the blood vessels in that patch return to their original size, become sealed, and are again closed. Finally, only a few patches remain to be cleared away. The flow then tapers off and ends. What had been a deep-red spongy lining is reduced to a smooth pink surface, ready for new growth. This is how menstruation begins and then ends, for the first time, in adolescence, and each time thereafter until menopause.

The Number of Days of Menstruation

The amount of the growth and shedding of the lining tends to be so consistent that most women find they always menstruate the same number of days. The average is four to five days. It is very normal for some women to menstruate only two or three days; for others—equally normal—it may be a full week or more.

The number of days between one menstrual period and the next is generally far less consistent than the number of days of flow. The average length of the cycle from day one of menstruation to day one of the next cycle is between twenty-six and thirty-two days. This is only an average, however, and almost all women occasionally vary at least two to three days; many vary by several days from time to time, and some are always quite irregular. The important factor to remember is that, throughout the years, each woman establishes her own general menstrual pattern, which becomes normal for her, but which should be expected to have some unpredictable variations at times.

One of the early signs of cancer of the cervix may be bleeding after sexual intercourse. One of the signs of cancer of the uterus may be spotting of small amounts of blood between menstrual periods. If any unusual bleeding occurs, you should report to your doctor for an examination as soon as the bleeding has been stopped for forty-eight hours.

It is important for you to wait the forty-eight hours so the cervix and vagina will not be obscured by blood and so a Pap smear or a uterine aspiration may be done. If there are fresh blood cells present, a Pap smear cannot be taken. Do not take a vaginal douche before the examination.

Premenstrual Syndrome

Premenstrual syndrome (PMS) is the name used for a variety of physical and/or emotional problems that may occur prior to a woman's menstrual period. At the same phase of each menstrual cycle, women with PMS may experience tension, depression, anxiety panic attacks, irritability, crying for no reason, fatigue, forgetfulness or mental confusion, clumsiness, and cravings for sweets, carbohydrates, salty foods, or alcohol. Other symptoms are: water retention, headaches, backaches, acne, cold sores, sinus problems, asthmatic attacks, and seizures. A woman may have only one symptom of PMS or she may have many.

Up to 90 percent of all women who menstruate have premenstrual syndrome to some degree. Approximately 10 to 12 percent of the affected women need medical treatment; 3 percent may be debilitated. For most, PMS is not too severe, but for some 20 to 30 percent, it is severe enough to cause serious disruption of their daily lives.

Women with PMS typically experience the feeling of being out of control. Tension from PMS may cause them to lash out at those around them with feelings of anger, bitterness, or resentment.

While as many as a hundred symptoms may be associated with PMS, no one symptom is unique to the syndrome. The key to determining whether or not a symptom indicates PMS is if it occurs primarily during the two-week period before the menstrual period begins. Keeping a daily calendar not only during menstruation, but for the entire cycle, is the simplest way to diagnose PMS.

No one knows exactly what causes PMS or why some women have severe symptoms while others have mild or no symptoms. Some researchers believe PMS may result from an imbalance during the last half of the menstrual cycle between the hormones estrogen and progesterone. Others think that nutritional factors may play a role. It seems probable that PMS has a variety of causes, which may explain the variety of symptoms and the fact that women experience PMS differently. PMS can appear in menstruating women of any age. It is most common during the later twenties and thirties. Some women first experience PMS after pregnancy or after they stop taking birth control pills.

PMS is not a character disorder. The symptoms that occur with PMS do not mean that a woman is weak or unstable or that she has lost touch with God. These symptoms are a result of physical changes, not an emotional or spiritual weakness. It is important for women to realize that PMS is not a sign that their body is abnormal but evidence that the hormones in their body are working.

Becoming aware of your own body and its unique reactions to your monthly cycle is the first step in dealing with PMS. Use this knowledge to effectively handle your emotions during menstruation. Understanding your body and how your hormones, diet, exercise, emotions, and spiritual life are interconnected helps reduce the stress associated with PMS. The importance of nonmedical treatment for PMS—limiting salt, sugar, caffeine; increasing exercise; and using certain vitamins regularly—should also be carefully considered. New research has shown that women who have four or more cups of a caffeinated drink per day may have five times the PMS symptoms. Making changes in your lifestyle is fundamental to reducing PMS symptoms. If these changes in diet and exercise fail to bring relief, there are some medications that may help. Taking a prostaglandin inhibitor, such as ibuprofen, one or two days before your period may reduce some symptoms. Natural progesterones have also been recommended for many women with PMS. Oral micronized progesterone is now available, as well. The usual dose of micronized progesterone is 100 milligrams a day but it can be increased to 300 milligrams a day or more if necessary. Progesterone produces a sedative effect, which may be its major contribution in helping PMS symptoms. There are a host of other medications that are being used to reduce symptoms, so check with your obstetrician/gynecologist for recommendations.

Following the recommendations outlined above and incorporating them into your lifestyle will be the start to living effectively with PMS and to maintaining better health in general.

Premenstrual Syndrome Considerations for Men

PMS is not easily predictable, and symptoms are rarely the same each month. But it does arrive about the same time each month, which allows men the opportunity to prepare for some shifts in emotions and moods. It is especially important not to tease or be condescending in any way. Many men make the mistake of blaming any of their wife's mood changes solely on PMS. They make remarks such as, "Isn't it that time of the month?" Derogatory remarks will not reduce the emotional tension. In fact they will more than likely make more unpleasant the already difficult period.

What will help is general kindness and a special sensitivity. Favorable remarks about your wife's appearance and increased physical touching in a nonsexual way will also be most pleasing. Help your mate reduce stressful situations and help with domestic duties. Criticism is certainly out of order and may be viewed as an all-out attack. Recognize that your wife's insecurity may be at a high level and affirm your love and commitment whenever it is appropriate to do so. Try to make your mate as comfortable emotionally and physically as is within your power.

PMS doesn't give a wife the right to be mean. She is responsible for her behavior and attitudes. But extra kindness and consideration will most likely help take the edge off her emotions, and this approach is the right and responsible thing to do. Listen closely to the things she says and try to help accommodate those special needs, which may vary or change from month to month. Remember you are building your relationship for a lifetime, so invest wisely with kind acts, wisdom, and patience.

Conception and Pregnancy

Fertilization takes place in the shelter of a mother's oviduct, which is the tube that leads from the ovary to the womb. This is the meeting ground for the successful union of the female egg and the male sperm cell.

Egg and Sperm

The round egg of the female is the largest single human cell, yet it is smaller than a dot (·). The male spermatozoon, sperm for short, is similar in shape to a comma (,). It is much smaller than the egg, so much smaller that 2,500 would be needed to cover a comma—and all the sperm needed to repopulate the world could be fitted into an aspirin tablet! The egg is so much larger because it is laden with food to sustain a growing embryo in its first few days. The relatively cumbersome egg is motionless, but the sperm is agile. With the lashing of its hair-fine tail, a sperm cell can propel itself ahead about one inch in eight minutes, which, for its size, is a much better speed than an athlete can match. At that speed, a sperm may reach the egg in an hour to an hour and a half. By way of comparison, an athlete would have to run 70 miles per hour for 250 miles to approximate the speed and distance traveled by a sperm.

Egg and sperm come together from opposite directions. At ovulation the immobile egg is thrust out of the ovary in a gently rising spring of fluids and is swept up by the fingerlike fringes (fimbriae) into the oviduct opening. It must be fertilized within twenty-four hours or it will disintegrate.

During this time, the egg will be in the midportion of the oviduct. The sperm may be waiting there or may arrive after the egg. Sperm cells have a longer life span than the egg. They stay alive and vigorous for two to three days and, according to some evidence, may survive even much longer. Sperm do not have to arrive exactly at the time of ovulation. They may arrive some hours before it, or after it, providing an approximate total of three to five days in each monthly cycle during which conception can occur (see figure 6).

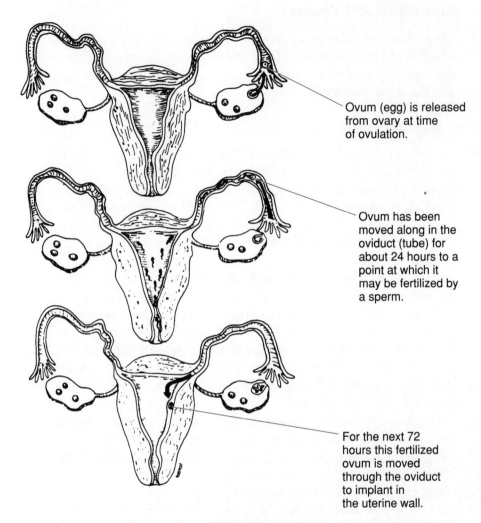

Ovum (egg) is released
from ovary at time
of ovulation.

Ovum has been
moved along in the
oviduct (tube) for
about 24 hours to a
point at which it
may be fertilized by
a sperm.

For the next 72
hours this fertilized
ovum is moved
through the oviduct
to implant in
the uterine wall.

Figure 6
The process of fertilization

When the egg is thrust out of the ovary in a gently rising spring of
fluids, it is swept up by the fingerlike fringes (fimbriae) of the
oviduct and carried along the tube. Note that the oviduct is not
attached to the ovary in any way; yet the tiny egg is miraculously
carried into the place where it can meet the sperm.

In sexual intercourse, the sperm are ejected in a somewhat force-ful fine stream that normally aims at the narrow entrance of the cervix and finds entry most readily at the time of ovulation, when the normally dense mucus at the entrance to the cervix is thinner and more fluid.

Fertilization of the Egg

Millions of sperm begin the journey, but a comparative few reach the tiny egg in the oviduct. Some sperm attach to the mem-brane, which covers the egg, and activate it, so that finally one sperm may enter and fertilize.

The one sperm that enters the egg loses its tail, which is ab-sorbed, and its head proceeds on through the food-rich substance of the egg. This one tiny sperm carries the father's threads of inheri-tance to the egg's center, where the mother's threads of inheri-tance lie. These chromosomes contain thousands of smaller units called genes that specify the inherited characteristics of the child. The male sperm carries the sex-determining chromosome. In a few hours, the threads of inheritance of the two parents become knitted together. In a few hours, the fertilized egg begins to divide and goes on to become a cluster of bubblelike cells.

The Nine Months of Pregnancy

By the end of the first week, the cell cluster comes to rest in the upper part of the uterus, where it clings and takes root. The nest-ing cluster finds nourishment in the lining of the uterus, prepared during the menstrual cycle. Toward the end of the second week, the cluster begins to form an embryo. Production by the woman's body of pituitary hormones is inhibited, so that ovulation is now suppressed, the lining of the uterus is maintained, and menstru-ation is postponed for the duration of the pregnancy.

During the first two months of pregnancy, the mother's breasts will enlarge and begin to be tender as a result of the change in the hormone level in her body. Morning sickness may occur tem-porarily. After about the twenty-seventh day, the placenta, the so-called afterbirth, which is attached to the lining of the uterus and is linked to the embryo by the umbilical cord, starts a variety of functions necessary to maintain the pregnancy. One of these functions is the production of the hormone chorionic gonadotropin. Since chorionic gonadotropin rises to a high level for a short period of time, its detection in urine serves as a test for pregnancy. This test can be performed in a few minutes with a high degree of accuracy. (This is the simple test that you can now do yourself with a kit purchased at your pharmacy.) Another function of the placenta is the production of progesterone. It takes over this important job as the ovary stops secreting progesterone. This hormone from the placenta is vitally important in maintaining the pregnant uterus and equally important in preventing the ovaries from developing another mature egg.

Quietly a tremendous change is taking place. The whole embryo is being formed from head to toe. Every feature and every vital organ starts to form in the first two months. The heart begins to beat on about the twenty-second day but it is still so small that it cannot be heard easily for another four to five months. At the end of the first month, the embryo is only about the size of a small pea. By the end of the second month, it is about one inch long and nearly weightless. At this time the embryo is called the fetus. It can move the arms and legs, turn the head, open and close the mouth, and swallow.

In the last three months of pregnancy, the reproductive system becomes stretched to its limits in size and in capacity for supplying nourishment. The baby gains about five to six additional pounds, some of it as a padding of fat. From the maternal bloodstream the baby also accumulates essential immunities to diseases. Its lungs mature, and its strength and coordination improve.

The uterus has now increased its capacity about five hundred times. In the ninth month a little understood chemical reaction occurs, which causes profound changes in the great muscles of the uterus. This is called labor. In the first stage of labor, the muscles of the uterus exert a force of about fifty pounds per square inch to push the baby out through the cervix. The narrow opening of the cervix gradually expands to let the baby's head and body pass through. Next, the baby's body stretches the walls of the vagina and reaches the light of day.

Birth

Birth is remarkable—all the more so because the reproductive organs, having performed an enormous task, very soon return to their former size and functions. Within about a month they are ready to begin again. The first ovulation after delivery is likely to occur about this time. Although nursing may hasten the return of the reproductive organs to their original size and may delay menstruation, it will not always prevent ovulation, as many people believe. Therefore, conception can occur before the first menstrual period after delivery. Most often the first period occurs about six weeks after delivery. This is about the time the new mother should return to her physician for her six weeks examination.

Immediately after the birth of a baby, the mother has a great drop in her estrogen level, for there is almost no estrogen produced by her ovaries. During pregnancy most of the estrogen was being produced by the placenta, which is no longer present. Some new mothers may feel very depressed after the birth of their babies because of this lowered estrogen level. Nursing also suppresses the production of estrogen, and if the baby continues to nurse for several months, thinning of the vaginal lining may result. This thin vaginal lining is like senile vaginitis older women develop in the menopausal years. A thin vaginal lining causes painful intercourse and requires the use of estrogen cream, placed up inside the vagina once or twice daily, until a few weeks after the baby stops nursing. During this time if there is any discomfort, do not neglect to use ample artificial lubrication before every sexual union.

The Male Reproductive System

To aid in understanding the anatomy of the male sex organs, please refer to the accompanying drawings (figures 7 and 8). There are three basic male sex organs:

1. The *penis,* with its glands and tissues
2. The *testicles,* also called the gonads or sex glands
3. The *prostate gland,* and *seminal vesicles*

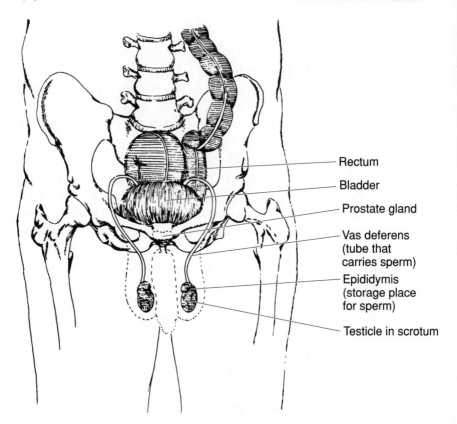

Figure 7
Front view of male reproductive system

In this view of the reproductive organs, notice the relationship
between them, paying special attention to the vas deferens and
its ready accessibility in the scrotum. It can be squeezed
between thumb and fingers and feels like a small cord. A section
of it may be easily removed in the vasectomy operation.

Penis. The most obvious fact about the penis is that it can be
distended with blood under mental or physical stimulus, so that
it becomes stiff or erect. The penis is made up of three columns
of spongy erectile tissue—the middle one containing the urethra.
The head of the penis is called the glans and is very sensitive to
touch. The glans contains many nerve endings, which help build
orgasmic tensions during sexual contact.

At birth the glans is covered by a fold of skin called the prepuce or foreskin. The foreskin requires special care to keep it clean and prevent accumulation of a greasy secretion called smegma. If the foreskin is too tight, it may interfere with erection and intercourse. For these reasons, the practice of circumcision shortly after birth has grown in popularity as a hygienic measure. Circumcision is the cutting off of enough foreskin to leave the glans exposed.

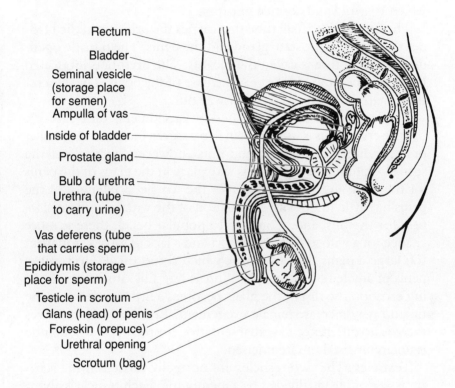

Rectum
Bladder
Seminal vesicle
(storage place
for semen)
Ampulla of vas
Inside of bladder
Prostate gland
Bulb of urethra
Urethra (tube
to carry urine)
Vas deferens (tube
that carries sperm)
Epididymis (storage
place for sperm)
Testicle in scrotum
Glans (head) of penis
Foreskin (prepuce)
Urethral opening
Scrotum (bag)

Figure 8
Side view of male reproductive system

Semen (the seminal fluid) is manufactured and stored in the prostate gland and the seminal vesicles where contractions force it into the urethra at the time of ejaculation. As you can see, any enlargement (hypertrophy) of the prostate gland may interfere with the flow of urine from the bladder.

For many years some peoples, by custom or religion, have practiced circumcision. It is interesting to note that this is the only
surgical operation mentioned in the Bible. About four thousand
years ago, God commanded that the operation be done on the
eighth day after birth. It is only in the last few decades that it has
been found that the eighth day is when blood-clotting and in-
fection-preventing factors are the most favorable in a baby's life.
Today, however, the timing of this operation is not as critical,
because we have modern surgical instruments and drugs with
which to avoid and control infection.

The urethra is a small tube that carries the urine from the bladder through the prostate gland and the penis. The outside opening of the urethra is called the meatus. The urethra is lubricated
by secretions from glands near the base of the penis. These secretions help the sperm make their way out.

The length of the unstimulated or flaccid penis varies greatly,
but the erect penis is usually from five to seven inches long. Smaller
or larger dimensions are not abnormal, however. Practically all the
sexually stimulating sensations take place in the glans of the penis
for the male and in the clitoris for the female. So, length of the
penis has little to do with stimulation of the wife or with satisfaction for the husband. Contrary to popular belief, there is more
chance for a wife to feel discomfort and a lack of satisfaction from
too large a penis than from one which is too small. However, a
penis of any length is capable of providing full satisfaction. During erection the rim of the glans becomes a little harder than the
tip and may increase female excitement. Recent research proves
there is no difference in sexual sensation for the male, whether he
is uncircumcised or circumcised.

Testicles. The two testicles are normally carried in the scrotum—a double sac divided by a membrane. Each testicle is about
the size and shape of the female ovary. Its main structure is a mass
of tiny, coiled tubes in which the male reproductive cells, called
sperm cells, are produced. The new sperm move off into other
small tubes that cover one side of the testicle in a bundle. This
bundle is called the epididymis. Then the sperm are carried to the
prostate gland in a larger and longer tube—the vas deferens—

which takes a roundabout course through the inside of the pelvis—about eighteen inches in all.

In performing a vasectomy for sterilization of the husband, a one- to two-inch section of each vas deferens is removed (see figure 9). This operation is described in chapter 11.

The vas from each testicle broadens out into a seed reservoir, or ampulla, just before it enters the prostate. Opening off these reservoirs are the seminal vesicles—large pouches on each side and behind the prostate. These fill with sperm and act both as storerooms and as a physical reminder of the need for sexual relief.

While in the storeroom, the sperm cells are joined by a lubricating prostatic secretion that helps them do their next job—swimming. Other similar secretions are added to make up the final seminal fluid, as the seed take the next step in their journey. During the sexual climax—the ejaculation—the fluid is forced from the storerooms through small tubes that meet in the ejaculatory duct, just before entering the base of the penis. The muscular contractions that take place in the prostate gland force the seminal fluid past the base of the penis, then through the urethral canal, and out the meatus (the outside opening of the urethra). This fluid, called semen, usually is projected forcefully enough to travel twelve to twenty-four inches after it leaves the penis. The contraction of the prostate gland provides much of the pleasant sensation of sexual climax.

Prostate. The prostate gland, approximately the size of a walnut, is located at the base of the urinary bladder. This gland literally encircles the urethra, the tube emptying the bladder, which is the only exit for urine from the bladder. Because of the intimate anatomic relationship between the prostate, the bladder neck, and the urethra, a benign enlargement of the prostate poses a concern regarding various degrees of bladder outflow obstruction. As we age, the prostate enlarges so that a man in his sixties and seventies will generally have a prostate two to three times the size of a man in his twenties and thirties. Due to the benign enlargement of the prostate, the amount of sperm often decreases and becomes more watery in consistency. In addition, the ejaculate exits the penis with much less force than in younger men.

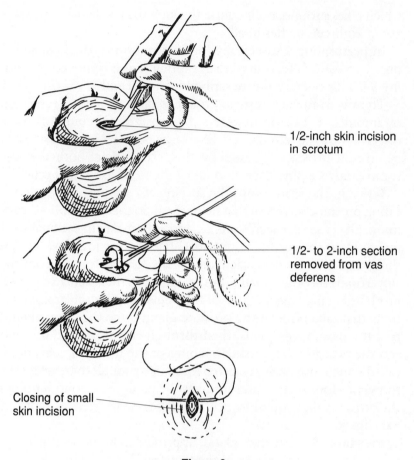

1/2-inch skin incision
in scrotum

1/2- to 2-inch section
removed from vas
deferens

Closing of small
skin incision

Figure 9
Diagram of vasectomy operation

A small amount of local anesthetic is injected into the skin of
the scrotum before the incision is made. This operation is
usually performed in the physician's office.

Many times enlargement of the prostate does not pose a problem. If the size of the prostate is such that the outflow tract, the
urethra, is compressed, however, there will be varying degrees of
urinary symptoms, such as a decreased stream and decreased frequency and urgency of urination. For most of this century this condition was treated with surgery, a prostatectomy (removal of the

prostate gland). Within the last several years, however, there are several medications that are extremely effective in minimizing voiding symptoms. These medications often preclude the need for surgery. Nevertheless, sometimes surgery is required and this is often done through the penis, an operation called transurethral resection of the prostate (TURP). Very often, after this operation, the man will experience a dry ejaculate. This happens because much of the seminal fluid comes from secretions of the prostate gland and during the TURP procedure, the gland is literally cored out so there is much less tissue to produce seminal fluid. In addition, the bladder neck region is resected and the seminal fluid that does enter the urethra will first enter the bladder in a retrograde fashion, rather than exiting directly through the penis. This will not interfere with the individual's ability to obtain an erection or experience orgasm; however, it will generally render a man sterile.

Pregnancies may be achieved through retrieval of sperm sequestered in the bladder following intercourse. Erectile dysfunction or impotence is very rare following transurethral surgery of the prostate and is more common following radical removal of the prostate, which is reserved for cancer of the prostate. Recent surgical techniques, however, have allowed the preservation of potency in 60 to 70 percent of the cases undergoing radical prostatectomy.

Prostatitis is an inflammatory condition of the prostate that can be caused by bacteria and nonbacterial agents. Often this will cause a temporary decrease in sex drive and in erectile ability. The bacterial prostatitis may require several months of antibiotic therapy to eradicate. Symptoms include low back pain, pelvic pressure, urethral discharge, and diminished libido (sexual desire). The prostate is tense and very tender, and often the male feels like he's "sitting on a hot potato." Conservative treatment measures are appropriate, consisting of antibiotics, very hot Sitz baths, and more frequent intercourse in an attempt to milk the prostate gland. Passive congestion of the prostate due to a buildup of seminal fluid because of prolonged intervals between emissions can produce prostatitis and its associated symptoms.

Prostate cancer generally has no symptoms and is discovered during the course of a digital-rectal examination and/or a periph-

eral blood sample that shows an elevation in prostate-specific anti-
gen (PSA).

The condition called hematospermia, which is blood in the
semen, is generally a benign condition due to small calcifications
occurring in the prostate gland and generally is not the harbinger
of anything serious.

Semen. Just past the prostate are the two openings of the glands
that secrete mucus to lubricate the urinary canal for easy movement of the semen during ejaculation. Some of this lubricating
fluid may escape from the penis during the erection before orgasm.
The fluid, with the secretions from the female vagina, helps provide easier entry of the penis into the vagina. This oozing during
excitement is natural and beneficial and does not mean that semen
is being "lost," nor is it a sign of sexual weakness or venereal disease. However, you must be careful, as there may be enough sperm
in this small amount of lubricating fluid to produce a pregnancy.
This is one of the reasons the withdrawing of the penis from the
vagina just before ejaculation is not an effective means of birth
control.

The semen is primarily protein, similar to egg white, and is not
dirty or unsanitary despite its distinctive odor. I do not advise a
vaginal douche after intercourse, but a few women may produce
a large amount of lubricating fluid, which when mixed with the
semen produces enough discharge material to be a problem. These
women may desire to douche after intercourse. Inserting a tampon a few minutes after intercourse or keeping a small hand towel
at the bedside are other easy solutions to the problem.

Male/Female Similarities

As we conclude this section on physiology, it is interesting to
realize that the female and the male sex organs develop out of the
same structures. The most obvious of these similar structures are
the clitoris and the penis. The clitoris repeats—reduced and modified—the chief elements of the male penis. The spongy tissues of
the clitoris that engorge with blood are similar to the glans of the
penis with its numerous nerve endings and great sensitivity. The
muscles at the base of the penis are repeated in the pubococcygeus

(P.C.) muscles surrounding the vagina. The female major lips are the counterpart of the male scrotum. In some degree, the meeting of the outer folds of the inner lips over the clitoris corresponds to the foreskin over the glans of the penis.

It is clear that the sex organs, both male and female, have other functions besides the propagation of the race. Even before the human being is fully mature and able to reproduce, the sexual glands (the ovaries in the female and the testes in the male) have begun their work of making a woman or making a man, as they manufacture some of the hormones that encourage and control the rate of physical development, mental growth, and psychological maturation.

As we describe sex technique and response in the next few chapters, you will appreciate the reason for this detailed study of the anatomy of the sex organs.

Three Physiological Phases

It is now known, thanks to the work of Dr. Helen Singer Kaplan and others, that the entire experience of sexual response involves three phases that are interlocking—but separate and distinguishable. This finding has been of great help in treating sexual disorders and solving sexual problems. The three physiological phases are *desire, excitement,* and *orgasm.* To use Dr. Helen Kaplan's metaphor, these three phases have a common generator but they each have their own separate circuitry. In other words, they are interconnected but governed by three separate neurophysiological systems.

Dr. Kaplan explains in her book *Disorders of Sexual Desire:*

> Sexual desire is an appetite or drive which is produced by the activation of a specific neural system in the brain, while the excitement and orgasm phases involve the genital organs. In both males and females the excitement phase is produced by the reflex vasodilatation of genital blood vessels. By contrast, orgasm essentially consists of reflex contractions of certain genital muscles. These two genital reflexes are served by separate reflex centers in the lower spinal cord.

An inhibiting switch may turn off any one of these physical responses in your system. Therapists are now trying to determine and treat specific causes of inhibition in each phase. One set of causes may inhibit orgasm. Another type of conflict may hinder erection. An altogether different group of variables may interfere with sexual desire (libido). The problem of low libido is the most difficult to treat, but therapists are making progress in this area.

In my own experience as a sex therapist and family doctor, most of the cases I have seen of inhibited sexual desire have one root cause: repressed anger and resentment that have led to depression and a chilly indifference toward the marriage partner. This indifference is most easily expressed through a disinterest in sex. In such cases, wrongs on both sides must be confessed and righted, and love must be restored to the marriage.

Love is always the truly magic ingredient that brings meaning and pleasure to sexual activity.

5

One Flesh
The Techniques of Lovemaking

Within the intimacy of their marriage and in the privacy of their bedroom, man and woman gradually learn the meaning of the Genesis pronouncement: "They shall be one flesh."

Please note that this is a *learning* process, with husband and wife progressively discovering how to provide pleasure for each other. They begin with some explicit information (the more the better); then with growing delight, they find out by experience and application of information just how to make love and impart maximum joy to their mate.

Several hindrances have blocked this learning process in the past. First of all, young couples were brainwashed by the romantic novels and movies that suggested that "it all comes naturally." Then many people have been defensive about their knowledge and skills as lovers, feeling that they must pretend to know it all or else admit to personal deficiencies.

Today more and more couples are seeking Christian counsel in the area of the sex relationship, because they do not want to depend on the trial-and-error process, which may or may not lead to satisfaction. They are beginning to understand that the Lord has designed blessing and pleasure for them and they do not want to miss out.

The first reason for marriage, according to Scripture, is companionship: "It is not good that the man should be alone" (Gen. 2:18). God designed marriage to keep people from being alone. If in any area—spiritual, psychological, or physical—the man and wife are not one with each other, then they are *alone* in that part of their life. Some Christian couples may be beautifully related in one mind and one spirit; they may have a good marriage in many ways, but their marriage remains incomplete and unfulfilled if they do not know how to please each other in the intimacy of their physical relationship.

Detailed how-to books on sex are readily available these days so that a great deal of information is at hand. Unfortunately these publications are sometimes medically erroneous and often crude and distasteful in presentation. Worst of all, they miss the mark for the Christian reader, who realizes that much more than a selfish seeking of physical sensation is involved. The discerning lover approaches the experience, knowing that the keenest pleasure comes from the exquisite joy of pleasing the beloved.

The act of love is experienced as a single ecstatic episode by the two involved, but medically it can be analyzed and divided into four phases, which reflect the physical changes that occur. Before we discuss them, let us consider the physical environment most conducive to a meaningful relationship. Most important is your need for privacy. In considering buying or building a home, you should pay close attention to having your bedroom and bath as isolated as possible from other rooms. Every master bedroom needs a good lock, controlled from the inside, of course. Every child should be trained not to disturb his mother and daddy when their bedroom door is locked. If a couple is to concentrate totally on each other (which is necessary for maximum enjoyment), they must be assured of protection from intrusion. Under no circumstances should you allow a child to sleep in the room with you, except perhaps a new baby for the first six months or less.

The question of lighting in the bedroom should also be considered. Some wives are better able to abandon themselves to maximum expression of enjoyment by having sexual intercourse in a room with very little or no light. However, the husband is greatly stimulated by seeing his wife's body and watching her responsive movements and expressions of delight. For this reason, you may wish to vary your settings between darkness and very soft light, even candlelight. Remember that the mystery of the body enhances the lovemaking experience.

Phase I: Arousal

This time of sexual stimulation, often called foreplay, can be delightful for both husband and wife, if the husband realizes that his tender skill at this point will prepare his wife for the love act itself. Most women like to be wooed and won. Let the man indicate by the way he approaches his wife that he is demonstrating his love for her, not claiming sex as his right. The husband must be careful not to appear hurried, crude, rude, mechanical, or impatient!

Sexual intercourse can be a joyful affirmation of the life two people share, or it can be a revelation of defects in their relationship. It will either draw a couple together or push them apart. Because your sexual relationship will tend to reflect your emotional relationship, it is important to realize that every meaningful, fully enjoyable sex act really begins with a loving, attentive attitude hours or even days before. Husband, you should be aware that your wife views the sex act as part of her total relationship with you, even though you, like other men, may think of it separately. When both partners assume the responsibility for giving of their total selves—physically, emotionally, and spiritually—sexual interaction becomes a dynamic way of fully expressing love for each other. *It is your daily behavior toward each other* that will measure the extent and depth of the pleasure you find in making love sexually.

Before beginning sex play, a bath or shower will show one's mate how important the event of physical unity is. When married, bathing at night before getting into bed makes good sense. When, during the day, will you be in as intimate contact with anyone as you are during the night when sleeping with your spouse? Bathing and shaving at night will show love, respect, and an anticipation of closeness.

Relaxed love play begins with kissing, embracing, petting, and fondling. The most effective touching for both man and wife in

the early part of sex play is a gentle caressing of *all* the body. All
includes everything and excludes nothing. Do not touch only
those areas that seem directly related to excitement. Your partner
may enjoy caresses on the inner thighs, the lower back and buttocks, the earlobes, or the back of the neck. Caressing varied areas
shows an interest in the whole person. As Solomon said, "Thou
art all fair, my love; there is no spot in thee" (Song of Sol. 4:7).
And his wife, the Shulamite maid, said of Solomon, "He is altogether lovely. This is my beloved, and this is my friend" (5:16).

Caressing each other should *never* be hurried. Only lust and
self-gratification are done in haste. Take the time to fully enjoy
each other! It is important to understand the timing of lovemaking. There should be a gradual building and intensifying of emotions and sensations. Do not stop or let up the stimulation once
begun, but continue in an ever-increasing arousal. During this
phase, a long hug or any period of stillness will serve to slow or
reverse sexual tensions, especially for the wife. The movement of
thigh against thigh, her breasts against his chest, and stroking each
other's back and shoulders are much more exciting than a clinging hug. Each part of the body moving against the spouse's body
will greatly heighten sexual tensions.

The union of marriage frees the couple to enjoy their bodies in
whatever ways are most pleasing, provided that both are being
pleased. Without restrictions (other than selfish acts that hurt the
partner or evoke distaste), the couple should feel free to experiment and to "know" each other in the most intimate sense possible. Love involves close bodily contact and the pleasure of seeing, touching, and enjoying with all the senses. Let this be your
guide in love play.

The very first sign of sexual arousal in the husband is erection
of the penis. This occurs within a few seconds after being triggered
by caressing, a stimulating sight, or an erotic train of thought. If
the stimulation continues, he progresses into the second phase after
only one or two minutes. But this second phase needs to be prolonged for ten to twenty minutes or more, if he is to receive maximum pleasure from orgasm. Erections will wax and wane during
a leisurely lovemaking experience, so that the wife may need to

occasionally fondle the underside of the shaft and the glans of the penis to keep the erection full.

Lubrication of the vagina within seconds may occur in the wife. This is only a beginning sign of arousal for her and does not signify readiness for intercourse. During this first phase, the inner two-thirds of the vagina begins to expand, and if the penis is introduced at this time, the woman may receive little sensation and the man may have less feeling of containment. It is not until the second phase that the lower vagina is prepared to grip the penis.

Phase II: Time of Increasing Excitement

Following the arousal phase, a gradual and not well-defined transition into the second phase occurs. This is often called the plateau stage. After the preliminary period of stroking the entire body, the husband may enjoy fondling his wife's breasts, and she may enjoy his caresses and kisses on the nipple area. At first, the nipple becomes more firm and stands out from the breast; then as excitement increases, the nipple may appear to be somewhat hidden by the swelling of surrounding tissues. This surrounding engorgement helps guard the sensitive nipple from excessive stimulation.

A gentle caressing of the genitalia will greatly increase sexual excitement at this point. Be creative and imaginative rather than rough, blundering, or predictable in your approach. Always remember that stirring the imagination helps bring about the most response in both men and women. Anything is permissible as long as it is desired by both partners, affords mutual pleasure, and does not offend either partner. The Scriptures tell us that the joyous sexual expression of love between husband and wife is God's plan. Hebrews 13:4 proclaims the fact that the marriage union is honorable and the bed undefiled. The word translated *bed* in the Greek New Testament is actually *coitus,* the word meaning sexual intercourse.

Song of Solomon (2:6 and 8:3) describes a position ideal for intensified love play. "His left hand is under my head, and his right hand doth embrace me," the bride says. (The Hebrew word translated *embrace* usually means to embrace lovingly, to fondle or stimulate with gentle stroking.) In this position, the wife lies on her back with her legs extended, comfortably separated, and her husband lies down on her right side, placing his left arm under her neck. In this way he can kiss her lips, neck, and breasts, and at the same time his right hand is free to fondle her genitals.

As excitement continues to rise, the clitoris swells and the labia minora (inner lips) at the entrance to the vagina become two or three times enlarged. The swelling and engorgement of the lower vagina reduces the diameter of the outer one-third of the vagina as much as 50 percent, which prepares the vagina to actually grip the penis. When the inner lips change color from bright red to deep wine or from pink to bright red, this indicates that orgasm will occur within sixty to ninety seconds, if effective stimulation continues. Other responses may be tensing of muscles, increased pulse rate, and a general flush of the skin, especially over the upper abdomen and the chest. There may be almost spastic contraction of some sets of muscles in the face, chest, abdomen, and buttocks. Voluntary tightening of the sphincter muscle, which holds the anus closed, and some voluntary contractions of the muscles of the buttocks may help heighten sexual tension.

While the man learns to control the timing of his response, the wife should learn to let herself go, trust her husband, trust her own body, and be as free as possible. As she concentrates on her physical feelings, she should learn to communicate her level of sexual excitement to her husband with looks, touches, and sometimes loving words. This helps the husband to properly time his lovemaking. One of the most common sources of sexual unhappiness is the failure of a woman to tell her husband frankly and clearly what stimulates her and when she is ready for a particular stimulation.

While the husband's caresses of the wife's genitalia are essential to bring on the wife's orgasm, the wife's caresses of the husband's genitals do not usually speed up the male orgasm. While excitement has been building in both partners, when the wife actually touches the husband's genitals, it is soothing and comforting to him.

The wife's very light gentle caressing should center around the inner thighs, the scrotum, and the under surface of the penile shaft. Stimulation here will help maintain the husband's erection. Touching of the scrotum should be very light, since the scrotum is quite pressure sensitive. Fondling the head of the penis and the frenulum on the underside of the penile shaft will greatly increase the husband's excitement but may also trigger ejaculation more quickly than desired. By fondling and lovingly touching her husband's genitals, the wife soothes him and quiets his responses, while her own excitement builds.

The clitoris, rather than the vagina, is the center of feminine response, and its stimulation will produce orgasm in almost all women. Increase of arousal will come from manual play at and alongside the clitoris more often than from placing fingers in the vagina. As excitement progresses in the wife, the shaft of the clitoris will enlarge and become firmer. The firm clitoris usually can be felt at the peak of the surrounding lips above the vagina. Before sexual excitement, it is very difficult even to find the shaft of the clitoris, and it is important to note that in 50 percent of women there is no discernible enlargement of the clitoris during sexual arousal.

If the husband has given his wife enough stimulation to build excitement, some natural lubrication may be brought to the outside from within the vagina. A well-lubricated clitoris will be much more sexually responsive to the husband's touch. If the wife does not produce enough natural lubricant, some artificial lubricant may be used to lubricate the clitoris and vaginal opening. (Be careful to warm the artificial lubricant by holding the tube, bottle, or applicator in warm, running water before you go to bed.) Applying the lubrication can in itself be exciting to the wife, as it shows her husband's tender care for her. Trying to stimulate a dry clitoris or inserting a penis into a dry, tense vagina indicates lack of understanding or selfishness and should be avoided. Clitoral sensitivity in some women increases to the point where direct stimulation may become unpleasant (too much!) or even irritating. Therefore, movement of the husband's fingers should be directed to the area immediately around the clitoris. A consistent and persistent movement of the husband's fingers alongside the shaft of the clitoris is usually most effective in heightening her excitement.

When the labia minora on each side of the vaginal opening engorge or swell, the husband receives an important clue as to how far along his wife is in her arousal. These inner lips may so engorge that they protrude beyond the outer lips. The husband can only judge when this occurs by learning how to detect it with the tips of his fingers, as he stimulates his wife. This swelling of the inner lips is the most easily observable physical sign, telling the husband that his wife is ready for insertion of the penis. Although this is one sign of readiness, the husband should never insert his penis until the wife signals him to do so. The penis is always inserted in the most gentle way, never followed immediately with vigorous thrusting, as this usually decreases arousal in the woman. Most couples have found that it is very useful for the wife to insert the penis. She knows exactly where it should go. This will avoid interruption at this very important time. Even after entrance of the penis, she may still need light caressing of the clitoris to increase excitement to orgasm. It is estimated that 30 percent of women always require manual stimulation of the clitoris to achieve orgasm.

Positioning of the couple's bodies should suit their own individuality. There need be no set patterns, although early in marriage, the bride, not having had her tissues stretched from childbearing, may find that some angles of penile insertion will cause discomfort. After several children have been born, the tissues around the vagina will be stretched, and the wife will then be more comfortable in varied positions. Remember, changing of positions may restore interest and encourage excitement, but these new positions must be comfortable and pleasing for both husband and wife. It is worth noting that the right rhythm of movement is just as important as the right position in attaining a satisfactory response for both partners.

The *male-above position* is by far the most commonly used and gives the husband freedom of movement plus greatest control of strength and rapidity of thrusting. Many couples consider this the most satisfying of all positions. The wife lies on her back with legs extended, comfortably separated. The husband lies on top of her, supporting some of his weight on arms or elbows, his legs inside hers. After insertion of the penis, her legs may be moved farther apart, closer together, inside his, or wrapped around his legs or up over his body.

To assume the *female-above position* the husband lies on his back, while the wife straddles his body and leans forward. *She* inserts the penis at about a 45-degree angle and moves back on the shaft, rather than sitting down on it. She then assumes whatever posture is most stimulating and comfortable to her. This position allows the wife by her movements to control the exact timing and degree of thrusting that affords her the most sexual response. The placement of each partner's legs will govern deeper or less deep penetration of the penis, depending on what is preferred. The female-above position gives the husband access to her breasts. He also has free use of his hands to better stimulate the clitoris, if necessary, while they are joined in sexual intercourse. This position is often advantageous for a large husband and a small wife, and is sometimes more comfortable as the abdomen enlarges during pregnancy.

The *lateral,* or *side-by-side position* is assumed by starting intercourse in the female-above position. The wife leans forward and shifts her body slightly to the right, placing her right leg between her husband's legs. Her left leg is then flexed over his right leg. Advantages of the lateral position are that each partner has at least one hand free for fondling and caressing. Each is free to thrust or rotate hips. Neither has to support weight with hands and legs and neither is being "pinned" by the body weight of the other.

The *male-behind position* is seldom used but may be tried on occasion and may also be used during late pregnancy. Both husband and wife lie on their sides facing the same direction with the husband in back of the wife. The penis is placed into the vagina from the rear. Disadvantages are that the penis does not contact the clitoris and the couple cannot kiss during intercourse. This position leaves the husband's hands free to caress the body and breasts and stimulate the clitoris.

We have described the basic positions here. Others are given in chapter 12 in the discussion of sex during pregnancy. By all means feel free to explore the pleasure of other positions that you imagine would be exciting for you and, of course, acceptable to your mate.

It should be understood that the size of the penis has nothing to do with how much either partner enjoys intercourse, as only

the outer two inches of the vagina contain tissue which is stimulated by pressure on the inside. Many men think deep penetration of the penis gives their wife greater stimulation, when it is
actually better contact with the clitoris that will increase her stimulation to the point of orgasm.

Phase III: Orgasm

The term *orgasm* comes from the Greek word *orge* meaning
excitement. In the woman, it has been described as a momentary
feeling of suspension, followed by a sensation of warmth starting
in the perineal area and pervading the entire body. Rhythmic contractions of the lower third of the vagina follow. There may be
from three to ten contractions over the period of a few seconds.
She can increase the intensity of the physical sensations by voluntarily strengthening her P.C. muscle contractions and adding
her own pelvic movements to her husband's, as she lets herself go
in seeking release. As her physical movements, her response to her
partner's stimulation, and her own mental concentration blend
into a total reaching for satisfaction, she comes to climax—often
an emotional mountain-peak experience, when the rest of the
world recedes and seems to stand still—a high point of feeling,
best described as *ecstasy.*

Sometimes a woman does not know if she has experienced an
orgasm. If you feel your vagina contracting involuntarily, if you
feel excited at first, and later feel calm and physically satisfied, you
can take this as evidence that you have had an orgasm, even though
perhaps a weak one.

The man's orgasm consists of involuntary muscle tension and
contractions, with sensation centered specifically in the penis,
prostate, and seminal vesicles. His orgasm is complete when he
has expelled the semen.

Husband, there are five things you can do that will increase the
physical intensity and pleasure of your orgasm:

1. Wait at least twenty-four hours after previous orgasm to allow
   the body to store a larger volume of seminal fluid.

2. Lengthen the foreplay and excitement period so that the penis can remain erect about twenty minutes.
3. Increase your imagination factor by seeing and feeling your wife's ecstatic response to your knowledgeable and skillful physical stimulation, which brings her to the point of maximum physical pleasure.
4. Voluntarily contract your anal sphincter muscles during your orgasm.
5. Increase the force of thrusting while your orgasm is in progress.

During these few seconds of intense sensation known as orgasm, both husband and wife experience various muscular responses, even facial grimaces. As they both move in rhythm, they usually grasp one another tightly. Men and women are sometimes unaware of their extreme muscular exertions during orgasm, but it is not uncommon the next day to notice muscular aches, particularly in the back and thighs.

As soon as the husband finishes ejaculation, he should begin manual stimulation of his wife's clitoris, so that she can have repeated orgasms. This is the way the woman is designed! She should not have to ask for this, as the whole sex relationship is a pattern of pleasing each other. This means it is not desirable to change pace by having to ask for something for one's self. It should be the natural desire of the husband to provide every pleasure he knows of, and the wife may be intensely pleased by this continuing stimulation.

While arriving at orgasm at the same time may be a goal for lovers, it is not nearly as important as aiming at mutual enjoyment. Some begin to experience simultaneous orgasms as they come to understand each other more intimately. What does matter is that both partners be fully satisfied in each sexual encounter.

Time is all important. Take time to thoroughly arouse each other physically. Take time to ensure the wife's orgasm and the husband's controlled, full response. Finally, after intercourse, take time to express your love and appreciation for each other.

Phase IV: Relaxation

Picture this final phase according to the poetic term one doctor has given it—*afterglow*. After intercourse is over, the fires of passion and pleasure settle down to a lovely, quiet glow. Let this be a time when the husband shows tenderness toward his wife with hugs, kisses, and love pats. The couple should continue to express their appreciation as they lie close in each other's arms and just enjoy each other's presence. This ensures a smooth transition to complete relaxation together. It may be as long as fifteen minutes before all the physical signs of arousal are gone, and in a younger man it may be as long as a half hour before the erection completely disappears.

You will find a unique joy in using all the skill you possess to bring pleasure to your marriage partner. In fact every physical union should be an exciting contest to see which partner can out-please the other. The husband should be the world's greatest authority on how to please his wife. And the wife should be able to say as joyously as the bride in Song of Solomon, "I am my beloved's, and his desire is toward me" (7:10).

6

Solutions to Common Problems

Couples hoping for good sexual adjustment in marriage are dismayed early in their relationship when, instead of pleasure, they find problems in their lovemaking. There are two basic problems, and virtually every couple encounters one or both of them, at least at the beginning. These are not as complex or as hard to solve as one might think. The real problem lies in the fact that these difficulties are often ignored or excused, until poor adjustment becomes an accepted, expected part of the sexual relationship.

Here are typical complaints heard in my office:

From a young woman: "His lovemaking just doesn't last long enough for me!"

From a weary husband: "It takes my wife forty-five minutes to come to a climax, if at all. I'm so tired after a hard day at work. It's hardly worth the effort."

From a mother of six: "There must be more to sex than babies and hang-ups! I almost never get any enjoyment out of our physical relationship."

From an older man: "I'd like to be a better husband. But our sex life was so unsatisfying to my wife for so many years that

91

she is completely indifferent now. I know it's not too late to learn . . . if only she wanted to learn with me."

I can assure any couple that it is not too late to develop a good sex relationship. I will show you proven techniques—almost wonder-working in their simplicity and effectiveness—to overcome these basic problems. Some effort will be required, along with the desire to reach sexual adjustment.

If you recall the poky tortoise and the excessively speedy hare of Aesop's fable, you will be able to picture both problems. The tortoise represents most often, although not always, the wife. By this I mean that a large proportion of women take a longer time to reach orgasm than do their husbands. Correspondingly, a large proportion of men are like the hare. They reach orgasm too quickly, before their wives are sexually fulfilled.

God in His great wisdom created most women to become more slowly aroused than men. This prevents the sex act from being just a mechanical process; instead, it is an opportunity to learn to interact—to give and to receive reciprocal attention in a way that both partners can be satisfied.

Before husband and wife can learn how consciously to adapt to each other's need, two conditions may become evident: orgasmic dysfunction in the woman and/or premature ejaculation in the man. This means that some women are very slow to reach orgasm, rarely reach orgasm, or may never have had an orgasm. In the case of men, premature ejaculation means the inability to control ejaculation for a sufficient length of time to satisfy the wife. When the latter condition is solved, the wife often has no difficulty in reaching orgasm.

It usually is possible for couples to solve these problem conditions with the use of some simple physical exercises, which they can do together. In the process of learning how to consciously slow down or speed up, they also develop valuable nonverbal communication skills and come to realize their dependence on each other. The result: a more harmonious marriage in every aspect.

Some readers who do not suffer from premature ejaculation or orgasmic dysfunction may be tempted to pass over the remainder of this chapter. Let me encourage you to read on. The exercises

I will suggest can improve *any* marriage. Every couple I have dealt with has had something to learn, either in control or in better use of what God has provided. Most have something to learn in the area of timing, adjustment, or rate of response. While the husband learns to control his speedy responses, the wife learns to intensify excitement so that she can respond to him more quickly and more fully.

Premature Ejaculation

Because premature ejaculation can be the primary cause of the woman's orgasmic dysfunction, we will discuss ejaculatory control first. Specifically, the term describes the husband who ejaculates before entering his wife's vagina, or ejaculates immediately after entry. It also refers to the husband's inability to control ejaculation for a sufficient length of time during intravaginal containment to satisfy his wife in at least 50 percent of their times of sexual intercourse. In other words, the husband arrives at ejaculation *before he wishes to do so.*

One main cause of premature ejaculation is poor learning at the beginning of marriage. A new husband who has built up great tension through the period of courtship and engagement may ejaculate when he takes his wife in his arms on their wedding night, and for many nights thereafter. Some men mistakenly feel that a quick release is a sign of masculinity. Thus they never realize the need to learn to control the timing of their ejaculation so that they can experience the joy and oneness that comes with consistently bringing the wife to orgasm during intercourse.

The problem of premature ejaculation is occasionally established from sexual experiences before marriage. Heavy petting with stimulation to ejaculation can form a hurried pattern of lovemaking. Premarital intercourse instills guilt about the sex act itself, and in such furtive acts there is the constant pressure to "get it over with" before discovery. This pattern of hurried ejaculation will usually continue after marriage, until the husband realizes that there is a need to change. A good sexual adjustment is always a learned experience. It does not come naturally.

The main difficulty with premature ejaculation is that it does not give full sexual satisfaction to the wife. When this problem persists, the pattern of the marriage is somewhat predictable. The wife feels that she is being inconsiderately used and that her husband is only concerned with his own pleasure and has no real appreciation of her sexual needs. She is left without a means of physical release and builds an increasing level of resentment at being *used* sexually rather than *loved* sexually. In the usual course of events, after a period of years, husband and wife both withdraw from some of the commitment of marriage; the man doubts his masculinity and the wife loses her confidence as a woman. As the man becomes more and more anxious about his failure to satisfy his wife, he may even lose his ability to maintain an erection. This is called *impotence*. A quiet but hostile marriage without sex may result.

Another problem of premature ejaculation is that a "satisfied" husband has a tendency to discontinue his physical attentions to his wife after his orgasm. Not only is the wife denied the feeling of sexual release in orgasm, but she may also have acute and chronic physical pain stemming from congestion of her pelvic organs, engorged with blood that is normally released with orgasm. Thus the wife is frustrated when he falls asleep at her side. He is snoring and she is fuming!

An occasional premature ejaculation can occur in any man, especially when there is sexual union after the husband and wife have been apart for a number of days. If this is the case, the husband should immediately begin to use his fingers to gently stimulate his wife's clitoris, since his penis will no longer have the firmness necessary to stimulate her to orgasm. Thus the wife is assured of her husband's concern for her complete sexual fulfillment.

The need to prolong erection and delay ejaculation is a problem that has been around for a long time. Until recently, a man's only solutions were to concentrate on something not associated with sex (sometimes difficult to accomplish while in the sex act), to take tranquilizers, or to apply some type of anesthetic cream or a sheath to the penis. None of these so-called solutions is completely effective or satisfactory. Recently physicians have begun prescribing Paxil which tends to delay ejaculation.

Sometimes the husband tries to solve the problem by using manual stimulation to bring the wife to a very high degree of sexual tension just before insertion of the penis. A disadvantage of this technique is that the wife is often so desperate to have her orgasm that her frantic thrusting produces almost instant ejaculation by her husband, while she still needs more time.

Many other factors may add up to produce an unsatisfactory sex relationship. Since the husband can be relieved by ejaculation, he may not see the need to change for his wife's sake. Researchers have found that many such men are selfish and do not consider themselves inadequate lovers, but blame their wives for not being sexy enough. The husband may assume that his wife also enjoys the relationship as it is; or he may assume that her slower response is all her problem. The wife may further complicate the situation by faking orgasm and faking enjoyment of sex to please her husband. The false idea that pleasure in sex is unnecessary for the woman, as well as the belief of some wives that sex is strictly a duty, has contributed greatly to the misery of the tortoise-hare relationship.

Recognizing and admitting that a problem exists is half the battle won. Too many couples simply go on for years accepting premature ejaculation, not even realizing that they have a problem. A few couples would rather not contemplate a change where they have failed so often in the past. It becomes easier and easier to remain in the same old rut, rather than get on the road to a solution.

The husband's problem is easier to remedy than the woman's; so, men, you no longer have to be the hare. With the methods we will discuss, you can slow down to be of greater help to your wife, and at the same time gain more satisfaction and confidence in yourself!

Although it is essential at the beginning for the husband to admit that he has the problem of premature ejaculation, both he and his wife should view this as a "couple" difficulty, requiring "couple" cooperation to find the solution. Husband and wife need to covenant together to follow through a relatively short program of practical exercises that will definitely help in a matter of a few weeks. In the course of these procedures they will learn the technique of *squeeze control,* in which squeeze pressure is applied to the erect penis. This technique causes no pain, since most of the pain-sensitive areas in the male genitals are in the testicles rather than the penis, but it does make the husband lose his urge to ejaculate, and often he loses some erection momentarily.

The squeeze-control procedure was presented by Masters and Johnson at the Reproductive Biology Research Foundation in St. Louis, where Gaye and I studied at one of their postgraduate workshops for counselors and educators in the field of human sexual function and dysfunction. I have adapted the material for my medical practice and for this book.

The wife must understand that the squeeze-control technique is not effective if done by the husband on himself. She must be involved! With her full cooperation and willingness to learn and apply certain basic principles, and with warm personal involvement expressed openly, this troublesome marital problem can be solved. Much greater sexual pleasure will be the reward for both partners.

Since the premature ejaculation problem may have been present for a long time, no couple should expect an immediate solution. It will take time to form new response patterns. Practice sessions of at least twenty minutes' duration should be carried out lovingly and leisurely with little attention given to the clock. It is important not to skip practice sessions and they should never be shortened to less than twenty minutes, unless an ejaculation accidentally occurs.

During the course of this program, one can get so caught up with avoiding orgasm that tension builds. Remember, there is no harm in an orgasm by mistake. Nevertheless, strictly avoid orgasm as a goal. Special objectives are given for each phase of the program. But always, learning physical communication and building sensitive understanding are of key importance. Each session should be a time of pleasure and enjoyment for both partners, never hurried and never tedious.

Repeat a phase at your practice sessions until you have mastered the objectives of that particular phase. *This means that you may spend a number of practice sessions on one phase before you are ready to go on to the next.* These sessions may take place on a daily basis or at two- or three-day intervals. I suggest that the total duration of the first four phases not exceed four weeks, as prolonging this time tends to lead to boredom.

Premature Ejaculation Control Exercises

Phase I. You may both be so "gun-shy" from the husband's quick sexual release that you have been avoiding touching as much as possible. You need to take the focus off orgasm and timing and concentrate on improving nonverbal, physical communication without seeking to reach orgasm. The objective of this phase: *To improve physical communication and learn to appreciate physical closeness with your mate.*

1. Spend time touching and fondling each other.
2. Do the things that physically please your mate, such as a scalp massage or stroking the back or neck, and so forth.
3. Avoid directly stimulating genital areas.
4. Do not have intercourse, but focus on improving physical communication with your mate.
5. Learn to appreciate and enjoy physical closeness.
6. Follow this procedure for at least the first two sessions.

Phase II. The objective of this phase: *For the husband to learn to recognize the physical sensation that comes just before ejaculation, so that he is able to communicate to his wife the best time to apply the squeeze.*

During this session it is vitally important that the husband concentrate completely on his own sensations. He is to block out all other thoughts, so that he will become keenly aware of the feeling that comes just prior to ejaculation. It may help if he closes his eyes. As soon as the husband feels he is nearing the point of ejaculation, he is to indicate this to his wife by some predetermined word or signal. She is then to quickly use the squeeze technique. This phase should be repeated during the daily practice sessions, until the husband can consistently recognize the sensation that occurs just before ejaculation (see figure 10).

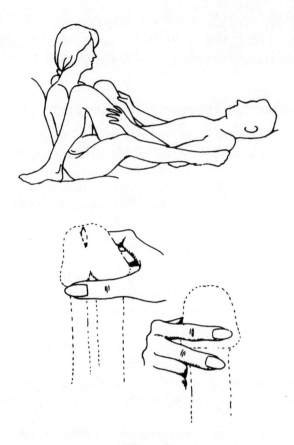

Figure 10
Positioning for premature ejaculation
training session using squeeze control

1. The wife is to sit with her back against the headboard of the bed, with her legs spread comfortably apart.
2. The husband is to lie on his back, with his head toward the foot of the bed.
3. The husband positions his pelvis between his wife's legs, with his genitals close to hers. With knees bent, his feet are to be placed outside her thighs (near her buttocks).
4. The wife now lovingly and gently caresses the man's genitals, paying special attention to the underside of the shaft or

the head of the penis, or wherever her husband directs, to encourage him to attain an erection.

5. As soon as the husband achieves full erection, the wife will begin the squeeze technique. She places her thumb on the underside of the penis, about one-half inch below the slit opening just where the shaft ends and the head begins. She then places the first two fingers of that hand on the opposite side of the penis, with one finger above the ridge and one finger below the ridge that distinguishes the head from the shaft.

6. She then squeezes her thumb and two fingers together with very hard pressure for about four seconds.

7. She then quickly releases the pressure.

8. After fifteen to thirty seconds, she manipulates him to full erection again and repeats the squeeze. The husband should inform his wife by word or subtle signals when he feels she needs to repeat the squeeze to delay his orgasm.

9. Repeat this procedure every four to five minutes for the entire twenty-minute session.

10. The husband may prefer to have a lubricant applied to his penis to more closely simulate the sensations felt during sexual intercourse.

11. Do not have intercourse or insert the penis into the vagina.

12. At the end of the session, stimulation should be continued to ejaculation.

13. It will be desirable for the husband to use manual stimulation of the wife's clitoris to bring her to orgasm *after* each practice session.

Phase III. The objective of this phase: *For the erect penis to remain almost motionless in the vagina for fifteen to twenty minutes before ejaculation.*

1. The husband lies on his back, and the wife stimulates him to an erection.

2. When he feels he is nearing the point of ejaculation, he signals his wife, and she quickly uses the squeeze technique.

3. She should repeat the stimulation almost to ejaculation and then squeeze the penis. This should be done several times.
4. Then the wife straddles the husband in a sitting position. Leaning forward at about a 45-degree angle, she very gently and slowly inserts the erect penis into the well-lubricated vagina, then moves backward comfortably onto the shaft, not just sitting down on it.
5. She remains motionless, giving her husband a chance to achieve control. If the husband loses his erection while the penis is in the vagina, the wife should raise her body and manually restimulate him to erection.
6. If the husband becomes aware that he is nearing the point of ejaculation, he should indicate this to his wife, so that she can raise her body and repeat the squeeze procedure. Then she gently reinserts the penis.
7. Husband and wife should be able to maintain this position with the erect penis almost motionless in the vagina for fifteen to twenty minutes before ejaculation.

Phase IV. Remember, it is important to wait at least one day before beginning a new phase. The objective of this phase: *To be able to keep the erect penis in the vagina with very gentle movements for about twenty minutes before ejaculation.*

1. Spend some time in loving foreplay.
2. Again assume the position of the wife straddling the husband and leaning forward to insert his penis.
3. The husband is to begin thrusting slightly, thus learning to tolerate gradually increasing amounts of movement of the penis in the vagina.
4. This gentle thrusting should be continued for fifteen to twenty minutes before ejaculation. Use the squeeze technique if necessary.
5. When this phase is mastered, the husband may now ejaculate with the penis in the vagina, but he is to continue concentrating on his own sensations, until each practice session is over and he has ejaculated. Then he is to take time to man-

ually bring his wife to orgasm. (Remember, this is still a training session.)

Phase V. The objective of this phase: *To learn how to have comfortable sexual intercourse in the side-to-side (lateral) position.* This position gives better control of movements by both husband and wife and allows the husband the best ejaculatory control.

1. Spend some time in loving foreplay.
2. Again assume the position of the wife straddling the husband and leaning forward to insert his penis.
3. Place a pillow under the husband's head and another one along his left side.
4. The wife brings her right leg to a straight position between his legs. She leaves her left leg on the outer side of his body.
5. At the same time, the husband moves his left leg out from his body, placing it flat on the bed, with knee bent.
6. The wife is to shift her entire body slightly to the right, while leaning forward with her left breast at the level of his left breast. She will now be partially supported by the pillow at her husband's left side. Additional comfort is achieved by another pillow for her head and shoulders.
7. It will take several practice sessions to learn to change easily into this side-to-side position and arrange the arms and legs in the most comfortable manner. (Once learned, this position is used by many couples most of the time.)
8. While in the side-to-side position, the thrusting should be gentle, so that the penis can remain in the vagina for twenty minutes before ejaculation.

Establishing Lasting Ejaculatory Control

Practice sessions should continue on a regular basis to maintain ejaculatory control.

1. Use the squeeze technique at least once a week for the next six months.

2. Once each month practice the squeeze technique for an entire twenty-minute session.
3. Good ejaculatory control is usually attained in three to six weeks.
4. Within six to twelve months the husband should be able to be consistently quite active in intercourse for ten to twenty minutes without ejaculation.
5. Complete control is attained when the husband does not have his orgasm until he chooses.

Prolonged emphasis on controlling orgasm in these practice sessions may sometimes cause a husband to have a temporary lack of ability to keep an erection. Do not be dismayed. It is just this portion of the husband's body demanding a brief rest.

As you read this detailed list of instructions for the practice sessions, the process may seem to be rather tedious. But any couple who recognize that premature ejaculation plays some part in their lack of maximum sexual fulfillment will find that a few weeks of mutual effort and discipline will lead to far greater sexual pleasure for the rest of their lives. It is a fact that few men possess the ability to delay their ejaculation as long as they would like. These training sessions, using the squeeze-technique procedure, can result in heightened pleasure for any couple desiring a better sexual relationship.

During the squeeze-technique sessions, the wife may discover that she is beginning to experience some new and pleasurable feelings. She begins to feel more sexual arousal. She may even experience her very first orgasm. Even if she has been able to reach orgasm before, she may now begin to enjoy multiple orgasms.

The Pubococcygeus (P.C.) Muscles

Just as the husband has shown an effort of sacrifice and love in gaining complete ejaculatory control, so the wife can also contribute to the relationship by attaining full control and strength in the pubococcygeus muscles, which surround the lower third of her vagina, in order to experience a much more intense sexual stimulation.

Before we discuss this important muscle group, I should point out that most of what researchers have called "orgasmic dysfunction" in women is not caused by a physical dysfunction. Most failure in achieving orgasm is related to the wife's attitude and thoughts. The next chapter will discuss this in detail. However, by undertaking these specific exercises to build up certain important muscles, the wife can usually begin to participate in and enjoy sex. These physical exercises, along with the restructuring of attitudes about sex, have had great success in treating "orgasmic dysfunction" in women.

Exercising to strengthen the P.C. muscles can be undertaken effectively, though other factors still may inhibit the wife's orgasm. While it is always desirable to treat the entire person—body, mind, and spirit—still, an improvement in just one area will improve the whole person to some degree. In fact it may be the one "missing link" that will trigger a satisfying sexual response. Even if the husband is uncommunicative and unwilling to share in the total improvement of sexual relations in marriage, the strengthening and toning of the P.C. muscles is done with exercises that the wife can perform by herself. This can be an encouragement to him and shows him that she really desires to help improve their sexual relationship.

Other important benefits of improved P.C. muscle control are:

1. Improvement of support of pelvic organs.
2. Improvement of urinary control.
3. Reduced extent of childbirth injuries to the mother.
4. Shortening of length of time in labor and delivery.
5. Increased safety for the baby during the birth process.
6. More effective natural childbirth. (The exercises are included in the YWCA classes for natural childbirth and in the International Childbirth Education Association programs of instruction, as well as in the Lamaze Method.)

In the early 1940s, Dr. Arnold H. Kegel, a surgeon and professor of gynecology at the University of Southern California School of Medicine, made a discovery about women who had trouble controlling their urine flow when coughing, laughing, or sneezing. It was found that this problem, referred to as *urinary stress incontinence,* could be helped by exercising the pelvic muscle group called the pubococcygeus muscles or P.C. muscles. In medical school anatomy books they are called the *levator ani muscles.*

The P.C. muscles are located above the legs and extend from the pubic bone to the coccyx (tailbone) in the back. They are like a sling and form the floor of the pelvis, also supporting and surrounding the outer one-third of the vagina, the neck of the bladder, and part of the rectum (see figure 11).

Dr. Kegel found that repeating specific exercises strengthens the P.C. muscles, with resultant stoppage and control of urinary stress incontinence. The exercises he prescribed to strengthen the P.C. muscles are called the Kegel exercises.

Further study by Dr. Kegel revealed that fewer than one in three women have adequate P.C. muscle tone. However, women who have poor muscle tone do not necessarily have urinary leakage. The strength of the P.C. muscles seems relatively unrelated to general muscular development of the woman. Since the P.C. is suspended between two solid nonmoving bony structures, its strength is unaffected by the use of other muscles. Therefore, a female athlete can have poor P.C. musculature, and a weak, inactive woman may have strong P.C. musculature.

The stretching that occurs during childbirth weakens the P.C. muscles. Uncontrolled urinary leakage most often appears after a woman has borne children, since much of the support for the bladder comes from the P.C. muscles. The urethra, or urinary passage, penetrates and is also supported by the P.C. muscles. When these muscles are weakened, poor urinary control often results. Under ordinary circumstances, even weak muscles can hold back urine; but under a stress like a sneeze, laugh, or cough, urine is sometimes allowed to escape. In less than two months most of the patients who followed Dr. Kegel's exercises were able to control their urine flow. Today these exercises are a standard technique for learning to establish urine control, and when these muscles are strengthened, there often is no need for surgical repair.

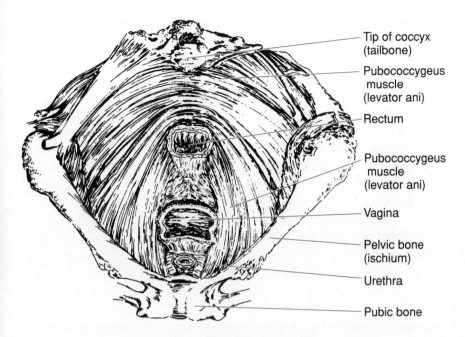

Figure 11
Pubococcygeus muscles viewed from below,
looking from front to back

Note the extent of the P.C. muscles, as they form a primary
part of the support for the reproductive organs, bladder, and
rectum. Weakness of the P.C. can result in chronic pelvic
discomfort or leakage of urine. Refer back to figure 1 in
chapter 4, to better visualize the location of the P.C. muscles.

For many patients, the Kegel exercises strengthen and build much better pelvic support than a surgical operation.

One patient reported to Dr. Kegel that for the first time in fifteen years of marriage she had orgasm in intercourse and suggested this welcome event might be connected with the exercises she had been doing. After following the exercise program, other women also volunteered the information that they experienced more consistent orgasm during intercourse or had orgasm for the first time.

Dr. Kegel finally concluded that strengthened P.C. muscles resulted in increased sexual satisfaction. This information, though new to our culture, had been observed by primitive and oriental peoples, as well as other cultures, who also noted the lessening of sexual satisfaction after childbirth. Certain "secret" sex practices in some primitive cultures depend on controlling and strengthening these muscles around the vagina.

Since Kegel's early efforts, research has revealed that sexual stimulation in the woman's vagina is much more related to *pressure sensitivity* than to *frictional sensitivity*. This stands to reason, because the P.C. muscle group is well supplied with pressure-sensitive nerve endings (called proprioceptive nerves) which do *not* respond to light touch or light friction. Thus, a strengthening and tightening of the P.C. muscle group around the outer one-third of the vagina can produce much more sexually stimulating pressure sensitivity for the woman during intercourse.

These pressure-sensitive nerve endings of the P.C. muscles are actually around but *outside* the vagina. A *firm* squeezing pressure on the penis within the vagina is needed to give greater sexual stimulation. A vagina that makes poor contact with the penis affords little sexual stimulation for the wife. It has been found that a larger object introduced into the vagina does not help increase sexual sensitivity, since sensitivity depends on *contraction* of the muscles—not stretching. Therefore, the size of the penis has no relationship to the wife's sensitivity. When the vagina is tightened to a firm channel by a strong P.C., however, thrusting of the male penis will also press and push the P.C. and give more satisfying stimulation to the wife. More stimulation results in reflex contraction of the vagina, which is part of the pattern that leads to orgasm for the woman.

In a woman who does not experience orgasm during sex, the P.C. muscle exercises can contribute to providing relief of pelvic congestion and muscular tension, which is a very frequent cause of low-back pain. The exercises are easy and not fatiguing—in fact if you tire while doing them, you are not exercising the right muscles.

Some women can easily contract the P.C. muscles when they first learn of their existence and may experience orgasm for the first time when they learn to use these muscles during intercourse. However, if the muscles are weak (as they are in so many women), action will have to be added to knowledge. The woman must learn exercises that can help her to both strengthen and control the P.C. muscles.

The P.C. Exercises

The following instructions are directed to wives who want to experience the benefits of these exercises. I will explain them to you as if you were a patient in my office.

You might have difficulty locating the P.C. muscles at first. Without instruction, it is more likely that only the weaker, external muscles around the vaginal opening will be contracted. This will tighten only the vaginal opening. Being told that the P.C. muscle group is more internal often causes the woman to contract muscles of the lower back, abdomen, and thighs. These muscles are not linked to the P.C. muscles, and contracting these may cause fatigue. The P.C. muscle exercise should be fairly effortless, though it may take some patience and concentration at first. After the exercise is learned, it's almost as easy as shutting your eyelid.

Since one of the functions of the P.C. muscles is to stop the flow of urine, it can be said that the P.C. muscles have been contracted if urination is interrupted. However, the less important external muscles can also shut off the urine flow; so the simplest method to determine if the muscles contract is to attempt to stop urine flow with the knees spread. In the sitting position on the commode, with knees widely separated (about two feet apart), allow the flow of urine, and then attempt to stop the flow without moving the knees. In nearly all women, this procedure exercises the P.C. muscles. Once you feel what it is like to correctly contract the P.C., you can do the exercise any time. The stoppage of urine flow during urination can then be used once in a while as a check to make sure you are contracting the right muscles.

Another way to tell if the P.C. muscles are being contracted is to see if the perineum rises. The perineum is the area between the anus and the vaginal opening. Use a mirror to observe the rise of the perineum or place one finger about an inch and a half inside the vagina and feel the muscle contract. When there is good P.C. muscle control, you should be able to squeeze this one finger very firmly.

After learning precisely how to contract the P.C., you can begin a program of exercising. Start with five to ten contractions on waking and every time you urinate. Hold each contraction for two seconds. When control of the P.C. muscles is improved, you should be able to release as little as a teaspoon of urine at a time, and the contractions should be easier than when first attempted.

In approximately four days, when you have confidence you are contracting the P.C. muscles, increase exercising to ten contractions about six times per day. If each contraction takes two seconds, the total time involved will be only two minutes per day. Over a four- to six-week period, gradually increase to three hundred contractions per day, which should require no more than a total of ten minutes per day. Better urine control and some sexual improvement may be occurring by now. About four more weeks (or a total of ten weeks) should complete the program. More planned exercise probably should not be necessary, since strong and well-developed P.C. muscles will keep the involuntary urine flow under control. Occasionally check to see whether you can still tightly squeeze one finger in the vagina.

Sexual activity also helps strengthen the P.C. muscles. Women are advised to start voluntary contractions of the P.C. during foreplay in order to heighten sexual tension before the penis is inserted. This helps condition the P.C. for involuntary contractions later in orgasm, and it also helps firm up the vaginal walls. By consciously contracting these muscles, the wife can have an earlier response and more intense pleasure. In the final spasms of each orgasm, the P.C. contracts by itself, involuntarily, four to ten times at intervals of four-fifths of a second. After these independent contractions, there is a tremendous feeling of release and lessening of tension, which signals that the wife's orgasm is over.

Most nerve endings in the body are sensitive to light touch; the nerve endings in the P.C. muscles, however, are sensitive to pressure. Obviously, the skillful use of the P.C. muscles during intercourse is included in God's design to give increased sexual stimulation to the woman.

P.C. muscle contraction can also provide the husband more pleasurable sensations during intercourse. When the wife develops voluntary control and when there is loving, verbal communication between the two, the wife can learn exactly when to contract the P.C. muscles to give him the maximum stimulation just before and during his orgasm.

Wives, you can see how important your involvement is and how necessary your helpful participation is in sex play, both for your husband's benefit and your own. Remember, as we have said elsewhere, that the vagina is *not* a passive receptacle for the penis. Picture it as an active, involved organ during sex. The role of the vagina was described many years ago by Dr. Theodore H. Van de Velde in *Ideal Marriage:* "The working of the . . . muscles . . . is an apparatus for gripping and rubbing the male sexual organ . . . by pressure and friction, to ensure this orgasm."

Ask yourself how good your P.C. muscle control is right now. The muscle should be able to grip the penis as tightly as a clenched fist.

Almost every woman can significantly heighten her sexual adequacy through understanding the Kegel exercises to condition, strengthen, and achieve voluntary control of the P.C. muscles. And some men have found more intense physical sensation in orgasm after strengthening their own corresponding pelvic muscles.

The few weeks of exercises for ten or fifteen minutes per day add up to very little time or trouble, and yet the rewards are great for both the wife and her husband. They enjoy more satisfying sex, and the benefits are lifelong. It all adds up to an experience that should be well worth the effort.

Here is a case history for your encouragement from Tim and Beverly LaHaye's *The Act of Marriage:*

One such case, a mother of five and married almost twenty-five years said, "Dr. LaHaye, it all seems so unnatural to me. If God wanted those vaginal muscles strong enough for me to get more sensation during lovemaking, He would have made them that way." I explained to her that He did originally, but her five births and natural aging process had so relaxed them, they were of little help to her and the older she grew, the more she would need them toned up through exercise.

Quite reluctantly, she went home to try, but she admitted she had little faith it would work. Fortunately, she did her exercises diligently and as she reported later: "Within one month I experienced sensations I had never felt before. Within five weeks my husband, who had been having a little trouble maintaining an erection, had noticed how much more exciting our love life became. Now we both think our next twenty-five years of lovemaking will be more exciting than the first twenty-five."

Along with the exercise, here are further suggestions for the woman learning to experience orgasm: The ability to build sexual tension or excitement after actual introduction of the penis must be actively sought and learned. You should keep anticipation and desire foremost in your mind, surrender to your own natural drives, and build emotional excitement, as well as physical stimulation, until your tension climaxes in release. Many women have found that they are able to reach a climax more quickly if they also tense the muscles of their legs, thighs, and lower abdomen, while concentrating on their own sensations, until they have orgasm.

Vigorous thrusting as soon as the male organ enters the vagina usually guarantees that the wife's sensation will be blurred and that excitement will actually decline.

A gentle introduction of the penis will almost always better meet the wife's needs. Both partners may wish to develop some mutually pleasing movements with the penis fully inserted—perhaps side-to-side movements, rocking motions, or hip movements, which help take some of the thrust away from the upper end of the vagina and direct the pressure to the more responsive lower vagina, which is surrounded by the P.C. muscles. The husband should be very sensitive and responsive to his wife's movements.

The art of lovemaking involves an enjoyment of each phase of the experience, seeking every pleasurable sensation, anticipating but not hurrying toward climax. As you learn this art together, your "tortoise and hare" problems will diminish and disappear!

7

For the Preorgasmic Wife
Fulfillment Ahead

This part of *Intended for Pleasure* is written especially for the woman who seldom or never reaches orgasm during intercourse.

I want to speak very directly with you who up to this time have been unable to enter into the sexual pleasure God designed for every wife. In the past, you would have been called frigid—a word that seems to denote an icy personality, unfeeling and self-contained. And you know yourself to be a warm and loving woman. It's just that you haven't been able to experience the thrills and excitement you've read about. You love your husband and you want all there is from marriage. Perhaps both of you are feeling discouraged because it hurts too much to go on failing, so why keep trying? Why not be content with just loving each other and settling for what must surely be second best? I assure you that you do not have to miss out on the pleasure of sex with your husband.

Nor do you have to think of yourself as frigid. Today we reserve the term *frigid* for a woman who finds the sex act distasteful, even offensive. The more accurate term for the woman who has never reached a sexual climax is *preorgasmic*, which implies fulfillment ahead; it's delayed, *but only for a time.*

Now, failure to achieve a sexual response may have stirred up feelings of frustration, self-doubt, and inadequacy in both you and your husband. This is an understandable reaction. When these feelings come from sincere attempts to express love to your mate, the wound goes very deep as you begin to sense failure in the very area in which you most want to succeed. Yet never forget that the warmth of your love does exist. It is the ability to express and receive this warmth physically that has become blocked by memories of previous failures, coupled with a lack of sexual knowledge.

Your problem may be rooted in the past, even before marriage, but psychological causes can seldom be exactly pinpointed, and the only purpose served by seeking the cause in your past is to find someone or something on which to place the blame.

The mature approach for the Christian couple is to realize that no matter what the cause, *God is able to meet your need in any situation*. You and your husband can start right where you are by asking God to raise your level of love and sexual interest for each other, and then both of you can enter into a mutual, loving cooperation in following some simple instructions.

Before I give you an effective (and pleasant) procedure—a series of training sessions—to solve this problem, there are principles to be underscored.

First, no matter which of you may seem to be the most at fault, both you and your husband will have to make a fresh start, as if you were just now getting married. Quit worrying about who might be at fault. This is not the issue. It is only important to discover how both of you can experience more pleasure in your sexual relationship.

So give each other a chance to make love without demand or criticism. This is not a time to keep score, but a time to practice and learn together without anxiety. This will be a period when you realize both of you have much to learn: You will learn to receive, and he will learn to give unselfishly.

Your goal will be to build up memories of pleasurable sexual feelings. When those are combined with some new experiences and a realization of your husband's loving desire to give you sexual pleasure, this will increase the number of signals to the brain, which can build up to an uninhibited sexual response.

Second, I want you to understand yourself. *Desire* is your ally. If you desire to have an orgasm, because you know it is your right, your provision from God, and because you want to keenly enjoy the most intimate times with your husband, then there is no reason why you cannot experience an orgasm. It will come.

But it will not come as a result of your exerting your willpower. Certain things must happen within your body as you are sufficiently stimulated, and orgasm will be the result. You can never work it up by trying. Yet intense concentration is an important key. I hope that does not sound like a contradiction. The concentration must be on your own feelings, your own sensations, your own desires, as you move with them and let them take you where they will.

Third, beware of factors that can break your concentration and keep you from reaching orgasm. What will break your concentration? You may find yourself becoming a spectator at your own lovemaking, critically watching yourself to see if you are "performing satisfactorily." Self-consciousness will interrupt your enjoyment and turn off desire, which may be only just beginning.

Or you may find yourself concentrating on your husband's reactions. You may start worrying: *He must be tired. . . . This isn't much fun for him. . . . I'm sure he wishes he had married someone more sexy.* And by that time another facet of self-consciousness will have spoiled all sensual delight, just as it was beginning to flower.

A third interruption in concentration may come from guilt feelings of a rather interesting variety. You may have overcome psychological hurdles in thinking of sex as a "bad thing," for you now realize it is God-created and God-ordained. But as you concentrate on your own wonderful new sensations and look forward to a climax, suddenly the thought comes: *I should be trying to please my husband. It's wrong just trying to please myself.* And again desire is aborted.

Let me give you true and sensible thoughts with which to program your mind before making love:

1. In these "training sessions" there is no need to judge yourself, for nothing at all will be demanded of you. The atmos-

phere will be relaxed and yet sensuous to permit *a natural unfolding* of the sexual response, which lies within you. *Natural* means that you force nothing, that you pretend nothing. As a matter of fact, it can be one of the most wonderful times of your life, when nothing is required of you but to *let yourself* find pleasure as it comes.

2. You may not realize how much your husband is going to enjoy these training sessions! They are purely *pleasure-oriented*. Couples have reported that their relationship became particularly close and romantic as they began to concentrate on each other strictly for pleasure, without pressure. As you cast off all self-consciousness, you will become more sensual and more desirable to your husband.

3. As you learn to respond by concentrating on your sensations, you *are* learning to please your husband! You cannot imagine how devastating an indifferent response is to a man who tries time after time to arouse his wife with lovemaking. You also cannot imagine the ecstatic thrills that come to a man when he sees his wife responding totally, enjoying every moment of their time together with a lovely abandon.

Now as you go into these training sessions, your husband will have the opportunity to show you his love, as he temporarily defers total sexual gratification. You will show him your trust, as you put yourself in his hands and risk being completely vulnerable and honest in this relationship.

Your training sessions should be in a very private place with no chance of interruption. Of course you will both be very clean and as rested as possible. I suggest that your husband have a clean shave and trimmed, smooth fingernails. If his hands are even slightly rough, he should use a generous amount of hand cream or lotion to make his caresses more pleasing.

All caresses must be gentle, never harsh, brusque, or forced. If they are light, fleeting, and teasing in nature, they serve to arouse the imagination to a much greater degree.

You will both take off all your clothes, and your husband is to use his fingers and his hands to touch, massage, and fondle your body anywhere you lovingly direct him, while you just relax and become conscious of the pleasure gained from his care and caresses. At first, use a gentle trial-and-error method, maintaining very comfortable positions in bed, and avoid any thought of hurrying or any feeling of need to satisfy your husband or any seeking for your own orgasm.

You should repeat these unhurried relaxed times of receiving your husband's caresses daily, for at least four days, for whatever period of time that gives you pleasure. For these times, you may wish to actually avoid touching the genital or breast areas. You should now both be discovering the most sensitive areas of your body. You should also be aware that you have permission to freely express your pleasure in sexual feelings without regard at this time for your husband's sexual needs.

These few sessions in which you and your husband touch and caress each other unclothed will help to establish or reestablish a healthy climate of physical giving and pleasuring. The absence of actual intercourse during these sessions will help reduce tensions that have built up in former experiences of coitus.

Also, during this period, you should learn to talk things over. You each should begin to learn to anticipate the other's physical wants and needs. Remember, if your husband tries a particular form of caress on you, it would be a good idea for you to recip-rocate. The idea that it might be pleasurable probably occurred to him because he would like the same caress returned!

You can begin touching your husband, and as you delight him spontaneously and without duty, you may find your own pleasure increasing.

Up to this time, you should not have directed your husband's hands to your breasts and genital area, but now you must follow some detailed directions for maximum pleasurable sexual stimu-lation. Your husband is to place himself in a sitting position with his back comfortably resting against pillows at the headboard of the bed. With his legs widely separated, you are to sit between his legs with your back against his chest and your head resting com-fortably on his shoulder, your legs spread apart and draped over his. This position allows him freedom of access for creative explo-

ration of your entire body. You should encourage specific direction for this by placing your hand lightly on his hand, so you can
show by slight increases in pressure, or by gentle directional movement, the "where and how" of your desires at any particular
moment. This will allow both of you to learn precise physical communication without the distractions of verbal request or detailed
explanation. At this time you should direct his every movement,
and he should absolutely refrain from any of his own ideas as to
what may be stimulating to you.

Your husband may feel that he should now stroke the end of
your clitoris, but this has been found to be too sensitive and tender an area. You will probably achieve much more pleasure by
well-lubricated stimulation along the shaft or sides of the clitoris
and around the upper part of the vaginal opening. Almost never
is there pleasure in introduction of fingers deep into the vagina.

Often you will want him to just lightly stroke your neck, your
earlobes, your breasts, your upper inner thighs, your buttocks,
and then return to those most stimulating areas, just above the
clitoral glans or just in front of the vaginal opening.

There is no hurry, and you should not at this point be attempting to force yourself to reach an orgasm. These are pleasurable
times, which may extend over a period of several weeks, when
both you and your husband are lovingly discovering exactly what
it is that excites you sexually, and learning to communicate with
each other physically and verbally.

If at any time you feel that you are highly aroused sexually, you
should try to continue increasing the intensity of the stimulation
with his hand or your hand, until you experience the intensely
exciting sensation of orgasm. The sensation is centered primarily
in your pelvis. While you are learning with your husband, you
should have complete freedom to stimulate your own clitoris, if
you feel it is needed to produce your first few orgasms. This will
help to start a pattern of response, which will later make it much
easier to experience orgasm in sexual intercourse. After you have
had several orgasms by manual stimulation, you should begin having sexual intercourse in the female-above position. Then use
whatever positions you desire.

Do not be concerned if your orgasm continues to come from manual stimulation of the clitoris. The idea that satisfaction for the wife comes from the penis in the vagina is only sometimes true. Your goal, now, is satisfaction given by a loving husband, and achieving the fulfillment of orgasm.

Also do not anxiously work toward simultaneous orgasm with your husband. This is wonderful when it happens but has been far overemphasized in current literature. The purpose should be pleasure for both partners during the sexual relationship.

Remember, skillful, gentle, appropriate stimulation of the clitoris and the nearby areas will almost always bring any wife to a higher level of desire and an experience of sexual release in orgasm.

You can see that the answer lies not just in collecting a group of new erotic techniques, but simply in learning to touch and enjoy each other, to communicate and discover how to please each other. As you learn to enjoy sex because of the wonderful sensations and the precious oneness with your mate—and not just because it is something that makes your husband happy—you will know fulfillment!

Now I want to describe for you some of the common physical conditions that may cause difficulty in achieving orgasm. Pain during intercourse will always inhibit pleasure and hinder sexual release. Painful intercourse is called dyspareunia, but this is a symptom, not a diagnosis. Any woman who has pain or other difficulty with intercourse should have a thorough physical examination, one that includes a pelvic and rectal examination. Since only a minority of doctors will ask a patient about the state of her sex life, you should never just hope the doctor will guess your difficulty. Take a deep breath, blush (if need be), and tell him what is wrong.

One common cause of pain is atrophic vaginitis, a thinning of the vaginal wall, caused by a lack of female hormones, especially estrogen. This occurs in menopause when the amount of estrogen is reduced, or it may occur at any age after removal of the ovaries or any time the ovaries are not producing enough estrogen. This thinning of the vaginal walls can be easily corrected by taking estrogen by mouth, by injection, or by applying estrogen cream up into the vagina. Atrophic vaginitis is the only physical sexual problem actually caused by the menopause and it can be prevented by maintaining the proper level of estrogen through the menopause years.

Another kind of vaginitis, which produces pain and burning in the vagina, is caused by infection—candidiasis, a yeast infection, and trichomonas, a parasitic infection, are the most common. These infections are contagious, may become chronic when ignored, and demand medical treatment along with a few days abstention from intercourse as well as the use of condoms for a week or two when intercourse is resumed. The husband and wife must take medication simultaneously to eradicate trichomonas infections.

Other causes of pain in intercourse that must be discovered and treated include a dropped-down uterus, known as uterine prolapse, and endometriosis, which produces irritation and scarring in the pelvis. A much less common physical cause of painful intercourse for the wife may follow childbirth during which a tear in the broad ligament has occurred. This ligament is one of the supporting structures at the side of the uterus. Pain is experienced on deep penetration of the penis, but it is very difficult for the doctor to find this injury until several months after childbirth. If you developed this pain one or two months after you had a baby, be sure to ask your doctor to check for this tear. The tear may need to be repaired surgically to provide relief.

Pain can also be caused by vaginismus, a term that describes the involuntary action of the muscles of the vaginal entrance, as they go into spasm when an attempt is made to insert the penis. This muscular spasm may be so severe that even the little finger cannot be inserted into the vagina. This painful condition usually starts right at the time of the first attempt at intercourse but it may occur at other times, such as after the birth of a baby, after a pelvic operation, or even at the time of beginning a second marriage.

Vaginismus can usually be eliminated in about one week with the following procedure. With the wife in position for pelvic examination on the examining table at the doctor's office, the husband is brought into the room and puts on a rubber glove. He is instructed to attempt to place one well-lubricated finger into the wife's vagina. This is to demonstrate to both husband and wife the severity of the spasm of these muscles around the outer one-third of the vagina.

Once the husband's index finger is in the vagina, this very firm, tense muscular contraction around the vaginal opening will become readily apparent. Like any muscular spasm, it will become painful if too much digital pressure is rapidly applied against it, but slow, steady pressure in the vagina downward toward the rectum over a matter of several minutes will allow the muscles to relax.

The husband and wife are instructed to take three or four graduated dilators home and use them in sequence once or twice per day. It may be best for the wife to insert the dilators herself at first, just until some confidence has been gained. These are called Hegar dilators, the larger size looking like a rod, a little bigger than a fountain pen; or you can use a readily available set of plastic rectal dilators, which can be obtained at most drugstores. Of course, they should be well lubricated before insertion. Once the dilator is in the vagina, the wife should let it remain there for twenty to thirty minutes. When it can be easily inserted, the wife should retain one of these in her vagina for several hours each night. By using these dilators once or twice a day, the woman is gradually becoming comfortable with the idea that something can be in her vagina, and that it does not have to hurt.

At some time during the week it may be possible for the husband to begin inserting the dilator rather than the wife. Most vaginismus is caused by psychological problems, and the husband's interested, loving cooperation and tender care of his wife is an important part of the treatment.

When the couple plan to have intercourse, the dilator should be inserted in the vagina and should remain in place until the wife feels it is time for penetration of the penis. Then she is instructed to assume the woman-above position, at which time she takes the dilator out of her vagina with one hand and within a few seconds inserts the well-lubricated penis with her other hand. It is crucial that this transfer require only a few seconds, because a longer interval than that may allow the vaginal muscles to go into spasm again.

This quick change is an essential step for at least the first few times that the couple has intercourse.

We have seen extreme cases of vaginismus at the clinic where not even the little finger could be inserted in the vagina. One couple had adopted two children after seventeen years of no intercourse. Another couple had gone fourteen years without intercourse. Both cases were resolved within six weeks with the use of graduated dilators.

If no regular dilators are available, a simple substitute for the Hegar dilators could be short, tapered candles in graduated sizes, the largest being just a little bigger in diameter than a fountain pen.

Pelvic congestion is one of the most common causes of low-back pain and pelvic pain and tenderness. In the plateau phase, the time of increasing sexual arousal, all of the wife's pelvic structures become engorged with blood under a significant amount of pressure. If she proceeds to a good strong orgasm, the involuntary muscular contractions close off the small arteries and open the venous system to produce drainage of this pooled blood in a matter of minutes. This leaves a distinct, pleasantly overwhelming sensation of comfort and warmth in the pelvic area, followed by a feeling of relaxation.

Each time the stimulated wife fails to reach orgasm, this represents some injury to the pelvic organs and to her emotions, often leaving her with nervousness, weakness, fatigue, and moderate to severe pelvic pain and low-back pain, which may become chronic. This also may lead to chronic vaginal discharge or heavy or irregular menstrual bleeding. Unfortunately many women undergo pelvic operations because of this pain. This repeated congestion may also contribute to significant enlargement of the uterus, which may fool a doctor into thinking that there is a disease requiring surgery. I suggest that you avoid surgery for pelvic pain until you have made every effort to learn how to achieve full orgasm on a regular basis.

With any of the chronic symptoms we have discussed, you should have regular pelvic examinations at least every six months to one year, since some physical condition could arise at any time, requiring medical treatment.

Most cases of failure to attain orgasm that I have seen began with poor preparation for marriage, a frustrating and fearful honeymoon, followed by a prolonged period of disappointment, blundering, and boredom in marriage that conditioned the wife to feel there was no hope for fulfillment.

This situation was often aggravated by the wife's failure to understand that it is man's nature to be adventurous. When a man realizes his wife is not being satisfied, this inclination is increased even more, as he attempts to please her. She begins to view his variety of approaches as distasteful, vulgar, or abnormal. Nothing will chill and remove the bright lustre of married love more quickly than a cool, silent, sullen, indifferent, or negative attitude toward the young husband's advances.

Applying the information given in this book, today's husband has the opportunity to become a skillful lover—one who can tenderly lead his wife into the richest pleasures of the sexual relationship. Remember: *Every wife should be given the opportunity to experience orgasm in every intercourse.* The relationship may be very loving and warm, but this is not enough. Fulfillment ahead! This can be yours!

8

For the Impotent Husband
Fulfillment Again

George C., a physically strong, hardworking man of fifty-three, had desired intercourse five or six times a week during his married life—until recently. His wife complained that he no longer showed an interest in her. She recalled that he had lost his erection a few weeks back, and they had terminated their lovemaking that night. They had never discussed it, but he had seemed indifferent since then. She also observed that he had taken on more responsibility in his job the past few months and showed an unaccustomed tiredness.

Greg H. and his wife slept in twin beds and were careful never to touch each other or demonstrate any affection. Over a period of time he had developed an inability to have intercourse. His wife felt sorry for him and "tried to make it as easy on him as possible by not bothering him about it."

Ralph B. desired his wife, but in the middle of their lovemaking his desire "short-circuited," as he described it.

Don Y.'s wife was highly demanding of her husband, often commenting on his failure to satisfy her. He soon found himself concentrating on his performance, rather than on his pleasure. Finally he could not perform at all.

Harry M. had been an alcoholic for some years. After experiencing several failures to obtain an erection, he became more and more fearful.

Joe S. and his wife had always had a satisfying sexual relationship but they both noticed a disturbing change in his ability to maintain an erection. They discussed it and then made an appointment to see their family physician.

Roger A. was in a state of depression and had no interest in sex at all. His wife could not tell the doctor which had come first, the depression or his indifference to sex.

All these men suffer from the disturbing condition known as impotence. Impotence is the inability of the husband to achieve or keep an erection sufficient for intercourse. In physical terms, the erect penis contains four or five times the volume of blood it has when flaccid. When the man experiences impotence (for whatever reason), the vascular reflex mechanism fails to pump in sufficient blood and hold the blood there to make the penis firm and keep it erect. A man may feel aroused and desire to make love, but his penis does not become erect. Another man suffering from impotence may be in the process of making love to his wife, when his erection disappears and he reacts with panic.

Some of the most discouraged men I see in my office are those who come because of impotence. Yet these men have reason to hope, because most of those who take constructive steps toward facing and resolving their problem will regain their sexual powers. Their marriages may be even better afterward, for solving the impotence problem requires a kind of loving cooperation from the wife that can greatly strengthen a couple's mutual understanding and enrich their expression of love.

While a very small percentage of men have never been able to experience an erection or ejaculation, the great majority of men seeking treatment for impotence have functioned at least fairly well, until they developed a difficulty. Impotence appears in all ages, all races, on every social level, and within every economic group. At the risk of oversimplification, I will observe that impotence *usually* is caused by a man's thoughts. Seldom does a man with a positive mental attitude toward sex suffer from the condition, although *every* man at some time or other loses an erection. Therapist Helen Kaplan asserts that approximately one-half of the male population have experienced occasional times when they lost their erection or could not even get one for intercourse.

In many cases of impotence, this rather common experience of erection loss sets up a vicious cycle of failure/anxiety/more failure/more anxiety, until impotence, rather than a pleasurable sex experience, becomes the conditioned response. Anxiety narrows into panic as the condition continues; and the keener the fear and psychic pain, the more the sufferer tries to escape by "turning off" to his wife, virtually trying to expunge sex from his life.

I particularly appreciate the opportunity to give this information on impotence to both husbands and wives who may be facing this problem. I intend now to talk to you, in the privacy of your own marriage, through the pages of this book. For others of you who have never experienced this condition, I suggest that you read carefully and be forewarned. Wise responses to a passing difficulty may save what could be years of grief if the temporary experience were allowed to become an established condition. The point is that in most cases this does not have to happen. An occasional experience of impotence may have no significance, unless the man or his wife views it as a serious problem. Of course, impotence that changes the sex life of a couple must be dealt with.

Why is this condition so extremely devastating to the man? Because it cuts away his self-esteem where he is most vulnerable. Historically, sexual ability has been viewed as the mark of the real man—the he-man. Impotence involves the organ of his body that most represents his manhood. Impotence threatens his ego with the thought that he can no longer satisfy the woman he loves. Culturally, men have been depicted as *always* ready for sex, continually on the verge of exploding with desire, as it were. This is something an ordinary man may feel he has to try to live up to, suspecting that his own intensity of ardor falls a bit below the standard. Add to this the increasing pressure today on the husband to perform, when many women are preoccupied with their own needs and loudly demanding all they think they have missed. Then the slick manuals on elaborate (and often uncomfortable) new approaches to sensation and all the magazine articles on the subject give the man the impression that the world is coming into his bedroom to check on his performance. All in all, a man may feel inadequate at best, and when the worst happens—impotence— the results are both frustrating and humiliating.

The greatest mistake a man can make when troubling impotence appears is to "try not to think about it." Some men who are free to verbalize their fears with a loving, understanding wife will overcome the difficulty without even considering the need for professional help.

If the condition persists, the man should see his physician and tell him specifically what the trouble is. When the doctor knows what the patient is there for, he will try to determine the real extent of the problem. The medical criterion for impotence is a patient's self-report of failure to achieve or maintain erection for successful intercourse in at least 50 to 75 percent of his attempts. (Occasional failures should *not* be viewed as impotence.)

Then the physician will give the man a careful physical examination and possibly will schedule urological and endocrinological studies to rule out organic causes.

Diabetes is suspected first because 40 to 60 percent of diabetics eventually become impotent regardless of their diabetic control. However, these men can continue to enjoy the sexual relationship because they can almost always ejaculate normally, even though they may be unable to have an erection. This, of course, means that both husband and wife will need to develop more enjoyable physical closeness and openness of communication, so that they can learn to provide the most pleasing manual stimulation for each other, leading to orgasm for both.

Researchers report that female diabetics usually do not experience a lessening of desire or orgasmic response, and there is no change in their vaginal lubrication during sexual activity.

Causes of impotence may be difficult to pinpoint precisely. About 75 percent of impotent men undergoing treatment are found to have some sort of organic condition that could contribute to the impotence. In fact impotence is sometimes of crucial diagnostic value since it may even be the first indication of an organic condition that definitely requires medical treatment.

However, in more than 75 percent of the men treated, mild to moderate psychological problems, such as inhibition, shame and avoidance, feelings of insecurity or personal inadequacy or guilt, anger and hostility, and a fear of intimacy, are definitely associated with the impotence.

Some Causes of Impotence

In determining the causes of impotence there are many factors your doctor must consider. Here are some of them.

Alcohol. The intake of alcohol sometimes provokes some sexual desire, but it takes away much of the ability to perform or enjoy sexual union. Because alcohol always acts as a depressant on the neurological system, it can inhibit a person's sexual functioning as much as it does his coordination or speech. The person who has lost control of his drinking (an alcoholic) almost never has normal sexual ability. Fifty percent of all practicing alcoholics are impotent. The male alcoholic retains a normal sexual desire but is apt to complain bitterly about his loss of ability to function sexually. This often drives him to seek even more escape through alcohol.

Fatigue. Simple fatigue is the most common cause of decreased sex drive in the normal man. Episodes of failing to achieve erection because of fatigue may trigger the condition of impotence. Many men come home from work with so much emotional or physical fatigue, they simply do not have enough energy available for a good sexual relationship. A relaxed attitude of waiting till one is rested and an acceptance of lessened sexual energy when one reaches middle age will avoid much of this difficulty. A wife can help by often initiating arrangements to retire at an early hour and by discouraging activities that keep her husband from getting enough rest.

Obesity. Researchers have found that when obese men (weighing an average of 250 pounds) went on a strict eight-week weight-reduction diet, their level of testosterone, the male hormone, rose significantly and in almost every case reached normal levels. Before losing weight, these men had had female hormone levels twice as high as those found in men of normal weight. The main source of excess estrogen in males is a chemical change occurring in a substance found in fat cells. This estrogen is believed to suppress the testicular production of testosterone needed for a male's sexual functioning. In addition to hormonal problems, obesity also drains strength, affects the physical union and contact of body parts, and sometimes lowers the individual's self-image and confidence.

Smoking and tobacco products. Recent studies comparing male smokers and nonsmokers have shown that testosterone levels in the blood were significantly lower in the smoking group but that they rose to almost normal levels after seven days' abstinence from smoking. Test results make it clear that heavy cigarette smoking decreases testosterone levels in otherwise healthy men. Dr. Alton Ochsner of Tulane University School of Medicine has said, "After very long clinical experience, I am convinced that smoking is one of the most frequent causes of impotence today, particularly among young people." Smoking is also a major cause of lung cancer and heart disease and responsible for strokes and poor circulation, decreasing vigor and blood flow to the penile area.

Drugs. Prescription drugs such as blood-pressure pills and certain other medications, especially those that produce a dryness of the mouth, can cause impotence in a man previously active sexually. Your doctor will be able to identify these for you, but here is a partial list:

Amphetamines	Monoamine oxidase inhibitors
Atropine	(Parnate, Marplan, Nardil)
Banthine	Narcotics
Barbiturates	Progesterone
Cortisone	Propantheline bromide
Estrogen	(Pro-Banthine)
Guanethidine (Esimil)	Psychotropic agents, including
Imipramine (Tofranil,	tricyclics
Presamine, Janimine,	Reserpine
Imavate, SK-Pramine)	Sedatives of all types
Methyldopa (Aldomet)	Tranquilizers

Note that the illegal narcotics and stimulants of today's drug culture are offenders. One would like to tell young couples that as they seek thrills in one area of life, they may be robbing them-

selves of some of the really great thrills available in a positive, growing sexual relationship in marriage.

Depression. It is important for the doctor to determine whether
the depression has brought on the impotence, or whether the condition of impotence has brought on the depression. A person who
is clinically depressed has a low appetite for food, sleep, pleasures,
sex, and for life itself. Most of this person's energy is directed
toward survival in the face of continuing despair, and it is understandable when there is no appetite for things normally enjoyed.
Appropriate counseling and medication are indicated and usually
produce positive results.

Sometimes a man will suffer depression because of something
that has happened in his life. It could be the death of a friend, or
the loss of a job, or any other disturbing happening. The depression may well trigger sexual inability but this should be only a
temporary situation. Sexual desire is sometimes absent for months
after such serious illnesses as a heart attack or a stroke, because of
the depression brought on by the illness.

Other negative feelings. Any negative feelings, such as anger or
jealousy, which break a man's concentration in lovemaking and
drain off sexual energy can bring on impotence. Putting biblical
principles into action will avoid much of this. If clashes in the marriage are handled in a constructive manner when they arise, unspoken hostility will not carry over into the sexual relationship. If a
couple feel free to make love when they go to bed, this is a good
indication that concealed anger has been dealt with.

Dismay over decreased vigor. The man over fifty must accept
normal changes in his sexual capabilities. If he tries to hold himself to his twenty-one-year-old performance, he will at times fail
and may experience acute anxiety. If he adapts gracefully to minor
physiological changes, he can enjoy sex for many years to come.
He should remember that what he has "lost" in youthful vigor,
he has gained in capacity to express his love in a mature, more
meaningful, and more skillful manner.

Any unusual stress. Any stress in a man's life can express itself
through impotency. After all, the very word *impotence* suggests
weakness, feebleness, helplessness, inability, and lack of power,

strength, vigor, and capacity. When these feelings attack because of stress, it is perhaps natural that they find the sexual function a vulnerable target. It will be helpful to remember that one cannot *will* an erection. A tense man trying to force an erection of his penis will be unable to do so. Relaxation and concentration on pleasurable sensations, without any feeling of forcing one's body to perform, will be the best and the only approach at such times.

Seeing sex as sin. Sometimes in a man's early upbringing he has encountered the erroneous belief that sex is sin, and later in life, after he is married, this may lead to unexpressed guilt, even fear of touching his wife. His normal sexual reaction, then, is short-circuited, and his conscious-mind censor refuses to let erection happen; instead, it represses the trigger mechanism. When he is asleep, of course, he will have nocturnal emissions, and sometimes in the morning, like most healthy men, he will have erections. His impotence is psychogenic, but it can be resolved with godly professional help and a right understanding of God's Word.

Poor learning experiences. Sometimes early in marriage men fumble and struggle in trying to insert the penis and in the process lose their erection. This may set up a sensitivity that produces impotence. The male feels foolish; his self-esteem is damaged. And besides that, he loses his concentration on sensation when he has to stop to try to find the place for the penis to go. This is why the wife should always assist in inserting the penis, even when there is no problem with impotence. She is the one who knows best where it belongs.

The Primary Problem

Beyond all other factors contributing to impotence is the primary problem: The husband is too intensely preoccupied with his ability or inability to achieve and maintain an erection. He is pressured by the fear of failure. He concentrates on his bodily reactions like a spectator at his own lovemaking until self-consciousness destroys all joy, abandon, and sensation of pleasure. He tries, without success, to command the sexual reflexes, but they respond only to desire and stimulation. He becomes like the person who "can't do anything right." "I'm all thumbs today," such a person complains, and from then on pays attention to his failures, not his successes. So the anxious lover fumbles and concentrates on his fumbles, until he is aware of nothing else. Self-consciousness is always self-defeating. It always produces an unsatisfactory state of affairs and never more so than in the lovemaking process. It opens the door to fear of failure, the true villain behind the scenes, and any cure must deal with this fear.

What has happened to the wife during the development of impotency? She is apt to be in one of three camps: (1) feeling rejected and taking the blame; (2) feeling rejected and reacting with hostility; or (3) trying to understand and wanting to help in the most mature and loving way possible—if only someone will tell her how.

I cannot emphasize enough to the wife that she very well may be the one who holds the key to the cure for her husband. The cooperation of a loving partner in restoring a man to sexual vigor cannot be overestimated. When I see such a wife ready to work with her husband—loyal and caring, more concerned about him than about her own ego—I have great confidence that the husband will be cured.

A woman who has difficulty accepting herself may view the husband's impotence as a personal rejection of her, when in reality it is another problem altogether. She may take it as proof of her own inadequacy as a woman, when instead it may in no way reflect her husband's disinterest. In fact men are most apt to fear failure with the woman they love, while they could perform effectively with a woman they are indifferent to. Someone has pointed out that *love* and *erection* are not synonymous words. Her frustrated husband may have a great deal of desire but no accompanying erection. So to such a woman, I suggest that she choose to think rationally about herself, her husband, and the situation. When she refuses to put herself down and instead puts herself at her husband's disposal, as they work together for a cure, she will take significant steps toward the kind of emotional maturity that will make her far more desirable than ever before.

I have noted that some of the women who complain most about their husband's not being able to satisfy them sexually turn out to be the least cooperative when it comes to working together to solve the problem. To the hostile wife, I should point out that she is only defeating herself, for she and the husband she is undermining are still one flesh in the eyes of God. In helping her husband, she will do a great service to herself and will perhaps find the love she inwardly longs for, as she learns to give.

To that woman who is mature, stable, sensitive, and accepting of her husband's needs, I say that she can work wonders—and she will! In the process, even without intercourse, there can be a good deal of mutual pleasure as well.

The two begin by admitting that they have a problem—a *couple* problem—which can be solved. As they move toward a solution, they will be ridding each other of the buildup of feelings of inadequacy. What a gift to give!

The solution involves three lines of approach, which we might call in easy-to-remember terms: *talk, touch,* and *teasing.*

Talk refers to the establishment of broken communication lines, lines that have been battered down by periods of indifference and frustration. The wife must help her husband put his fears into words. The conspiracy of silence is now broken, and the man must be able to express how he feels. As each is open to the feelings of the other, a climate of understanding and tender togetherness grows.

Touch refers to physical communication, which may also have broken down as each moved to his or her own side of the bed after periods of frustration. The husband and the wife must begin again to enjoy the fun and pleasure of affection, of cuddling and caressing and sleeping close together.

Teasing suggests the kind of sexual relationship that can begin to develop, even though the husband is still unable (or thinks he is unable) to gain an erection. The couple should agree to spend time together pleasuring each other without any demand for intercourse. The husband should use the new communication lines to tell his wife exactly what gives him pleasure. Her body is available to him, and his body is available to her. Let them enjoy caressing each other in love play without expecting anything further. The wife should demand nothing of him in terms of arousal; some therapists suggest that the couple agree to prohibit intercourse and orgasm for several days. They should simply relax together in a warm, intimate situation, while he learns to let his body take over with the proper responses. In this setting of leisurely erotic stimulation without sexual intercourse, the penis erection will wax and wane. The husband will discover that once an erection is obtained, it will come back if it goes away. To observe it come and go is an important part of the training process for both husband and wife, as they gain experiential knowledge that with loving cooperation the erection will always return.

When the time seems right, the husband will find delight in satisfying his wife by stimulation of the clitoris. When he feels ready for intercourse, the wife should be prepared to insert the penis. Even if it is only partially erect, she can "stuff" the penis in the vagina, and the subsequent stimulation will often increase and maintain the erection.

It has been found that the male-above position is usually the most satisfying and stimulating position for men experiencing difficulty with erection.

The lovemaking process should never be rushed. There is enough time to regain full sexual powers, and the love play should be carried out in a most pleasurable, leisurely, and sensual manner. Privacy should be ensured. The wife should wear her most appealing gown (which may be no gown at all), and the husband should use the endearing names he once called her. Some names can be very unstimulating. (Have you ever heard a man call his wife *Mom?* Too often, if he calls her this, he will subconsciously visualize her as mother, thus losing sexual interest.)

Once gentle stimulation and erotic encounters have turned the tide, remember that success breeds more success. The husband should realize, however, that fears of failure in sexual performance could come back at any time, perhaps when he is in a stress-filled situation. He can find a cure the way he found the first one—by turning to his wife, sharing his fears, finding.comfort and pleasure in her body, relaxing and refusing to *demand* any performance from himself.

The wife must be careful not to make him feel inferior, never to put him under pressure, never to judge his sexual performance. She must be responsive and seductive, yet not come on too strong. Together they can make the most of their sexual relationship—perhaps finding far more pleasure in each other than they ever did before the difficulty developed.

Other Treatments

Medical treatment of the erectile dysfunction generally consists of one or all of the following: taking the patient history, physical examination, and appropriate medications. A good history and physical examination are paramount to help determine the cause of the impotence. Should a treatable condition be found, appropriate medications or changing medications would be in order. Sometimes a specific cause is not found, even when the patient continues to manifest organic or physical impotence. In those cases one or several of the following therapies may be tried.

Initial treatment of the condition may consist of using a mild vasodilator such as Yohimbine in an effort to improve penile blood flow. It is important to remember that this is not specific for the blood vessels of the penis and there may be side effects associated with its use, such as dry mouth, dizziness, and upset stomach. This medication has about a 30 percent objective response rate.

Those who may not be able to tolerate Yohimbine or fail to respond to it may need to consider a vacuum system. There are approximately ten manufacturers of various vacuum systems. All the vacuum systems work in basically the same way. They create a negative pressure around the penis and literally draw blood into the penis until the penis becomes very tumescent. At this point the individual places a rubber ring or rubber band around the base of the penis, trapping the blood in the penis and providing an erection lasting for up to thirty minutes. Then the rubber band is removed. Patients who are taking anticoagulants or have local skin diseases in the genital region, which may worsen with use of this suction device, should not use the vacuum system.

Another treatment that is becoming increasingly popular is penile injections. Medications that have been included in this form of therapy are papaverine, phentolamine (Regitine), and prostaglandin (Caverject). Of these drugs, only Caverject is approved by the Food and Drug Administration for use in the treatment of impotence. The individual learns to inject a measured amount of drug into the corpora cavernosum within the shaft of the penis, which produces a very prompt erection lasting on the average between thirty and ninety minutes. This drug has proved to be safe and reliable in approximately 70 to 75 percent of men. Contraindications to the use of penile injections include concurrent anticoagulant therapy or existing scarring of the penis such as Peyronie's plaque. Long-term effects can include scarring, which may result in an irregular curvature of the penis. If this should develop, it is advisable to immediately discontinue penile injection therapy.

The most definitive treatment to date is penile implantation. There are basically three types of penile implants: a pair of malleable rods, a self-contained pair of inflatable prosthetic cylinders, and a three-piece fully inflatable prosthesis. These prosthetic devices must be surgically implanted. Two of the most common complications consist of infection or mechanical failure. Both occur less than 5 percent of the time. If infection should occur, the device would have to be removed and at a later date, a second device could be implanted. Infections are slightly more common in diabetic men. If the device fails, a re-operation is required to correct the defect and/or repair part or all of the prosthesis. Nevertheless, sexual satisfaction rates on the order of 90 to 95 percent for both men and women are quite common with penile implantation.

Penile re-vascularization has failed to provide satisfactory return of potency in the majority of men. It has been used in individuals who have rather discreet localized arterial blockages or in those individuals who may suffer from significant venous incompetence. In this operation, the penis is re-vascularized with a neighboring blood vessel, such as the inferior epigastric artery, which is located in the lower abdomen. Basically the artery is retunneled into the penis to provide new blood flow. In case of venous incompetence, the large dilated veins that drain the penis are literally tied off or ligated.

A rate of cure of impotence of 50 to 75 percent is reported by secular therapists. I have no exact statistics to quote, but I have observed a rate of cure that is much higher for the Christian husband who claims and uses his extra resource against the main villain—*fear* of failure. God has given us resources far greater than the spirit of fear, and resting in that knowledge will provide the Christian husband with a stability and relaxation that can go far in solving almost every impotency problem. The Bible says, "For God hath not given us the spirit of fear; but of power, and of love, and of a sound mind" (2 Tim. 1:7).

Every situation of life in which we see our own inadequacy can be an opportunity to see the power of Christ undertaken for us. No need is too small or too great for our God to meet, we discover, as we count on Him!

9

The Power
of Sexual Intimacy

When our Creator devised the one-flesh relationship, He placed within it the potential for a sexual intimacy that could bless marriages almost beyond belief. This potential has not always been understood, but today therapists and researchers are discovering that *genuine* sexual intimacy has a remarkable power to heal, renew, refresh, restore, and sustain the marriage relationship.

But, one may ask, Isn't *every* sexual encounter an expression of intimacy? After all, what could be more intimate than the sex act? The ancient Romans had a gloomy proverb that suggests the answer: *Post coitum omnis animal triste.* "Every creature is sad following sexual intercourse." In other words, in the vastness of the universe, a small attempt at closeness has been made. Two have tried to cure loneliness through the temporary joining of their bodies. But in only a matter of moments, even the attempt is over, and one is alone again. For men and women trying to smother their loneliness and anxiety with casual sexual encounters, sadness and a gnawing sense of emptiness are the logical outcome; such intercourse is devoid of the real, sustained intimacy possible only between a husband and wife who are committed to each other.

Too often, impersonal sex happens *within* marriage. Then the loneliness becomes even more acute for married people who remain unsatisfied in their longing for a deep, shared closeness, in which each act of intercourse reaffirms and renews an intimacy that is always there.

Real sexual intimacy links marriage partners with strong strands of caring that are deeply emotional, mental—even spiritual—and also intensely physical; thus closeness does not occur only at times of intercourse. Because of the God-designed one-flesh relationship, real intimacy between husband and wife always has sexual dimensions, whether they are having sex or just talking; snuggling close in their sleep or dressing together for the day; working in the garden side by side or engaged in prayer. It is all *lovemaking*.

The practice of tenderness; loving gestures; frequent, affectionate, physical touching; shared thoughts; exchanged feelings; mutual supportiveness and trust; the valuing of each other's bodies, almost as if the other were one's own; shared laughter; a closeness so substantial and abiding that no one else can interfere with it—all this adds up to continuous sexual interaction in a deeply satisfying form. It is the mating pattern of true sexual intimacy.

This intimacy has its roots in the sense of belonging that two people nurture and develop over a period of time. In our book *Love Life for Every Married Couple,* we shared what one couple, married more than twenty-five years, had told us about the development of their relationship, as they cemented the sense of belonging into their marriage. They said:

> On the way to our June wedding, we thought we had everything going for us. Our friendship was warm, our romantic feelings even warmer, and as for the fires of passion, they were just waiting for the match! After we settled into married life, the companionship and sexual desire and romantic thrills were still there. But it was all a little less perfect than we had expected because we were such imperfect people. The pink glow of romance hadn't prepared us for that! We weren't Christians then so we didn't know that *agape* love could glue us together. Fortunately, something else brought us through those first rocky years when wedded bliss almost got buried under the un-bliss. You might call what developed between us a sense of belonging. We had decided right from the start that it was us against the world—two people forming a majority of one. So whatever happened, or however much we clashed in private, we stuck by each other. We were like a brother and sister on the playground. We might scrap with each other, but let an

outsider try to horn in and he had to take us both on! If one of us
hurt, the other wiped away the tears. We made a habit of believing in
each other while our careers got off the ground. We showed each
other all the kindness that two impatient young people could be
expected to show—and then some more. It really wasn't long until
we discovered something stupendous about our relationship. We
found we belonged. We came first with each other, and always would.
Because we belonged to each other, no one could spoil our love and
togetherness from the outside. Only we could do that, and we weren't
about to! It was too good to lose. A lot of people seem to spend their
whole life looking for a feeling of belonging. Maybe they don't know
that marriage is the best place to find it.

Intimacy is rooted in this security of belonging but it must be
nourished by an ongoing sexual relationship that is sensuous and
satisfying, characterized by tenderness, and by the feeling both partners receive of being loved for themselves. When sex is experienced
in this way, a cluster of emotional benefits appears: relief from hurts,
a welling of joy and optimism, a sense of security and peace.

When this kind of intimacy is sustained, husband and wife
become so close emotionally that they are alert and responsive to
fluctuations of feeling in the other, always concerned about the
other's well-being, finely tuned to what the partner needs.

Partners may become angry with each other—this happens
occasionally in any interpersonal relationship. But the situation is
rather quickly resolved, because they cannot bear to have their
state of intimacy disrupted. Afterward, sex becomes a means of
joyous reunion.

Developing real sexual intimacy carries a couple safely through
the traditionally dangerous waters of the first several years of marriage; the seventh year, when outside temptations are said to be
greatest; the middle years, when the children leave home and partners are thrown back on their own relationship; the hard times,
when outside pressures and problems become acute; the periods
of physical illness or disability, when sexual intimacy makes it possible for the couple to adjust to new conditions in their sex life;
and on through old age, when sexual intimacy continues to be
enriching, pleasurable, and very reassuring.

But the other side of the coin is also true. Because sexual intimacy *is* so important as a constructive, integrative force, when it is disappointing or absent altogether, it has an enormous potential for disruption of the marriage.

The warning signs indicating the failure to develop a rewarding sexual intimacy are: boredom with the marriage, disinterest in sex, a feeling of frustration because "the honeymoon is over," and the temptation for one or both to look elsewhere for the intimacy they crave.

Here are some factors that will hinder the development of sexual intimacy in any marriage.

Hindrances to Intimacy

The Habit of Criticism

Many couples not only freely criticize each other in the hope of bringing about improvements in the other's appearance or behavior, but they also fall into the habit of unconscious criticism—constant carping on a small scale—woven into their daily conversation. This is not an environment in which intimacy can flower.

Listen to yourselves. If there is habitual criticism, you can do something about it, even before your partner decides a change is needed. On your part, totally refrain from criticism, no matter how much you want to retaliate. Instead, replace those critical words with positive words of praise and encouragement. It can reverse the whole trend of your relationship, and you will begin to see just how impoverished the two of you were before, when you were unable to sit down and just enjoy talking with each other in an atmosphere of open sharing.

Bottled-Up Anger and Resentment

Anger and hostility, no matter how veiled or repressed, will kill any growth of loving intimacy. Marital boredom is often the mask that hides a world of rage and resentment never openly expressed. This happens when a couple fail to resolve issues as they arise. Sometimes they will opt for a strained politeness, refusing to deal with the cause of tension. Sometimes they resume a marital front, pretending that the clash never happened, but the bad feelings are still there. The issue may still be there, too, waiting to trouble them another day.

An argument, distasteful as it seems at the time, is better than chilly silence, because an argument does represent a reaching out to the other person. The underlying desire of the two arguing is that their position will be understood and accepted by the other. Arguments sometimes bring about a new understanding between husband and wife.

A rousing "fight" can be better than repression of opinions and emotions, which produces resentment, leading to indifference. Indifference is the true enemy of love. At least the couple are still directed toward each other when they are fighting!

Two ground rules should be observed for constructive communication: (a) an agreement that both will keep talking, until they resolve the problem and understand each other; (b) an agreement to limit the discussion to the present conflict, not bringing up past failure on either side.

Failure to Communicate

There really cannot be intimacy without communication—a sharing on both verbal and nonverbal levels. One partner may actually attempt to keep the relationship superficial, because he or she is afraid of intimacy, afraid of closeness developing.

Most people, however, can learn to communicate with practice, if they really want to. Communication requires a listening love, as well as a willingness to be vulnerable—to try to put into words what one is feeling and trust those words to the partner's understanding.

Lack of Trust in One's Partner or Oneself

Mutual trust is one of the essentials of intimacy. It takes time and care to build this trust. But a different problem arises when an individual does not have a good feeling about himself. This can cause fear of intimacy, because intimacy is reciprocal. To be intimate is to *exchange*, which means that one must have something to give. A person with a low self-image may feel that he or she has nothing to give and may try to hide this "fact" by distancing himself or herself from family and friends. Sometimes people shrink from deep emotional involvement because they have been hurt by close relationships—often this happened when they were children and too young to understand and work out the problem. The pain that lingers from these experiences can be healed by replacing the remembered pattern of pain with a whole new pattern of pleasure in emotional closeness. This, again, takes time and loving patience on the part of the mate who must woo and win the other's confidence. But it can be done (and must be done), if the two are ever to enjoy an intimate relationship.

Anxiety about One's Physical Appearance

There is a direct correlation between a negative perception of one's body and inhibited sexual intimacy. Free sexual interaction, or even the intimacy of sharing a bedroom, cannot be enjoyed when a person is embarrassed about his or her body and trying to keep it covered at all times. The natural sexual responses of the body are also inhibited when a person is concentrating on his or her physical imperfections, rather than erotic and pleasurable thoughts. It is amazing but true that many people feel quite unlovable, just because of some aspect of their body, and they are convinced their partner has the same negative feelings toward their appearance. The one thing the partner can do is communicate his or her appreciation verbally for every part of the mate's body, always praising, never tearing down.

The individual with this anxiety concerning his or her appearance should look on it as a spiritual problem. Of course, if any practical improvements can be made, they should be. But the person needs to meditate on two scriptural principles: (1) God has given me these attributes. "I praise you because I am fearfully and wonderfully made; your works are wonderful, I know that full well" (Ps. 139:14 NIV). Therefore, I need to take the best possible care of my body and develop a positive feeling toward what God has given me and the way He has made me. (2) The Lord planned that husband and wife are to be "naked and unashamed" before each other as part of the one-flesh relationship (see Gen. 2:24–25). Therefore hiding my body from my mate is not scriptural.

"Spectatoring" during Lovemaking

"Spectatoring" is a therapist's term for apprehensively observing one's own behavior during lovemaking because one is so anxious about performing well sexually.

This can be remedied as an understanding partner helps the person turn his or her attention to sensual feelings and the pleasure of nondemand physical caressing.

Because intimacy is a mutual experience of sharing, it is difficult to enter into the enjoyment of it when you are self-preoccupied. Switching your attention to pleasuring your partner and enjoying the way your partner pleasures you will build intimacy and do away with anxious self-consciousness.

De-emphasizing the Value of Sex

The sexual relationship within marriage is one of the most profound, rewarding, and mysterious of all experiences. But, strangely, some people think of sex as an immaturity that should be outgrown. In some marriages one or both partners may consciously de-emphasize its value and turn their attention elsewhere. This is, of course, devastating to the rich, sexually dimensioned intimacy God planned for husband and wife.

Predictable, Mechanical Sex

An emotionally enriching intimacy is always a sign of life. Sex that is as routine as brushing one's teeth and as mechanical as mailing a letter is a sign of a dying relationship. It may be revived by emotional preparation for physical sex, by varying times and places and approaches for sex, and by emphasizing tenderness and sensuousness rather than a technique that is goal-oriented to quick orgasm. A man can have a sexual experience that lasts a scant two minutes but this would be cheating both himself and his wife.

Lack of Sensitivity

Intimacy grows as we show our sensitivity to our partner's needs. An insensitivity to needs and desires, particularly in the sexual relationship, can be quite detrimental to the development of intimacy. One traditional example often cited is the husband who demands sex right after an unresolved argument, with the children playing in the next room, and a neighbor at the front door! Or the wife who interrupts her husband's impassioned lovemaking to go take meat out of the freezer or check on a sleeping child! Therapists call behavior that hinders a satisfying sexual experience "sexual sabotage." If you want to develop intimacy, you will pour yourself into understanding your partner's needs and meeting them in sensitive, loving ways.

Absence of Nonsexual Physical Touching

To enjoy intimacy with your mate is to "be in touch." This means *physical* touch, as well as the ways you touch emotionally, intellectually, and spiritually.

I have observed that married people need physical touching of an affectionate nonsexual nature to retain the feeling of being in love. Emotional/sexual intimacy cannot grow unless you touch often, gently, sensitively, freely, without fear of rebuff or misunderstanding. Intimacy requires cuddling, snuggling, sitting close to each other, holding hands, and kissing as a part of your daily life.

Too often after marriage, couples use touch only as a sexual signal, but this should not be. Sex cannot be expected to meet all your needs for physical contact and affection. To build intimacy you must "keep in touch" every day.

Too Much Television

Television watching may seem less significant than other factors we have mentioned. However, television promotes passivity; people wrapped up in watching T.V. have neither the motivation nor the energy to develop an intimate relationship. It can become so hypnotic that one does not realize how much time is being given to T.V. viewing.

It can turn into a source of real friction. One partner stays up to watch the late-night programs and then expects the other to still be alert and ready for lovemaking when he or she comes to bed. Sometimes television viewing is used deliberately as a means of avoiding sex.

So weigh your priorities and decide which you would rather have: a life spent passively staring into a television screen or an intimate relationship with your marriage partner.

Up to this point you and your partner may have developed no more than a fraction of the intimacy you both are capable of. Use the spiritual dynamic of hope, and look on your untapped potential for warmth, caring, and tender sharing as an area where you can grow together as you consciously seek to build a lasting intimacy. This kind of growth does not happen quickly, but gradually, the way people themselves grow. And you will find, as you make progress, that coming to know a loved one intimately is never boring! The rewards will speak for themselves.

Prescription for Intimacy

We could give you endless lists of suggestions for building sexual intimacy in your marriage but we are going to prescribe only three things. These are broad guidelines that reflect what therapists call the three functioning aspects of human intimacy: *love, sensuousness,* and *sexuality.* The first guideline has to do with love, for that is the only way to build trust.

Establish Mutual Trust

You cannot build intimacy when you are trying to protect or defend yourselves. You cannot build intimacy when you are afraid of exposing your needs and frailties. You cannot build intimacy unless you feel safer with your partner both emotionally and physically than with anyone else in the world.

Intimacy grows only in a place of safety. Because human behavior is organized around the seeking of pleasure and the avoidance of pain, you must treat your partner in such a way that he or she will always identify you with pleasure, not with emotional pain.

When husband and wife are afraid of hurt, rebuff, criticism, or misunderstanding from each other, they will find it difficult to touch affectionately or share freely. God's Word shows how to establish the trust that builds intimacy in two concise statements: (1) "Love covers over a multitude of sins" (1 Peter 4:8 NIV). (2) "Love builds up" (1 Cor. 8:1 NIV). In other words: (1) Overlook mistakes and never criticize. (2) Always encourage and give your partner the precious gift of sympathetic understanding.

Criticism can be the death blow to love and intimacy. It never changes anyone for the better. It only succeeds in putting miles of emotional distance between a husband and wife who are longing inwardly for closeness. Praise on the other hand has power to enhance the relationship, while strengthening and inspiring the individual to higher attainments.

To give your partner unconditional love (that love we call *agape*) is the very best way to win his or her trust. If you want to find out how to love unconditionally, please read chapter 10 of *Love Life for Every Married Couple*, "The Agape Way." Also reread chapter 3 of this book.

Learn to Enjoy Sensuousness

Sensuousness is defined by therapists as the need to be held, fondled, caressed, and touched. It should not be confused with sensuality, which is a preoccupation with the physical, as opposed to the intellectual and spiritual. We are speaking simply of the importance of touch, as a means of meeting a human being's deep needs, and as an essential way of developing intimacy in the marriage.

In *Love Life* we have given twenty-five suggestions for nonsexual touching, which any husband and wife would do well to put into practice. Some individuals are hungry for more touching and they will gladly have sex, just to be held and caressed. Others do not understand what their true need is and they may try to use sex as a substitute for sensitive, affectionate, physical fondling and closeness. Then there are those who believe they "are just not affectionate." These must learn to enjoy sensuousness through the loving, patient persistence of the partner and the practice of nonsexual physical touching.

Sensuousness is also important in the enjoyment of sex. Almost every square inch of the human body has the ability to become erotic, and partners should use their hands and fingers to touch, stroke, massage, and caress all parts of the mate's body. Exploring every part of the body with loving hands (including tracing the beloved's face in the dark with sensitive fingers) will increase the sense of intimacy.

As sensuousness is learned, the husband may discover that sex can be much more leisurely than he imagined and that being sexually passive occasionally can be very enjoyable, as his wife caresses him in ways she has discovered will please him. Sensuousness requires the capacity to enjoy tenderness, and the man who has thought of feelings of tenderness as somehow feminine will have much to learn in experiencing this aspect of intimacy.

Relate Sexually as Lovers

After sex most men want reassurance that they have been good lovers, and most women want reassurance that their husband has been pleased, enchanted, and satisfied. But research indicates that a great many people just turn over and go to sleep without saying much of anything!

If you want to build intimacy, you will need to begin to relate to each other sexually as lovers, not as disgruntled moms and dads who occasionally have sex because it's a habit—or duty.

What are some of the characteristics of sex between marriage partners who are lovers? First of all, when they have sex, they are often reenacting the time when they first fell in love—the drama of their courtship—and this recalls the freshness of youth. These feelings can be recaptured each time they shut out the world to come together sexually. The husband can experience the thrill of conquest whenever he makes love to his wife; she can glory in his pursuit; and he can savor her melting response.

Because the husband is a lover, he shows capacity for tenderness and caring and the ability to express his feelings without embarrassment, along with masculine characteristics that please his wife, such as confidence and strength. The wife responds in turn. She is thrilled by his slow, sensual approach and by a romantic atmosphere and she lets him know it.

Lovers avoid dull routine in their sex play. They practice variety—variations in time or setting, variations in love play, variations in frequency, position, and mood. Sometimes their sex is fun; sometimes it is intensely passionate; sometimes it is leisurely and tender. Variety *is* the spice of lovemaking.

Lovers enjoy each other as man and woman. They spend time together—preforeplay time—taking walks or perhaps just talking in front of a fire in the fireplace, when they can be alone. They go away together for a night or a weekend or a few days to refresh themselves and renew their relationship.

Lovers learn to subtly or directly communicate their desires hours beforehand, to give both time to prepare emotionally, to look forward to the experience, and to fill their minds with exciting ideas of how to make the lovemaking experience more beautiful and prolonged.

After the climax, when both have been satisfied, lovers want to remain close to each other with lots of gentle stroking, murmuring, kisses, and embracing. They sometimes want to maintain the warm glow with conversation of a special nature. Nothing mundane is allowed! No talk of home repairs or money problems or Johnny's bad report card. In the relaxed afterglow of lovemaking, while still in each other's arms, they want to talk about each other, perhaps the history of their love affair. They may share conversation that is intimate or especially uplifting—perhaps expressing dreams and goals they would mention at no other time. It is a time for private laughter, and always for complimenting each other as lovers—thanking the other for the beautiful experience—and perhaps praying together before they fall asleep with gratitude for the way God has blessed them, even in their lovemaking.

For the Christian couple sexual intimacy always has spiritual dimensions as unity with the beloved is experienced and the two reach the highest possible degree of closeness physically, mentally, and spiritually. For this couple there is no sadness after intercourse, but two hearts singing as one with joy and praise!

It is our prayer that you will experience the pleasure of sexual intimacy in your own relationship.

10

The "Perfect" Wife
by Gaye Wheat

This will not be one of those very serious lectures on how to become the *perfect* wife! I don't want to imply that I have somehow attained that state or that it is possible for you to get there by following ten easy steps and putting forth a little effort.

The chapter title with *perfect* in quotation marks should suggest that we will be using *perfect* in a somewhat different manner than that which the dictionary decrees with its list of lofty definitions:

"Without blemish or defect." *(Who, me?)*
"Completely skilled." *(Hardly!)*
"Thoroughly effective." *(Maybe occasionally.)*
"Having all the qualities necessary . . ." *(Well, no.)*

But then that last definition gives pause for thought: *Having all the qualities necessary* . . . to assure your husband that you're the perfect wife for him. There it is! Exactly what this chapter is about.

We know we aren't perfect wives. And our husbands know it too. But it is possible to keep them so happy that they think of us as perfect, because in the details that matter most to them, we have learned to please them! Now I am not talking about devious dealings or cute manipulations designed to befuddle our husbands into adoring us. They are not that easily fooled. And, more important, there is a better way to please them—a way that God can honor, because it is rooted in the New Testament principle of servant-hood: "Ourselves your servants for Jesus' sake" (2 Cor. 4:5).

Of course this does not mean that we are to behave like menials around our husbands. To serve my husband for Jesus' sake does not demand that I be servile and abject like a Babylonian slave or an eighteenth-century washerwoman. *It begins with the attitude of thinking about him, instead of being preoccupied with myself.* It includes looking for ways, all the time, to help him and please him. In the words of Proverbs 31, this kind of wife will do her husband "good and not evil all the days of her life." The behavior that pleases him flows out of an inner attitude that I have already cho-sen for myself—the attitude that my husband is the king of my household and the king of my marriage. Next to the Lord, he is the one I want to please the most. He is my top priority, right after Christ. So it is my joy and privilege to treat my husband as my "lord." And here I am in good company, for Peter in his first epistle instructs the Christian wives to adapt themselves to their husbands, their beauty "the unfading loveliness of a calm and gen-tle spirit, a thing very precious in the eyes of God" (1 Peter 3:4 PHILLIPS). He goes on to point to Sarah as a good example: "Even as Sara obeyed Abraham, calling him lord" (1 Peter 3:6).

The rewards of this attitude have been mentioned earlier but they are worth repeating: The more you please your husband, the more he is going to be eager to please you. The more he attempts to please you, the more you are going to be happy and satisfied, and you are going to try even more to do the things that make him happy. This is the glorious cycle of response that we could call a circle, for a circle never ends. Once you step into that circle of love, you will not want to move out, and although your hus-band may still know your limitations only too well, he will feel that whatever you do is *all right*. You have proved yourself to be just the right wife for him.

When it comes to the sex relationship, we *must* be pleased our-selves in order to please our husbands. Men who rate their sexual experience as outstanding say it's because of the pleasure they receive from seeing their wives excited and thrilled. Most husbands realize there is far more to sex in marriage than having their biological needs met by a passive, tired, or bored but submissive wife. They want to see their wives sent into ecstasy by their lovemaking; and yet, according to statistics, less than 40 percent of married couples consistently enjoy maximum fulfillment and orgasm in intercourse.

Because I speak at seminars on sexual technique in marriage, women often talk to me about their disappointments and their longings in this area. They know they don't have a good sex relationship but they suspect everyone else does. And they are *not* happy.

On the basis of our counseling experience, as well as the evidence of the Scriptures, Dr. Wheat and I believe that good sex is a must for a good marriage. It may not be the most important thing, but if either partner is deprived of sex or dissatisfied with it, then it becomes a major issue. A *satisfactory* sex relationship strengthens any marriage. In fact a oneness in this intimate area often indicates that every part of the marriage will be reinforced.

Even though sex is such a public topic these days, women who have been married for thirty years still come to me and they don't know whether or not they have ever reached a climax. All the general discussion of sex in the magazines has not helped them. They need to understand the specifics of the sex experience, with its arousal, response, and climax, and that is why we have made this book so very specific.

The factual, physiological information, correctly put into action, will take care of less than half the problem for dissatisfied women and their husbands. What is left unsolved falls into the categories of attitudes and communication. Some counselors have suggested that as much as 80 percent of the difficulty lies in these areas.

Attitudes and Communication

Evaluate Your Attitudes

I have this suggestion for those of you who are longing for a better sex life, or for you who admit (without longing) that it isn't all that great for your husband. Take stock of your own attitudes first! This calls for some time alone, when you can honestly evaluate your attitudes toward sex and toward your husband as a lover. Before you are done, you will find that you are taking a long look at your self-esteem as well, for that too occupies a place in the total picture.

Begin with your attitude toward sex in general. When you read the word *sex,* what do you think about? What image comes into your mind? Something warm and loving and tender and yielding? Or perhaps something a bit distasteful, or even unpleasant?

What was your attitude before you were married? Did your mother tell you everything you needed to know beforehand? Did she tell you *anything?* Perhaps you thought your husband would know it all, and yet he didn't. Do you still have sexual inhibitions? Do you endure sex as a duty or anticipate it with delight? Are you warm and responsive to your husband's lovemaking or do you scoot over to the other side of the bed, hoping he won't show any interest?

Did your honeymoon experiences disappoint you or turn you off, establishing an unhappy pattern that has not yet been broken? I cannot count how many women have told me their first experiences in marriage were very disappointing: "The moon did not glow . . . the stars did not fall . . . and no lightning flashed at all!" Can you accept this disappointment, which perhaps still programs your reactions, by understanding that the difficulties you and your husband experienced were probably due to a lack of information and hopes too high for the moment you had been waiting for? Although romantic literature has implied that as soon as you are man and wife all your sexual responses are automatically released, this is just not true. The sex act is not instinctive. It takes time to establish a truly great sex relationship.

Here's a way of evaluating your contribution to the physical love relationship, suggested by Shirley Rice in *Physical Unity in Marriage.* She says that we women should try measuring our *physical* love for our husbands by the yardstick in 1 Corinthians 13, the great love chapter. See how you do. Remember we're talking now about *physical* love. Is yours patient and kind? Never envious or jealous? Not possessive? Not conceited? Never rude? Never indiscreet? Not insistent on its own right? Not self-seeking? Never touchy, fretful, or resentful? Does it pay no attention to a wrong suffered? Nor count up past wrongs? Does it not rejoice in wrong-doing, but in the truth? Does it always believe the best of him? Does it never fail?

What a strict measuring stick! We are just not capable of that quality of love without God's power. But the point is that we can have the enabling of God's power as women born again in Christ to remake and transform every wrong attitude we have found in ourselves during this evaluation time.

Let's continue the evaluation by considering just how we look at *ourselves*. Do you accept yourself the way you are? Or do you feel inwardly that you are unattractive? Either overweight or underweight? You think perhaps your hips are too big or your legs too skinny? Or you don't have enough bust? (And you know how men seem to look at full busts.)

When you and your husband make love, are you anxious to keep covered with a long gown, or to turn out all the lights, so that he won't see your deficiencies or blemishes? And doesn't this affect your behavior during the process? You aren't quite free; you never quite forget yourself and how you look!

Most of us know that we do not have figures to compare to the legendary Marilyn Monroe, so it is hard for us to accept the fact that our husbands might think that we with our ho-hum bodies are beautiful or desirable. I believe this is a bigger issue with most women than they will ever let on. The problem is compounded if you have the kind of husband who never says anything encouraging or complimentary to you. A woman who feels beautiful is going to be beautiful for her husband when they are alone together—and much more uninhibited in lovemaking. You and I should remember that our husbands chose us, above all others, and that if they get the loving response they want, they'll never think about our imperfections.

While we are evaluating, it is time for every woman to ask herself if she accepts her husband just as he is—not only in appearance, but with the kind of temperament, strengths and weaknesses, and even the earning ability that he possesses. You see, this has a definite effect on the way you respond to him in lovemaking, or the way he approaches you. If you cut him down in word or thought, your relationship will be damaged. After acceptance of your mate just as he is, it is time to concentrate on his strengths and focus your thoughts on them. How about a few compliments for him? As women, we may expect to be always on the receiving end. How about telling him how glad you are that he knows how to repair your car or your washing machine himself? Or how much you appreciate his kindness to your parents? Or how you admire his good taste in clothes? Or how wonderful it is to have such a physically strong husband, or a husband who gives you such wise advice when you need it? Or whatever applies to your own man. It is all a matter of honest appreciation, which you pass on to him, instead of keeping it to yourself. The couple who appreciate each other and *show it* have every reason to expect a wonderful sexual relationship. Difficulties in their situation are more apt to be only physical in nature, matters of adjustment, which can be readily solved by applying proper information.

Communication

After evaluating attitudes, you need to consider your communication. Sex without communication has little to commend it. Your communication may be of the nonverbal kind during the lovemaking process itself. Perhaps you have learned to do what the sex therapists suggest—to put your hand lovingly over your husband's and show him where you want stimulation. And if he is too rough or too gentle, to show him again with your hand over his. There are ways of telling him when you are ready for intercourse without saying a word. But even before you make love, you may need to communicate your needs to your husband, frankly and clearly. He may have needs to tell you about too. If you want to reach orgasm and are not doing so, ask him to give the manual stimulation that will bring you to orgasm. It is amazing how silent we women are on something as important as the sex act in marriage. We *wish* in silence or we *suffer* in silence or we *hope* that this time he will be different, that this time he will think of doing that which we long for him to do. Why not just tell him?

While we are speaking of communication, let me caution you about one thing that is better left uncommunicated. Some wives, out of a desire to please their husband (or for other reasons), have pretended for years that they are wildly enjoying lovemaking, when really they never even reach orgasm. Now with all the talk in magazine articles about attaining orgasm, they realize that they could have it after all—if only their husbands knew what to do. But the poor men think they have been doing it all these years. Some women, in an attempt at honesty, tell their husbands they have been faking a response. The results of this can be almost disastrous. We have known husbands whose egos were crushed by this revelation. When they found out that their wives had been pretending all along, they were so disgusted they would have nothing further to do with them. Realizing that the wife has been living a lie, a husband may well wonder what other areas of the relationship have been dishonest as well. I believe that the husband, in most cases, is better off not knowing. If you have painted yourself into a corner by pretense, you'll have to work yourself out of it with wisdom and a lot of prayer. Make some graceful suggestions to your husband concerning techniques you've read about, without implying that he has failed to arouse or satisfy you all this time. As these techniques are tried, you may find pretense becoming a wonderful reality.

Attitudes and Action

After evaluation time is over, action should begin. You may feel, as some women have expressed to me, that even though you know your attitudes are not right, you just *can't* change them. The woman who says she can't, *can't*. She is already committed to failure.

On the other hand, the woman who has the enabling power of God within her *can* change. How does it happen? By turning your attitude over to the Lord and then beginning to be and say and do what you know is right. Realize that as you please your husband, you are both obeying and pleasing the Lord. Let it be a love offering to both. The Lord will not *make* you do anything; He will not change you without your cooperation. You are not a robot or a puppet on a string. But if you know the attitude you should have, then you have to say, "Okay, with God's strength operating in me, I am going to be different." And then begin to *do it*. How does a woman quit biting her nails? Not by saying *I can't,* but by quitting. The principle is the same in changing your attitudes toward love, sex, marriage, and your husband.

There are a number of things you might consider to make sex more enjoyable for both of you. First, let me suggest the "tool" of anticipation—particularly if you have had some faulty attitudes concerning the sex experience. A period of romantic anticipation for sex, building up all day and ending happily in bed, can very much enhance the love relationship. Your husband has the opportunity to stir your interest and increase his own anticipation. For instance, if he gives you a very meaningful kiss when he leaves for work and then phones you sometime during the day, just because he's thinking of you and missing you, the stage is being set for a responsive welcome to his lovemaking after the children have been put to bed. If your husband does not yet know that response is greatly influenced by preliminary courtship, perhaps that is one of the things you will need to communicate to him. Along with mental anticipation, make some definite plans to take care of meals, children, and responsibilities so that you will have uninterrupted time to spend with your husband at the end of the day.

The best way to change your attitude about sex is to start thinking and acting positively, for better feelings always follow correct action. If your problem is that it takes you so *long* to get aroused, then start anticipating early in the day. Begin concentrating on the thought that sex with your husband is pleasant. Later when lovemaking occurs, keep thinking: *This is pleasing to my body. This is pleasing to me. This is what God created for me. I want to please my husband; this is going to be a happy experience. I am going to feel sensations that are pleasant and wonderful. . . .* This will greatly help you unless your husband just does not provide any wonderful sensations. In that case, offer him this book to read, so that he can learn how to pleasure his wife!

If you want to be able to enjoy sex for what you receive from it as well as for what it does for your husband, you are going to have to take the responsibility for your own sexual pleasure and not hesitate to communicate your needs to your husband. You are going to have to be very open with him, if you hope to develop the abandon that will give you the most pleasurable sex. Both of you need to establish that rejection of a particular form of love play is not rejection of the *person,* only the *action.* Each of you must be willing to give and to receive suggestions to increase excitement. We women do not hesitate to communicate our need for a new dress or a new carpet, but when it comes to our sexual needs, we seem to clam up. Do not ever think a problem is too small or insignificant to be discussed.

While in the process of lovemaking, concentration is most important. Even though you have been building anticipation and practicing new attitudes, you will find that you can be easily distracted and then have to start all over again in seeking arousal. You cannot allow yourself to lie there thinking about the problems of the day or about the fact that you forgot to take the meat out of the freezer. You need to keep your mind and body working together. Concentrate on whatever will arouse your desire. Think of the joy you are experiencing as you and your husband possess each other.

Be active, not passive, and you will enjoy lovemaking more. If you are active, your attention is less likely to wander. Do not be afraid to caress your husband while he is caressing you. When you abandon yourself to pursuing release, you will become more aware of your sensations, and your body will automatically begin to move about to help increase stimulation.

By the way, have you ever initiated sex? Almost every husband finds this an exciting development. The occasional husband who feels threatened by it is often one who fears his own sexual inadequacy. Tim Timmons in his Maximum Marriage Seminars says, "Sweep him off his feet . . . go get him . . . *go after him.*" Without saying one word, you can let your husband know that you think he is wonderful, and that you find him physically attractive and desirable.

Perhaps there has been a difference of opinion on what frequency of intercourse is desirable. Whatever the two of you together prefer certainly is "normal" for your marriage. If you think your husband seems to require sex a lot more than you do, ponder this illustration: If you were in the desert and you were thirsty, you'd think about a glass of water, wouldn't you? But if you're standing by the refrigerator, and there's an opportunity to push a button and get a glass of ice-cold water, and you know you can push the button and get it any time you want to, the need for a drink is not nearly so urgent. Maybe the reason your husband seems never to think of anything besides sex is that he's "in the desert" and "thirsty."

Sometimes you will be very tired and feeling as sexy as an old sock, but your husband will approach you with desire. Secular therapists say a wife should be able to respond, "Sorry, but I'm just not up to it tonight." My own opinion as a Christian wife is that we can depend on the Lord to give us the strength and ability to be as warm and responsive as our husband desires, no matter how tired we are. As we commit this in prayer, trusting the Lord to give us the strength to meet our husband's needs, we often find not only that we can do it, but that we enjoy the experience as well. The heart of the matter is attitude. Please do not be like the lady who told me grimly, "I have never *refused* him." And yet it was obvious that the refusal was there in her heart and even in her voice.

If you find rebellion rising within because of counsel that seems to stress submission to your husband and thus goes against your natural inclination, remember that submission to our God and to our husband is a supernatural work, the result of our own choice of action *plus* God's power. Psalm 40:8 says, "I delight to do thy will, O my God," and this is the point a wife must reach. Submission is always done *by* you, not *to* you.

Ritual can become a hindrance to sexual enjoyment. If you and your husband have been having sex always at the same time and exactly the same routine, try a different time and a different approach. As the wife who usually schedules the activities for the family, you can plan times when you and your husband will be rested and ready for each other. Your husband needs energy for a good sexual relationship, and you can sometimes protect him from the exhaustion that comes from adding social activities on top of his daily work load.

Your Appearance

Both of you will enjoy sex more if *you* feel that your appearance is at its best. Of course, this is not always possible, especially at those times when lovemaking occurs spontaneously. But at bedtime your husband will enjoy seeing you at your bathed and prettiest feminine best. And your confidence in your own desirability will rise accordingly. A filmy nightgown creates an aura of loveliness. There are some "granny" gowns that even Granny would not wear, and your husband's old college T-shirt probably doesn't do much for a woman either. However, if that is what your husband wants you to wear, then by all means sleep in it. Some of you may be thinking that your husband couldn't care less what you wear to bed, just so you take it off at the right time. Nevertheless, a clean, perfumed body attired in a feminine gown tells him that you care enough about your time with him to be your most appealing and desirable. Now we all know that a husband is greatly stimulated by seeing his wife's body, but there can be too much of anything, even nudity. Going about the house nude or only scantily clad is not a good practice. As a wife once told me, "A little something left to the imagination is especially enticing."

Of course your appearance for your husband at any time becomes an important issue. We have here some clues for the wife who *wants* to please her husband. Look pretty. Keep smiling. Don't complain. Receive your husband with open arms!

There are other ways to please, so simple that you already know them. But we all need reminding. Give extra attention to the beauty and comfort of your bedroom. Keep the house picked up late in the afternoon, so that there will be an appearance of order, even if you have not had time to clean. Freshen up yourself too before your husband comes home. Serve broccoli, if that's his vegetable, and leave off the green beans, which he detests. Wear the clothes you know he likes. If he prefers to stay up late at night, try to squeeze in an afternoon nap and stay up late with him. If he enjoys baseball, learn to like it. You don't do these things because you are a doormat, but because you *want* to enjoy his world with him. Most important, a wise wife will not argue. She will keep her husband peaceful and satisfied and happy by gracefully conceding to his wishes, or deferring to his opinions. When the issue is an important one, it can be discussed and decided on its merits. A husband usually welcomes the thoughtful opinions of his wife. To remind ourselves to listen more and talk less is always good advice for the wife. And all this fits with the admonitions in God's Word for wives to adapt themselves to their husband.

If you want to stay beautiful for your husband, you'll be careful not to let yourself go as you get older. If your husband does not want you to be fat, you will avoid adding those ten pounds a year. A physical fitness program with your husband will not only allow you time to enjoy each other's company, but may add quality of life to your golden years and even sexual energy by increasing maximum blood flow to the extremities.

More important, do not neglect inner beauty. Alice Painter says that when a woman is sixteen, she can't help it if she isn't beautiful. But if she is sixty and not beautiful, it's her fault! A woman who is miserable on the inside will show it in her wrinkles and her countenance. She will show it in her actions, pushing others away. She will reveal it in her voice, which may be loud and strident or whining and complaining or ridiculing in tone. The woman who is loved and knows she is loved, who loves the Lord and loves her husband, *will* be lovely.

The Security of Christian Love

I have been asked how my marriage has changed since Ed and I became Christians years ago. There is no comparison! Before that time, of course, we were both self-centered. We did not have the kind of sex relationship spoken of in this book because we just did not care that much about pleasing each other, and we were quite ignorant of the meaning of sex in God's Word. We got along well together but we did not share our innermost feelings with each other.

Now that we are Christians, I know that the love Ed has for me is the same kind of love that Christ has for me. I am safe and secure in that love. I know that I can always talk to my husband, and that I can trust his wisdom as the spiritual leader of our family. As we have become so used to pouring our hearts out together in prayer, we now are free to communicate about anything to each other. We are not afraid to expose ourselves and our faults, because we know that we accept each other, just as we are, with all our frailties and faults and good points. How wonderful it is to know that I am not loved based on my performance: No matter how poorly I perform, I am still going to be loved. And that *has* to make me perform better.

Is it a perfect relationship? Of course not! I still have attitudes rise up within me that are not right. Then I have to back up and start again, turning it over to the Lord, knowing that I don't *have* to act this way as a Christian. I don't *have* to let my old nature be in control and I need not choose to be childish and peeved about some insignificant thing that my ego felt as a slight. Actually, when I stop and consider a moment, I know that my husband was busy or occupied and that he did not mean whatever was said or done. As a Christian woman, I am free to be obedient to God and pleasing to my husband. I do not *have* to behave in any other way.

I would like to think that the husbands are reading this chapter, and that they will begin to show their wives how much they love them and appreciate them—not just in the bedroom, but at any time, with hugs and pats and kind, complimentary words. *Many a man does not realize that the wife he has is a reflection of his own behavior toward her.*

Children and Priorities

Two things should be said about the children in this discussion of sex and marriage. First, they should be in the proper place in the line of priorities. Our husbands must come first and the children after that. Some women put the children ahead of the husband; then when the children are grown and gone, the husband and wife have no basis for communication with each other. Second, our home is where our children first pick up attitudes concerning sex. The best sex education they can receive is to know that Mother and Dad love each other and to see this love expressed in tender, considerate ways.

Here is an example to show how a child's attitudes are influenced: Suppose that you are standing at the kitchen range preparing supper, and your husband walks by and pats you on the behind. You turn around and in a rebuking tone say, "Quit that!" Little Johnny and Susie, playing nearby, observe what has taken place. Do you see the lesson they have just learned? But now let's play the scene again. Suppose your husband walks by and pats you on the behind, and you turn around and grin at him, maybe reach out, and both of you put your arms around each other and exchange a kiss. He goes over to sit down and read the newspaper, and you hum a little tune while stirring the food. What a different lesson the children have just learned!

Yes, your children will observe your actions and absorb your attitudes. If they see that you and your husband have a warm, demonstrative relationship between you, they will be more likely to grow up to be affectionate themselves and to have a healthy attitude about sex. Perhaps later on you will have the privilege of helping to prepare them for marriage.

Advice for Brides

Recent brides have told me that they wish someone had shared a few suggestions with them. For this reason, I want to include the following hints:

- Make all your wedding preparations far enough in advance so that there are no last-minute details for which you are responsible.
- Both the bride and groom should be rested. This means no girl talk until the wee hours of the morning of the wedding and no bachelor party the night before.
- Plan a *short* trip for the first night.
- Be certain to pack a tube of artificial lubricant.
- Have a small towel handy to absorb the secretions.

- Decide beforehand what you both expect on the wedding night. Will you slowly and lovingly undress each other, or will you (the bride) come floating into the bedroom in your gorgeous white negligee and sweep him off his feet? The barrier of seeing each other naked is best broken at some time during your first night together.
- Take a shower together at least once on your honeymoon trip.
- Take along a candle for a romantic atmosphere.
- Relax and anticipate the cherishing and possessing of each other.

I have a choice Father's Day card from Hallmark that goes to my husband every year because the message is so perfect. It says:

> To my husband, who still gives me
> protection
> attention
> security
> grocery money
> and . . .
> GOOSE BUMPS!

And he does! I want you to discover that the principles in this chapter work when they are put into practice and that as you learn to please your husband and to be pleased by him, you'll have all the goose bumps you could want. It begins with you and your attitude.

11

Planning and Achieving Parenthood

> Lo, children are an heritage of the LORD; and the fruit of the womb is his reward. As arrows are in the hand of a mighty man; so are children of the youth. Happy is the man that hath his quiver full of them.
>
> Psalm 127:3–5

Every baby born should be considered a gift from God. Of course I am totally opposed to abortion unless the life of the mother is threatened. And it is my personal conviction that when both partners are knowledgeable and maturing Christians, they should have as many children as they feel they can properly train for a productive Christian life.

Husband and wife can know a special joy as they share together in the total preparation of their children for lives of individual service to God. Each child is launched out into the purpose of God as an arrow from their quiver.

God clearly pronounces blessings on parenthood but, as many of you have discovered, parenthood involves giving and more giving, without thought of receiving in return. One finds that the rewards God promised come spontaneously but not on demand.

163

If parents want to manifest unselfish and godly love for their children, they will pour their lives into bringing them up according to the Lord's instructions, which have been so clearly spelled out in the Bible. Dads and mothers who themselves are becoming emotionally mature in Jesus Christ will be free to love and give to their children, without exacting something in return. It is these people who can expect all the joy and satisfaction God promised.

When I speak of giving, I am not referring to materialistically pampering the child. A parent must give *himself;* he or she must be willing to invest all the patience and love and self-control he or she can imagine—and then some. Only those who give openly are open to receive, to receive the gentle trust of the little child; the warm, appreciative respect of the young adult; or the tender moments of the growing years in between.

The Bible describes the godly family in Psalm 128:1–4:

> Blessed is every one that feareth the LORD; that walketh in his ways. For thou shalt eat the labour of thine hands: happy shalt thou be, and it shall be well with thee. Thy wife shall be as a fruitful vine by the sides of thine house: thy children like olive plants round about thy table. Behold, that thus shall the man be blessed that feareth the LORD.

During the engagement period a couple should discuss their views on having and rearing a family and should be in harmony concerning the various issues involved, *before* their wedding takes place. Their ideas may change later, but if they are growing together in their marriage, their views will take on a similar shape as God guides them.

This chapter is included to give information to those people who are considering the many aspects of family planning. It is estimated that in the United States today, some 15 percent of marriages are childless because of an infertility problem. Another 10 percent of married couples have fewer children than they want. Later in the chapter we will give you practical advice on methods a couple can use to increase their chances of achieving pregnancy. If there are no physical abnormalities, some simple procedures can more than double the chances of becoming pregnant.

However, since more than three-fourths of all couples do not have problems with infertility, most of the questions a doctor is asked concern methods that will control the number of pregnancies and the spacing of children. As I discuss various methods with you in answer to the questions frequently asked, please understand that I am not recommending these methods, but only giving you medical information. Family planning is a private matter for which you and your partner must take full responsibility. The decision is yours. You must determine if you want to use an artificial means of contraception, a natural method of avoiding pregnancy, or no method at all.

In making your decision, keep this statistic in mind. During a year of unprotected intercourse 80 percent of couples of childbearing age will conceive. Here are other factors to be considered:

1. *It is desirable for a newly married couple to have some time for adjustment to each other,* learning to communicate and to share their lives with each other before accepting the responsibilities of a young family. On the other hand, having children right away will certainly discourage self-centeredness for any young couple.

2. *The health of the wife is a most important issue.* Without some means of family planning, a woman may be capable of bearing twenty children. For instance, a forty-two-year-old wife was recently featured in the news because she had borne twenty-one children in twenty-five years—all single births. She had spent the equivalent of almost sixteen years in pregnancy! Such continuous childbearing could hardly be recommended as best for the health of most women. Mrs. Wesley had 19 children and two of them, John and Charles, were great men used by God to turn England back to true Christian faith.

3. *It should be recognized that fear of pregnancy often inhibits enjoyment of the sex relationship.*

If a couple decide to postpone pregnancy, how do they find out which contraceptive method is right for them? There is no method that is perfect for every couple all the time. A method that is satisfactory for one may not be suitable for another. Also, a couple may wish to change methods as circumstances change or as their own personal convictions change.

The first consideration obviously is *safety*. The method chosen must be as harmless as possible. Present medical research is bringing to light some health risks in popular contraceptive methods, and you need to be aware of these. Some methods are not suitable for women who have a past history of certain medical conditions or current health problems. Other women may find that a particular method causes them some degree of physical discomfort. In these cases, your doctor should be the one to advise a method that he believes will be safe for you.

Because of the rapid advances in research and changes in government regulations, contraceptive information must be often updated, particularly in the area of statistics and side effects. I encourage you to talk this over with your own physician.

The second consideration is *effectiveness,* which depends in large part on the user. Those couples who are careful to use a method properly and regularly will have far greater assurance of success than those who use it carelessly or irregularly. For example, when I give you statistics on surprise-pregnancy rates for specific methods, the first figure given will represent the *method*-failure rate when followed precisely, and the second figure will indicate the range of the *user*-failure rate, reflecting the varied amount of care and caution taken by individual users.

The third consideration is the matter of *motivation*. Some methods require more time and thought. Indeed, the natural family planning methods demand painstaking record keeping, as well as time devoted to study and understanding of the factors involved. Also, about ten days of abstention from intercourse will be necessary for the absolute effectiveness of those methods. So determine your degree of motivation *before* you decide on a certain method.

The fourth consideration is the matter of *your own personal taste*. Any method that you find unpleasant, uncomfortable, or embarrassing—for whatever reason—will not be right for you.

As I discuss various means of contraception, remember that I am not endorsing any particular method, although I would like to discourage you from several that are either potentially harmful or ineffective.

I am going to describe the contraceptive methods used today, explaining how they work, giving current statistics on their effectiveness, and pointing out some of their advantages and disadvantages. We will consider the artificial methods (the pill, RU 486, the IUD, the diaphragm, vaginal spermicides, and the condom), then the surgical methods (vasectomy and tubal ligation), and conclude with natural family planning.

Other birth control methods that are currently in use are female condoms, jelly, sponges, vaginal contraceptive suppositories, cervical caps, Norplant, and sterilization (minilaparotomy and laparoscopy). A detailed explanation of these and other methods can be found in *1250 Health-Care Questions Women Ask*, 2d edition, by Dr. Joe S. McIlhaney Jr., as well as information pertaining to in-vitro fertilization (IVF), embryo transfer, and other procedures.

The probability of pregnancy from *any one act of intercourse* without a contraceptive will be from 3 percent to 20 percent, depending on the time during the menstrual cycle that intercourse occurs.

Oral Contraceptives—"The Pill"

The oral contraceptive method known as the pill is based on the discovery that the hormones estrogen and progesterone in the right combination can actually prevent ovulation. These are the same hormones that halt ovulation during pregnancy. Therefore, some women who begin taking the pill experience symptoms like those in early pregnancy, such as breast tenderness, a full feeling, or morning sickness.

The contraceptive tablet is taken every day for twenty-one days. To start out, a woman takes the first pill five days after the start of her menstrual period. She then takes one pill every day, until she has taken twenty-one pills. Then she stops taking the pills, and within two or three days her period should begin. Seven days after taking the last tablet, she begins taking the pill again for twenty-one days, and repeats the cycle. This routine continues month after month, for as long as the woman wishes to prevent pregnancy.

The pills are basically composed of two hormone substances, closely resembling the natural hormones estrogen and proges-terone, which are normally manufactured by the ovaries in the woman's body. They signal the body not to produce an ovum, and thus none is present to unite with the male sperm released during intercourse.

It is important to understand that as long as a woman is taking the pill, it is the *pill* that controls the timing of her menstrual cycle, not her own hormones. Since not every woman has the same response to a particular hormone dosage, there may be times when some bleeding or spotting will occur between menstrual periods. There also may be some increase or decrease in the amount and duration of menstrual bleeding, or a woman on the pill may com-pletely skip periods at times. If you do miss a period while taking the pill, you must still continue your same schedule dosage to be assured of protection against becoming pregnant. If you skip two periods while taking the pill regularly, return to your doctor for a checkup. Usually the pill makes menstruation more regular and menstrual cramps are almost always eliminated.

We know of no harm in continuing your pills a few extra days if you occasionally desire to postpone a menstrual period. The delay of the period may be particularly desirable if the husband has a job that allows him to be at home at irregular but predictable times. To regulate the time for onset of your menstrual period in this way, you must confirm from your doctor that you are taking the *combination* pill that has both estrogen and progesterone in each tablet.

If you decide to discontinue the tablets, ovulation usually will begin again in the first menstrual cycle after the tablets are dis-continued. However, some women have difficulty in resuming ovulation and menstruation. It may take up to ninety days to ovu-late again.

Many women ask if taking the pill will delay the menopause. The use of the pill may in some instances cover up the onset of menopause, but there is no evidence that its use will delay it.

What about discontinuing the pill to become pregnant? Some experts recommend that to be on the safe side, women should wait three months before attempting to become pregnant, using an alternative form of contraception in the meantime such as the condom or diaphragm.

The pill is the most effective of the artificial contraceptive methods, with less than one pregnancy occurring per one hundred women per year. However, mounting evidence concerning serious risks for pill users is being reported in medical literature. One of the most disturbing conclusions was made by researchers involved in a continuing study of forty-six thousand women in Great Britain begun in 1968. As reported in the *Lancet*, a leading British medical journal, the study's authors conclude that pill users in general face a 40 percent higher death rate than women of the same age who have never used the pill.

The United States Food and Drug Administration has warned of a definite relationship between the use of the pill and blood-clot disorders. Death from blood-clot complications occurs in three out of every one hundred thousand women taking the pill.

To put this into perspective, consider the mortality rate resulting from pregnancy: 22.8 deaths per 100,000 women, and the mortality rate from abortions: 100 deaths per 100,000 women. Statistically, the pill is less of a hazard to life and health than is smoking, driving, or swimming. For example, a woman who drives twelve miles on an urban freeway takes all the risk of dying that she would if she used oral contraceptives for her entire reproductive life, approximately thirty years.

However, the woman who smokes should realize that the pill is extremely dangerous for her—so much so that the experts today assert that any woman who wants to use the pill should give up her smoking habit. Otherwise, she must choose another means of contraception. It is known that the incidence of fatal blood clots and strokes quadruples in smokers, ages twenty to thirty-four years, and is twenty-five times higher in smokers, ages thirty-five to forty-four years. So if you smoke, do not use the pill!

Strong evidence also links birth-control pills with an increased incidence of gallstones in younger women. Oral contraceptives are suspected of causing ten thousand new cases of surgically documented gallstones in the United States alone. Another study of 16,638 women over ten years reports that a number of specific diseases, including malignant melanoma, may be linked to the pill.

Some research results are admittedly inconclusive, however, because of lifestyles among the users, which may influence the results. For instance, researchers point out that girls now using the pill seem to have earlier and more frequent sexual activity, and this may account for their strong tendency to have more cervical cancer.

In light of these findings, the individual woman must weigh the health risks of the pill against its effectiveness and convenience as a birth-control measure.

Lesser side effects of the pill may include nausea and vomiting, but these problems can often be overcome by taking the pill after dinner, when food in the stomach can slow its absorption and help avoid unpleasant effects. The symptoms usually disappear within a few days, as the body adjusts.

If any of the following conditions occur, the woman using the pill should consult her physician: frequent or persistent headaches; discoloration of the skin; unexplained pains in the chest; unusual swelling of the ankles; shortness of breath; disturbance of vision, such as seeing double or seeing flashes of light; unusual, persistent, or unexplained pain in the legs; lumps or growths in the breast; frequent or persistent vaginal bleeding.

Oral contraceptive pills are presently the most popular form of birth control in the United States. However, the associate executive director of Planned Parenthood of New York City predicts that in the future women will use the pill for much shorter periods of time. She believes that very few women will remain on oral contraceptives for as long as fifteen years.

Advantages of the Oral Contraceptive

1. When used properly, the oral contraceptive is the most effective reversible contraceptive method known.
2. It is a simple, sure means of contraception. No special preparations are necessary at the time of intercourse. The woman is protected at all times.
3. It does not interfere with the spontaneity and pleasure of lovemaking.
4. No measuring or fitting needs to be done by a physician.
5. In most cases the woman's menstrual cycle becomes more regular.

Disadvantages of the Oral Contraceptive

1. There are some possible long-term health risks.
2. Some women may experience adverse reactions.
3. Minor discomforts, such as nausea or tender breasts, may occur.
4. It may be difficult to remember to take the pill. (It is advisable to take it as part of your daily routine, such as when brushing your teeth at night before going to bed.)
5. It must not be taken by women breast-feeding an infant because the added estrogens may decrease or stop the production of breast milk.
6. The pill requires a doctor's prescription.
7. The low estrogen pills may allow fertilization but prevent implantation.

Statistic: Less than one surprise pregnancy per year occurs per one hundred users of the pill.

RU 486

Used by some women as a means of "birth control," the RU 486 pill chemically induces an abortion and is therefore not a means of birth control but an abortifacient.

Intrauterine Device (IUD)

The IUD is a soft, flexible, plastic loop or hook-shaped plastic rod, which must be uncoiled, placed into a tube like a soda straw, and inserted by a physician through the cervical canal and up into the uterine cavity, where it returns to its original coiled shape. Some IUDs are now made of stainless steel. Others have a fine threadlike copper wire wound tightly around the shaft. The small amounts of copper released in the uterus are thought to alter the functions of the enzymes involved in the implantation process and may also interfere with sperm transport within the uterus. The copper's benefit begins to weaken in two years, and the IUD must be replaced. Another IUD, shaped like a T, releases a small amount of progesterone into the uterine cavity for one year, and then must be replaced.

No one knows exactly why the IUD is effective, but some researchers believe that it hastens passage of the ovum through the cavity of the uterus, not allowing time for it to be implanted to start a pregnancy. Others believe that the IUD causes a local inflammatory reaction inside the uterus, so that the fertilized ovum is unable to implant because the uterine lining is improperly developed. Some feel that the IUD may produce a very early abortion. In one experimental series, rape patients received insertion of copper-bearing IUDs between twenty-four and forty-eight hours later, and no pregnancies resulted.

The main complications and side effects of all IUDs are pelvic inflammatory disease (two to three times normal), septic abortions, perforation of the uterine wall, embedding in the uterine wall, fragmentation of the IUD, exposure to radiation to locate lost IUDs, and ectopic pregnancy. While the overall mortality rate for IUD use is lower than that for oral contraceptives, IUD users experience seven times more disease.

Pelvic infections occur in about 4 percent of all women who have IUDs inserted, some of these very serious, some requiring hysterectomies, and some eventually causing sterility from inflammation and scarring of the fallopian tubes. Even the newest IUDs can cause infection and should not be used by women who want a future pregnancy. If a woman has used an IUD, her chances of being infertile are doubled.

Accidental pregnancies in women with IUDs carry an unusual risk of being ectopic; in other words, the ovum may be implanted in the fallopian tube. The chances of this happening are ten times higher with IUD users than with non-IUD users, and spontaneous abortions are three times higher than they are in pregnancies not complicated by an IUD.

Recent data suggests that infections related to ectopic pregnancy pose the greatest single danger of death for IUD users. IUDs significantly increase the chance of abnormal pregnancies, if conception does take place, but the death rates associated with pregnancy are also dramatically increased. One type of IUD was permanently removed from the market in 1975 for these reasons.

It has been documented that using an IUD increases the amount of menstrual flow in most women, and the pattern of menstruation also seems to begin earlier and end later, extending the menstrual period by two to four days each month. Researchers estimate that 10 to 20 percent of women are forced to discontinue use of IUDs within two to three years after insertion because of excessive uterine bleeding. Many more who keep their IUDs may develop iron deficiency because of chronic increased loss of blood, and some may become anemic. Another unpleasant side effect may be a vaginal discharge—watery, clear, mucuslike, and odorless.

An estimated 10 percent of IUDs are expelled during the first year after insertion. Expulsion is most likely to occur during a menstrual period. Attached to the IUD is a firm nylon thread, which protrudes from the cervix into the vagina about one inch. The woman can touch this thread to be certain that the IUD is in the proper place. When necessary, this thread is used to remove the IUD. If tampons are used during the menstrual periods, care should be taken each time a tampon is removed to be sure the thread attached to the IUD did not become entangled, so that the IUD is pulled out along with the tampon.

The easiest time to insert the IUD is during menstruation, when the cervical os is slightly more dilated, and it is the best time because your doctor can then be sure that you are not pregnant. The IUD should never be inserted immediately after the birth of a baby. Always wait at least two months, preferably longer.

If you are using an IUD, it should be checked by your physician every year or two. If you have excessive bleeding, heavy vaginal discharge, pelvic pain (especially with fever or persistent spotting of blood between menstrual periods), see your physician immediately.

While the IUD offers a high degree of effectiveness as a contraceptive, we now know that it can and sometimes does tamper with the delicate internal mechanism of the woman's body to a serious extent. I cannot recommend it, and I *discourage* its use.

Advantages of the IUD Method

1. Once the IUD has been inserted, little or no thought need be given to contraception.
2. It can be left in place for several years.
3. Most women find the procedure for insertion relatively painless.
4. It is one of the most effective birth-control methods—second only to the pill.

Disadvantages of the IUD Method

1. There is a high risk of disease, possibly resulting in death.
2. There is a higher risk of abnormal pregnancy.
3. There is a 10 percent possibility of expulsion of the IUD from the uterus.
4. Some women experience heavy bleeding or vaginal discharge.
5. This method may produce an early abortion.

Statistic: One to six surprise pregnancies per one hundred users per year occur with this method.

Vaginal Diaphragm with Spermicides

The vaginal diaphragm was developed as the first medically accepted contraceptive device. By the 1950s at least one-third of the couples using contraceptives depended on the diaphragm. The pill, however, was hailed as the perfect contraceptive, and when it became available, the less convenient barrier methods quickly lost favor. Many couples are returning to the diaphragm because of its proven safety. Used with a contraceptive cream or jelly, it is an effective means of family planning and remains one of the safest of all methods.

The diaphragm is a strong but lightweight dome-shaped rubber cap, from two to four inches in diameter. Its rim consists of a ring-shaped, rubber-covered metal spring, which is flexible, so that the whole diaphragm can be compressed and passed easily into the vagina. When released in the upper portion of the vagina, it covers the cervix like a dome, acting as a barrier to prevent sperm from entering the uterus.

Because the distance from the back wall of the vagina to the pubic bone varies from woman to woman, diaphragms are made in a variety of sizes, and the doctor must measure this distance to determine the proper diaphragm for a woman. It must also be refitted every year or two, or whenever the user gains or loses ten pounds. When you get your first diaphragm, you should receive insertion instructions from your physician. Practice insertion and removal at the doctor's office, until you know exactly how to do it. It is simple after you know how!

You will need to insert the diaphragm prior to intercourse, but to be less distracting you may put it in as much as two or three hours beforehand. If the diaphragm fits properly, neither you nor your husband should be aware of its presence.

To be truly effective, the topside of the diaphragm next to the cervix *must* be covered with a spermicidal jelly or cream made for this purpose. If extra lubrication is desired during intercourse, choose a jelly. Otherwise, use a cream. The spermicidal preparation will kill all sperm on contact, but the diaphragm must be left in place at least six (preferably eight) hours following intercourse to be sure that all sperm are destroyed.

Whether or not intercourse actually takes place, the diaphragm may safely be left in place for twenty-four hours or even longer. However, if intercourse takes place more than three hours after the diaphragm is inserted, an additional amount of contraceptive jelly or cream should be inserted into the vagina with a vaginal applicator, just before intercourse.

Check your diaphragm for holes by holding it to the light. Properly cared for, a diaphragm has a life of several years. Proper care includes the following:

- Do not use Vaseline as a lubricant because the petroleum base will rapidly deteriorate the rubber dome.
- Do not wash it with extremely hot water.
- Dry the diaphragm thoroughly after washing.
- Do not use perfumed soaps on it.
- Do not store it near a source of heat.
- Keep fingernails short to minimize the risk of tearing the diaphragm.
- After use, examine for flaws, such as separation of the rim from the cup.

When you go in for your routine pelvic examination, take your diaphragm and ask your doctor to determine if you still need the same size.

The diaphragm has no effect on future fertility and is a well-established, proven method with high effectiveness when used properly.

Advantages of the Diaphragm Method

1. The diaphragm may be inserted as much as three hours before intercourse, so that it does not need to interfere with lovemaking.
2. Neither husband nor wife should be aware of its presence during intercourse. It does not interfere with sexual sensation.
3. If properly cared for, one diaphragm can be used for several years.

4. If the couple want intercourse during menstruation, the diaphragm will help keep blood out of the lower vagina. The contraceptive cream need not be used during a regular menstrual period.

Disadvantages of the Diaphragm Method

1. The diaphragm requires measurement and fitting by a physician.
2. Inserting the diaphragm—when intercourse was not anticipated—may become a distraction.
3. The necessary contraceptive jelly or foam is sometimes considered greasy and messy.
4. Some women may have an aversion to inserting the diaphragm into the vagina.

Statistic: Two to twenty surprise pregnancies per one hundred users per year occur with this method. The high user-failure rate includes those who failed to use the necessary contraceptive cream and those who failed to use additional cream when having intercourse several hours after insertion of the diaphragm.

Vaginal Spermicide Method

Spermicidal products are sometimes used by themselves as contraceptives. Available in the form of suppositories, foam, cream, and synthetic gel, they contain chemicals which, when placed in the vagina, will kill sperm without harming vaginal tissue. The foam, cream, or gel base also provides a barrier over the cervix that helps prevent sperm from migrating into the uterus.

The spermicides are applied with a slim, plastic vaginal applicator, which automatically measures the proper dose. But it is important to remember that the preparation must be used before each and every act of intercourse. To allow time for all sperm to be killed, the user must wait at least six (preferably eight) hours after intercourse before douching, if you douche at all.

If you use foam, it should be deposited high up in the vagina near the cervix, not on the external vulva, and should be inserted

by the wife just before lovemaking, and no more than fifteen minutes before intercourse. Shake the can or prefilled applicator twenty
times before using, to make sure that the foam will have the consistency of shaving cream and that the spermicide will be well
mixed. Always keep a spare container of foam on hand.

Vaginal spermicides have been used for many years and are quite
safe. The foam is considered slightly more effective than the jellies or creams and also has the advantage of being less messy. A
variety of spermicides can be obtained at your drugstore without
a prescription. You will need to carefully follow the enclosed
instructions.

Advantages of the Vaginal Spermicide Method

1. Spermicides can be bought without a prescription.
2. No fitting is necessary.
3. There is nothing to remove after intercourse.
4. No serious side effects are known.

Disadvantages of the Vaginal Spermicide Method

1. The spermicide must be used just before intercourse.
2. It may occasionally cause an allergic irritation in the vagina.
3. A greater volume of discharge is present after intercourse.

Statistic: Two to twenty-nine surprise pregnancies per one
hundred users per year occur with this method. This user-
failure rate indicates that this method is far less effective if used
incorrectly.

The Condom

The condom (also called a prophylactic, pro, sheath, or rubber) is a thin sheath of latex or lamb membrane that fits over the
erect penis to receive the semen and to keep any sperm from entering the vagina during sexual intercourse.

Around the world the condom is still the most widely used,
effective birth-control measure. It is also the safest, for only one
mild side effect has been reported, that of an occasional skin rash

from the rubber condom. (Switching to the kind made of lamb membrane easily solves the problem.) The condom also plays a significant role in preventing the spread of venereal disease and herpesvirus 2.

Despite all these advantages, the condom has had a rather unsavory reputation in the United States until the past few years. The sale of condoms for contraceptive use was outlawed on moral grounds by most state legislatures beginning in 1868 and by Congress in 1873. More than two hundred cities also passed anti-condom laws. Many of these went beyond banning the sale of a condom for contraception; they even made it a criminal offense for one person to inform another that using a condom might prevent pregnancy! These laws have been declared unconstitutional, and today a new generation of married couples are benefiting from this safe, simple, and practical means of family planning.

But how effective is it? The condom has also had to overcome a reputation for unreliability. Years ago many condoms burst with use, or were found to be flawed. In 1938 the FDA estimated that three out of every four condoms then on the market were defective.

Today the situation is totally different. Every manufacturing company claims that each condom is individually checked before it is rolled and packaged. Rigorous testing is required by the FDA and, in addition, the FDA picks condom lots at random and subjects a sampling of them to leakage tests. Tests made by consumer groups in the past several years also indicate that today condoms are "virtually free of shortcomings" in the preventing of pregnancy.

As with the other barrier methods (diaphragm and spermicides), the effectiveness of the condom depends on the motivation of the user and the conscientious care taken. But the latest studies show the *method*-failure rate (when the condoms are used correctly during every act of intercourse) as only 1 percent. To appreciate how low this percentage is, let's put it into perspective. It means that one pregnancy will occur in every one hundred women who use the method for one year. Assuming two uses per week for each woman, that means one pregnancy will occur in ten thousand occasions of proper use.

Spermicidal foam is often recommended as an extra precaution, and when spermicide and condom are used together, it is considered very effective.

Here are a few simple instructions for successful use of the condom:

1. Do not wait until the time of ejaculation to put on the condom. That may be too late, since the initial lubricating fluid (which seeps from the penis before ejaculation) may contain sperm that will find their way into the vagina during genital closeness.

2. Fit the condom over the erect penis during foreplay and weave this into your lovemaking as an erotic experience, rather than a last-minute distraction.

3. Place the rolled condom over the tip of the erect penis and unroll it all the way up the shaft to the base of the penis. Note that the condom will unroll only one way. An uncircumcised user should retract the foreskin completely, when rolling the condom over it, as this will allow greater sensation.

4. Allow one-half inch of space at the end of the penis as a reservoir, where the semen can collect in the condom. Otherwise, the semen will provide so much lubrication to the shaft of the penis that the condom might slip off. Squeeze the air out of the reservoir as you put the condom on, so there will be room for the semen. Condoms can now be purchased with reservoir ends—a nipplelike extension on the tip to hold ejaculated semen.

5. Inadequate lubrication may be a significant cause of tearing of the condom. Either use lubricated condoms (you can obtain them in a variety of styles—some totally lubricated from end to end—others only at the tip and part way up the shaft), or use a nonallergenic lubricant, such as Astroglide. Do not use Vaseline or cold cream because these products weaken the latex rubber. If contraceptive jelly or cream is used for added protection, it will also serve as a lubricant.

6. After ejaculation, withdraw the penis promptly, before the penis shrinks enough so that the condom may slip off. Grasp

the ring of the condom firmly when withdrawing the penis from the vagina to prevent spillage.

7. If the condom should slip off during intercourse, grasp the open end of it and pull it out of the vagina with care, so as not to lose the contents. Then the wife should immediately fill the vagina with contraceptive foam (which should be kept on hand for such emergencies). If foam is not available, she should douche immediately with warm (rather than hot) water and lather externally with soap and water.

8. Dispose of the condom in the trash or garbage, not in the toilet. Condoms can clog plumbing.

9. Each time intercourse is repeated, a clean condom must be used.

10. Sunlight or fluorescent light accelerates the deterioration of the latex rubber, as does high temperature (such as in the glove compartment of a car parked in the sun or in a man's wallet). Condoms packed with a window in the wrappings should not be left in sunlight or fluorescent light, and sealed condoms should not be stored in places where the temperature may be high.

Condoms are readily available today at drugstores and other retail stores. They may be purchased without a prescription, and there is no need to consult a physician. Some are manufactured with textured surfaces, which increase sensation for the wife. Some men prefer the lamb-membrane condoms, which are thinner and provide more sensation for the husband. These are two or three times more expensive than the latex condoms. Because there is a slight decrease in sensitivity to the penis sheathed in a condom, some husbands report that they are able to prolong their intercourse to add to their wife's satisfaction and their own pleasure.

The condom method offers special advantages for men who are able to get an erection but have difficulty maintaining it. The roll at the base of the condom exerts a slight tourniquet effect on the veins of the penis, which helps keep the erection.

We have mentioned the value of condoms worldwide in preventing the spread of venereal disease, which is at epidemic proportions. But the condom method is also helpful for the married couple who want to continue intercourse, even though one partner is being treated for an infection, such as trichomonas. Some doctors recommend that couples use condoms for intercourse during late pregnancy to aid in preventing amniotic fluid infections. The wives of uncircumcised men are slightly more at risk of developing cervical cancer, and condom use may offer them some protection.

So in spite of its humble appearance, its nonclinical sources, and the unsavory reputation it once had, the condom is the safest of contraceptives, the simplest to use, the most practical for good health and hygiene, and it is quite effective *when used correctly.*

To summarize the barrier methods—condom, spermicide, and diaphragm—experts say that, when used correctly, they are at least 97 percent effective versus the 99.6 percent effectiveness of the pill.

Advantages of the Condom

1. The condom is convenient and easy to use.
2. It is extremely safe.
3. It is very effective, if used consistently and correctly.
4. It is inexpensive.
5. It is available without a prescription and without seeing a doctor.
6. It ensures the husband's involvement in the contraceptive process.
7. It helps protect against sexually transmitted infections.
8. It helps the man to prolong intercourse, enhancing pleasure for both partners.

Disadvantages of the Condom

1. Some people are afraid the condom will interfere with sexual pleasure.
2. The condom can be put on only after an erection occurs.
3. There is fear that there may be a small undetectable pinhole in the condom, which would allow pregnancy to occur. It has been estimated, however, that a pinhole would con-

tribute less than one in two hundred thousand chances for a pregnancy.

4. All condoms "leak" one to five microns. This does not hinder their ability to prevent pregnancy, but it means that they are not a sure way of preventing the transmission of the AIDS virus. Sperm is five hundred times larger than the AIDS virus.

5. The *user*-failure rate is quite high, indicating that the condom must be used properly to be effective.

Statistic: One to thirty-six surprise pregnancies per one hundred women per year occur with this method.

Vasectomy

We have been describing the artificial methods of birth control, methods that can be discontinued any time the couple wants to conceive. There are two surgical methods of birth control—the vasectomy for the husband and tubal ligation for the wife—that must be considered permanent and irreversible. Neither of these should be chosen unless husband and wife are both *very* certain they will never again want to have a child.

Vasectomy has become an increasingly popular form of sterilization; approximately five hundred thousand vasectomies are performed each year. The surgery is so simple that many men return to work the following day.

The traditional method of performing the vasectomy has been to use a scalpel to make an incision in either the front or side of the scrotum. Recently the nonscalpel technique is becoming increasingly popular with its advantages of minimizing tissue injury and avoiding potential complications. The procedure itself takes approximately fifteen minutes to perform, usually in a doctor's office under local anesthesia.

Basically the procedure interrupts the transport of sperm cells into the ejaculate. All other aspects of lovemaking, namely libido, erections, ejaculations, and orgasms will be maintained. If there is difficulty with erections following vasectomy, this is entirely psychological and will pass in due course. There has been some concern recently with regard to possible problems of atherosclerosis and prostate cancer. The American Urologic Association states, however, that vasectomy remains a very safe and reliable means of sterilization. There are no potential health hazards that should preclude having a vasectomy.

Vasectomy is becoming a much more common birth-control method than tubal ligation because of its overall simplicity, easy recovery, and the fact that general anesthesia is not necessary. Some men will deposit sperm in a sperm bank prior to vasectomy, guarding against the possibility they may at a later time want to impregnate their wife. Anyone who is considering this should investigate the availability in their locale regarding sperm banking and maintenance of sperm on deposit prior to vasectomy.

Reversal of vasectomy is successful approximately 75 to 80 percent of the time. If a reversal should fail, epididymal aspiration or intratesticular harvesting of sperm cells may be performed in conjunction with in-vitro fertilization of the female egg in an attempt to successfully impregnate and conceive a natural child. While these procedures are becoming increasingly popular, they are prohibitively expensive at present and often are not covered by health care insurers.

After a vasectomy has been performed, sterility is not instantaneous. There is risk of pregnancy as long as there are sperm in the ejaculated fluid. Time is not the main factor, but the number of ejaculations is. Semen is examined after ten or twelve ejaculations. If any sperm are left, semen is reexamined after five more ejaculations. It is possible to be sterile within one week, but it may take six to eight weeks, or even longer, for this to occur. Never depend on your vasectomy for birth control until at least one semen specimen is found to be sperm-free.

Probably the greatest misunderstanding about vasectomy is fear that it will adversely affect a man's sex drive. While all the possible psychological factors cannot be predicted, the vasectomy does *not* have any physical influence on a man's sex drive or his ability to perform. The tubes that have been cut have no function other than to transport the microscopically small sperm cells from the testicles. The fluid material that is ejaculated comes from the seminal vesicles and prostate gland, so that the amount of ejaculation fluid released after the vasectomy is not visibly decreased. The physical sensations and enjoyment during orgasm will remain the same.

Advantages of Vasectomy

1. Vasectomy is the simplest means of permanent sterilization for couples who definitely want no more children.
2. A couple need no longer use other methods of contraception.
3. Vasectomy is relatively painless and takes only a short time to perform.

Disadvantages of Vasectomy

1. The operation required to reverse the surgery is expensive, difficult, and sometimes unsuccessful. Permanent sterility must be expected.

Tubal Ligation

A tubal ligation is a surgical operation performed by a doctor to prevent a woman from being able to become pregnant. This is done by cutting and tying off each of the two tubes that carry an ovum from the ovary to the uterus. If the ovum cannot get to the uterus and sperm cannot reach the ovum, then there is no chance for the woman to conceive.

A tubal ligation must be performed in a hospital under anesthesia. There are three methods of performing a tubal ligation:

1. With an incision in the abdominal wall
2. With an incision through the back of the vagina
3. With a special instrument called the laparoscope

Many tubal ligations are now being done using the first method, because the operation is performed within twenty-four hours after the birth of a baby. The uterus is enlarged during pregnancy; therefore, the tubes are raised high in the abdomen, making it easier to reach the tubes within the first day after delivery. When a woman has a tubal ligation performed shortly after she has given birth to a baby, it is relatively easy for her and rarely prolongs her hospital stay more than a day or two. If the birth is by caesarean section, a tubal ligation takes only a few minutes more at the time of the caesarean section and does not prolong the hospital stay at all.

A description of the surgical operations for tubal ligation is given in chapter 4 in the section discussing the oviducts.

The tubal ligation has no physical effect, other than to prevent pregnancy. There is no change in the woman's menstrual cycle, and personality and sexual responsiveness will be generally unchanged. However, some women, relieved of their fear of pregnancy, become more responsive sexually.

Because of its simplicity and lower cost, vasectomy is usually chosen by most couples who desire a permanent form of birth control. However, personal preferences sometimes favor the tubal ligation, especially when it is to be done following the birth of a baby, and particularly when the woman's health seems to indicate an avoidance of pregnancy in the future.

Advantages of Tubal Ligation

1. After tubal ligation there is no need to interrupt lovemaking with the use of contraceptives.
2. The sterilization procedure is permanent.

Disadvantages of Tubal Ligation

1. Tubal ligation is considered a major operation and carries some operative risk, as well as considerable expense.
2. There is always the initial risk of problems with bleeding, infection, or poor healing.
3. There will be pelvic discomfort for a few days.
4. Only under rare circumstances can a woman get pregnant again, if she later decides she wants to have another child. Reversal of a tubal ligation is extremely expensive.

Natural Family Planning

Three commonly known biological facts provide the scientific basis for natural family planning, in which pregnancy is spaced or controlled without using any of the artificial contraceptives.

1. A woman normally produces only one ovum during each menstrual cycle.
2. The ovum has an active life of only about twenty-four hours, and it is only during this twenty-four hours that it can be fertilized by the male sperm.
3. The male sperm is capable of living for only about forty-eight hours after it is released into the vagina. It is only during this two-day interval that it can fertilize the female ovum.

The conclusion from these three facts is that there are really only three days each month when intercourse can lead to pregnancy—the two days before the ovum is released and the full day afterward. If a woman could avoid having intercourse during this time, then, *theoretically*, she would be in no danger of becoming pregnant.

The idea behind all natural family planning is that a woman must simply refrain from having intercourse on the days when she can become pregnant. What makes this simple idea so difficult to put into practice, however, and what limits the effectiveness of this method, is that no fail-safe way has yet been found to determine just which days are safe for intercourse. The old rhythm method simply assumed that most women would be safe one week before their period, during their period, and for about five days after their period. However, the method-failure rate for the rhythm system was quite high.

Today more and more couples are learning to use what has been called the sympto-thermal method, because it is far more precise in predicting the fertile period each month. Understanding and carefully charting your own monthly cycle is the key to successfully using this method. The sympto-thermal method is equally helpful when you want to conceive a child and may aid in selecting the sex of your baby through careful planning and accurate timing.

The sympto-thermal method is based on the fact that during a woman's periodic monthly cycle, certain bodily signs occur just before, during, and after the fertile phase of her cycle. The couple using this method learn to observe and interpret the signs to avoid sexual intercourse during the fertile time.

This method includes calendar calculations, daily temperature taking, cervical mucus observations, and observation of other signs that indicate the time when the woman is ovulating (releasing the ovum).

Calendar watching with daily record keeping is important, because ovulation usually takes place between twelve and sixteen days before the beginning of a woman's next menstrual flow. The problem lies in knowing for sure when the next menstrual period will begin. The number of days between periods may vary from one cycle to another and may vary at different times of a woman's life. Irregularity in the menstrual cycle is common among very young women and also in the years prior to menopause. Menstrual irregularities may occur when a woman experiences physical or emotional stress—or at any time.

A woman must learn just how much variation there is in the length of her own menstrual cycles. Over a period of months a pattern does emerge. With this detailed record, a woman can begin to predict the first day of the next menstrual bleeding, called day one of the menstrual cycle. When such a record is available, she can subtract fourteen days from the next predicted date of onset of menstruation to find the day of ovulation. Then she should avoid the four days just before ovulation and the three days after it.

But this is only part of the sympto-thermal method. The time of ovulation can be predicted with greater accuracy by keeping a daily record of body temperature. This can be done with an ordinary fever thermometer, but it is easier to use a basal body temperature thermometer, which is specially marked to measure even very slight variations in temperature between 96 and 100 degrees Fahrenheit. A woman using the basal thermometer takes her oral temperature as soon as she awakens in the morning, *before getting out of bed*. It is best to take it at approximately the same hour each morning and to keep the thermometer in the mouth for a full five minutes. Generally a slight dip in temperature below a level that has been constant for a week or ten days provides a signal that ovulation has begun.

This dip in temperature is usually followed in the next twenty-four to seventy-two hours by a rise of one-half to three-quarters degree. This is caused by the hormone progesterone, produced by the ovary after ovulation. The temperature elevation persists until menstruation begins. After two days of elevated temperature above the basal level, it may be assumed that a safe period has begun.

This careful, written record of body temperature provides a check on the accuracy of the calendar record. It should not be used alone, however, because illness or activity may cause fluctuations in daily body temperature that have nothing to do with the time of ovulation. To be useful, it is essential that daily temperature readings be made under the same conditions and at the same time every morning.

The third aspect of natural family planning involves observing the cervical mucus. At the time of ovulation it appears as a lubricating vaginal discharge. The first symptom is a feeling of wetness more profuse than in the normal vaginal secretions. In some women, the mucus may continue to be watery. But for many others, as ovulation approaches, the mucus produced by the cervix becomes like raw egg white, clear, almost transparent, and very slippery.

At this point, a woman can perform a simple test, sometimes done in fertility-clinic laboratories, to determine fertility. She may take a drop or two of the cervical mucus and place it on the flat side of the blade of a table knife. With the knife resting on a level surface, she should place the flat side of another table knife flat on top of the glob of mucus and carefully raise the top blade straight upward, while keeping it level. In the stretch phenomenon known as *spinnbarkeit*, the mucus at the time of optimum fertility will cling to the upper knife and stretch upward like a thread to a length of four to eight inches. For practice, one can try using a drop of raw egg white, but note that it stretches only about one inch.

This test for fertility is largely the product of clinical research by Doctors John and Lyn Billings, an Australian husband-and-wife team, who emphasize careful teaching of how to recognize the mucus symptom. They suggest a detailed record be kept of the cycle, whether it be a dry day, a mucus day, or a day of menstrual bleeding.

One must not depend solely on the cervical mucus test to determine days of fertility because vaginal infections, intercourse, or douching will drastically change the consistency of the mucus. The factors that help pinpoint times of fertility are the day on the menstrual calendar, the basal body-temperature curve, and the consistency and stretchability of cervical mucus. It is important to consider all these factors together, rather than attempting to pinpoint times of fertility by using only one or two of the factors.

The sympto-thermal method uses these factors as well as other bodily signs of ovulation to come up with a rather precise time of ovulation. Those who use this method claim that when it is intelligently practiced, the success rate is equal to artificial contraceptive methods. However, natural family planning does require about ten days of abstinence from intercourse every month, to be sure of complete protection. The supporters of this method say that this period of abstinence can be a time of courtship, renewing the romance of marriage, and anticipating the time when husband and wife can come together again sexually.

I have known couples who discovered a new togetherness as they noted the intricacies of the wife's reproductive cycle and as they planned for and anticipated times for making love. The information gained from the sympto-thermal method is also extremely valuable when a couple is ready for parenthood and is seeking the time of maximum fertility.

For an excellent explanation of the sympto-thermal method, I suggest the book by John and Sheila Kippley, *The Art of Natural Family Planning*. It gives thorough instruction in every detail of this rather complex method. The theology of the book is oriented toward members of the Roman Catholic church, since much of the research was encouraged by them. It can be obtained by writing The Couple to Couple League, P.O. Box 111184, Cincinnati, OH 45211 (513-471-2000).

It will take some months of study and practice before you are prepared to follow this method precisely and successfully. In a study of 1,247 couples of varied backgrounds using the sympto-thermal method, a surprise pregnancy rate of 11 percent was found. This rate should be understood in light of the admission of some couples who said they took chances with intercourse during times that possibly were unsafe.

The Douche

The word *douche* comes from a French word meaning to gush or pour. It is a mistake to douche after intercourse in the hope of washing out sperm that have already been deposited—even if only minutes earlier. Sperm are deposited at ejaculation in a forceful spray that lands at or slightly into the opening of the uterus. An average sperm travels an inch in eight minutes. Therefore, some sperm will probably have penetrated beyond the reach of the douche fluid. Furthermore, the pressure of the douche water may push some droplets of semen farther into the cervix without harming the sperm.

It is not really necessary to douche at any time. The vagina is well supplied with glands and a surface that produces its own fluids, which are sufficient to cleanse the vagina, much as tears are designed to cleanse the eye.

Almost all odor from the female genital area comes from fluids that have dried on the outside of the vagina. So, thorough washing with soap and water is all that is needed to remove almost any odor. Additional cleansing can be done simply by cupping your hands and splashing clean water up into the vaginal opening several times.

The morning after intercourse some women find the vaginal drainage of their own secretions mixed with their husband's semen to be uncomfortable. If this is a bother, they may sometimes want to use a cleansing douche.

Proper procedure for douching. You may use any one of several solutions for douching:

- two tablespoons white vinegar to two quarts of water
- two teaspoons of salt to two quarts of water
- just plain water
- one of the commercial preparations, following label directions

The two main types of douching equipment are the bag (or fountain) and the bulb syringe. The bag type can be hung from a wall hook, so that it is about two feet above hip level. Never hold the lips of the vulva together so that you put water into the vagina under pressure. Water can be forced up through the cervical opening and possibly out the fallopian tubes, causing an inflammatory reaction, which could become a severe pelvic infection.

The douche liquid should be at a comfortable temperature and should be allowed to flow in gently, until the vagina feels slightly distended. Then, allow the fluid to gush out. Repeat this procedure, until you use all of the two quarts of solution.

After each use, your douche equipment should be washed thoroughly with soap and water, rinsed, and dried. Do not allow the equipment to touch a wall as it hangs to dry. Some vaginal infections come from candida (monilia) growing on damp bathroom walls. Your douche equipment should never be used by anyone else and, of course, it should never be used for enemas.

The decision to douche is a personal preference, but you should understand that it has little value as a form of birth control.

Coitus Interruptus (Withdrawal Method)

Coitus interruptus involves the withdrawal of the penis from the vagina just prior to ejaculation. This method attempts to prevent pregnancy by depositing the semen outside the genital tract.

The withdrawal method is discussed in chapter 38 of Genesis— the only direct reference to birth control in the Bible. Verses 8 through 10 read:

> And Judah said unto Onan, Go in unto thy brother's wife, and marry her, and raise up seed to thy brother. And Onan knew that the seed should not be his; and it came to pass, when he went in unto his brother's wife, that he spilled it on the ground, lest that he should give seed to his brother. And the thing which he did displeased the LORD; wherefore he slew him also.

We know that the Hebrew custom of that day dictated that if Onan fathered a child by Tamar, his dead brother's wife, the child would not legally have been his, but would have been considered the child of his brother. Even though Onan complied with the command to marry his brother's wife, he perverted the purpose of the marriage, which was to produce a child; he deliberately disobeyed this order given by his father, Judah; therefore, he did not fulfill his spiritual and moral responsibility to his dead brother. It was not just the physical act, but the spiritual disobedience that displeased the Lord. This disobedience demanded the most severe discipline God could give.

Requiring Onan to marry his brother's wife apparently was done for two reasons. The first was to provide an offspring for the deceased brother and preserve his name and his memory and to provide an heir for his property. The second reason was to serve the interest of the wife; otherwise, she would be destitute. I think we can be safe in assuming that when a fellow in that day was considering marriage, his brothers were very much involved. They probably gave a lot of help in choosing a wife!

Today coitus interruptus is frequently used by those who have convictions against using artificial contraceptives. Unfortunately it is one of the most *in*effective of all methods. This is because some sperm are usually present in the slight lubricating fluid secreted from the penis during sexual excitement before ejaculation. Only one sperm is actually needed to fertilize the ovum and that one may be well on its way before ejaculation occurs. To attempt to use this method the man must withdraw completely from any contact with the woman's genitalia before he actually ejaculates.

Coitus interruptus is not only ineffective, but it is undesirable, because it imposes great restrictions on both partners at the very time each should feel the most free in the sex act.

Abstinence

The one method of birth control that the Bible forbids is continuing abstinence in a marriage. As 1 Corinthians 7:3–5 tells us,

> Let the husband render unto the wife due benevolence: and likewise also the wife unto the husband. The wife hath not power of her own

body, but the husband: and likewise also the husband hath not power of his own body, but the wife. Defraud ye not one the other, except it be with consent for a time, that ye may give yourselves to fasting and prayer; and come together again, that Satan tempt you not for your incontinency.

Couples should strive to be sensitive and considerate of each other's sexual needs and desires and to satisfy them regularly and lovingly.

For the Infertile Couple: Achieving Parenthood

Sex is intended for pleasure, and one of the sweetest pleasures comes as children are born. Young couples yearning for a family and failing to produce a child should find out why. There may be an infertility problem, and in at least a third of the cases this problem can be overcome.

Doctors define infertility as failure to conceive after one year of regular intercourse without the use of contraceptives. Infertility should not be confused with sterility, which is an absolute inability to reproduce. Infertility simply means the failure to achieve pregnancy within a specified period of time.

Studies have shown that 66 percent of pregnancies occur within three months of the initiation of unprotected intercourse. Within six months of such continued exposure, 75 percent of the women have become pregnant, and by the end of one year about 80 percent of the women have conceived. The remaining couples may want to seek help. Examination and counsel by their own physician might be all that is necessary.

The essentials of fertility are normal ovulation, unobstructed fallopian tubes, and normal semen. These factors must be present for pregnancy to occur:

1. The husband must be able to produce a normal number of healthy, motile (or mobile) sperm cells.
2. The sperm cells must be able to be discharged through the urethra during ejaculation.

3. These sperm cells must be deposited in the female, so that they reach the cervix, penetrate the cervical mucus, and ascend through the uterus to the fallopian tube. This must occur at the proper time in the menstrual cycle for the ovum to become fertilized.

4. The wife must produce a normal, fertilizable ovum, which must leave the ovary, enter the fallopian tube, and become fertilized.

5. Once conception has taken place, the fertilized ovum must begin to divide. After four days this tiny cluster of cells should drift down the fallopian tube and move into the uterus, where it becomes implanted in a properly developed lining membrane and there undergoes normal development.

If a couple are unable to achieve pregnancy, it is because a breakdown has occurred in one or more of these essential factors. Infertility is usually not the result of defects in only one partner, but the result of several factors, often minor, in both partners. In seeking help, both husband and wife should begin by having a complete physical examination, asking their doctor to search for any condition that might keep them from having a baby.

The physical examination of the wife includes a routine pelvic examination, with special attention to possible fibroids, polycystic (enlarged) ovaries, and vaginal and cervical infection.

It may be that the hymen is still intact, indicating that semen has never been deposited at the cervix. It is possible for infectious organisms to produce substances that injure the husband's sperm as soon as the semen enters the vagina. The cervix of the uterus may be obstructed by thick or heavy mucus. Tumors in the uterus (fibroids) or an inflamed lining membrane could be the problem. An improper tilt or position of the uterus can be a barrier to the path of the sperm. The tube where ovum and sperm meet can be blocked by mucus or obstructed by scar tissue from an earlier infection. The ovum itself may not mature properly because of an endocrine disturbance.

During a physical examination of the husband, any of the following problems may be easily detected: undescended testicle, very small or atrophic testicle, varicocele, or prostatitis.

A testicle will not be able to produce sperm if it has not descended into the scrotum by the age of puberty. (Generally one should try to surgically correct an undescended testicle by the age of five years.)

A varicocele is any unusual dilation of the veins in the scrotum above the testicle. Almost always (85 percent of the time) it appears only on the left side and is often detected only when the man is in a standing position. It is seen as a bluish, irregular swelling above the testicle in the upper part of the scrotum. The condition is similar to varicose veins found in the legs. This does not always produce infertility; many men with varicocele have normal semen quality. If a man with a varicocele has a decreased sperm count and lowered sperm mobility, significant improvement occurs 80 percent of the time when the varicocele is removed.

Prostatitis (described in detail in chapter 4) and epididymitis (infection of the area where sperm is stored) pose a threat to fertility, possibly due to a chemical alteration of the seminal fluid or to obstruction of the genital ducts by scarring.

Fertility is often influenced by one's general health, so the physician will look for any kind of chronic infection, malnutrition, anemia, or a metabolic problem. We know that endocrine disturbances, particularly hypothyroidism and deficiencies in the hormones from the pituitary, adrenal, and reproductive glands can definitely affect fertility. Vitamin A is needed to maintain the production of the sperm. B complex vitamins are essential to pituitary function. Vitamin C (ascorbic acid) is thought to be involved in preventing sperm destruction. So both husband and wife will be encouraged to follow the basic rules of good health, with a balanced diet, as well as adequate exercise and rest.

The physical examinations of husband and wife may be only the beginning of the physician's search to help the couple. It is no simple matter to pinpoint the cause or causes of infertility.

Although infertility has traditionally been regarded as a female problem, it is traceable to the male in 30 percent of childless couples. In an additional 20 percent, the male is a contributing factor. (The Bible long ago recognized the possibility of the barren male: "Thou shalt be blessed above all people: there shall not be male or female barren among you" [Deut. 7:14].) If the couple must be referred to a specialist, the husband will be studied first, since his evaluation is less time-consuming and less expensive.

Infertility, however, is always viewed as a couple problem, and each couple is thought of as a "reproductive unit." The family doctor will attempt to rule out other obstacles to conception before the husband is referred for a full fertility workup.

For instance, has the couple tried for *one full year* to have a child? The length of time is important in diagnosing infertility. How frequent has their intercourse been? Once every two weeks sometimes is not often enough to determine infertility. Have they been using any kind of artificial lubricant during intercourse? Some lubricating jellies are spermicidal. So is petroleum jelly (Vaseline). And any cream, jelly, or lubricant will interfere with the mobility of the sperm. The use of artificial lubricants, particularly those that kill the sperm, will cause temporary infertility, but the situation can be easily remedied.

Has the wife been douching before intercourse for the purpose of cleanliness? This will have an undesirable effect on the sperm, changing the normal acidity of the vagina, so that normal sperm function and mobility are altered. Was the wife using oral contraceptives prior to the start of unprotected intercourse? (There is now strong evidence that after long-term use of the pill, the return to normal ovulation may be quite slow.)

The doctor will turn his attention to sexual dysfunction as a possible cause of infertility. Is there in reality an impotence problem? Or retrograde ejaculation, where the man feels that he is ejaculating, but the semen goes into the bladder, rather than through the penis?

The husband's occupational history must be considered, as well as his recent emotional and psychological history. Diminished fertility often results from strong physical or emotional stress or from a buildup of psychological tensions. Fortunately fertility seems to often be restored when the stress is reduced.

Certain environmental agents, such as heat and radiation, may contribute to male infertility. One important function of the scrotum is to keep the testes about 2.2 degrees cooler than the abdominal cavity. But the husband may be inadvertently heating the scrotum to body temperature level by wearing tight bikini or jockey-type underwear, or by taking long, hot tub baths. In primitive tribal rites, the men sit in a cold stream before having intercourse! Heat can reduce the sperm count enough to cause temporary infertility, but by wearing loose-fitting clothing for a few weeks, a normal sperm count will be restored.

Radiation exposure, either medical or occupational, may be the source of infertility. The germinal cells of the testes are extremely sensitive to radiation. Depending on the dosage, however, fertility may be restored.

A particular medication may be at fault. Most of the anticancer drugs inhibit the production of sperm, as do certain cortisone drugs, antimalarial compounds, diuretics, nitrofurantoins (used to treat urinary infections), and some drugs used in treating depression. Taking testosterone will tend to shut off production of the hormone that, in the male, stimulates cell function and development. It has even been considered as a male contraceptive!

A past infection may be the hidden cause of infertility. For example, mononucleosis or a prolonged fever can cause temporary male infertility, but this will not show up for three months or so after the illness.

Response of the sperm count to therapy cannot be expected for at least three months. This three-month time frame should always be kept in mind. It takes the testes seventy-two days to produce the sperm, and another ten to fifteen days are required for the sperm to travel a circuitous route to the seminal vesicles.

If all the family doctor's lines of inquiry prove to be unproductive, the husband will need to go to a urologist or fertility clinic for semen analysis. Semen is analyzed for sperm numbers, mobility, shape, and form, as well as for the volume of seminal fluid. Sperm count may be highly variable when different samples are taken from the same man. Sperm mobility is estimated in terms of the speed of forward progression. Sperm shape and form is highly variable, and a 100 percent normal sample is never seen. Deformities are found in up to 15 percent of the sperm of fertile men. If more than 60 to 70 percent of the sperm are deformed, the chances of fertility are considered remote. Satisfactory mobility and normal shape are actually more important than the sperm count itself. In other words, the issue is quality, not just quantity.

In years past, normality was defined as 60 million or more sperm per milliliter (about one-quarter teaspoon) of semen. Today, even if there are as few as 30 million sperm per milliliter, the patient can be considered fertile if mobility, form, and structure are normal.

The *average* volume of semen ejaculated is 3.5 milliliters, or a little more than three-quarters of a teaspoon. The couple wanting to conceive should remember that multiple ejaculations (four times within forty-eight hours, for instance) will definitely reduce both the sperm count and the semen volume.

If the average volume of semen has a normal sperm count, about 210 million sperm cells will be ejaculated during the usual sexual intercourse. This may sound like a great many, but from among this entire group of sperm, only 50 to 60 percent are fully mobile. As the sperm begin a progression toward the point of fertilization in the outer third of the fallopian tube, there is a considerable loss of mobile sperm. The vaginal secretions alone will destroy a large percentage of sperm, and the remaining sperm will be reduced in number, as they travel toward their ultimate destination—the membrane covering the tiny ovum. In the final act of fertilization, a certain number of sperm must attach to this membrane and activate it, so that finally *one* sperm may enter and fertilize. You can see that millions of moving sperm are necessary for fertilization, even though only one sperm ultimately connects.

Some recent research has indicated that conception is even possible with as few as 20 million sperm per milliliter by using specialized procedures to make the best use of the sperm that are produced.

Postcoital tests are routine in an infertility study. The test is performed at the time of ovulation and involves microscopic examination of the cervical mucus a few hours after sexual intercourse.

This allows a direct look at the moving sperm to determine how their mobility is affected by the cervical mucus.

If the infertility has been caused by an acidity in the mucus that immobilizes sperm transportation, the woman should douche with a sodium bicarbonate solution (one tablespoon baking soda in one quart of lukewarm water) thirty to sixty minutes before intercourse. This will greatly improve the chances of sperm survival. Women with vaginitis need the sodium bicarbonate douching because it not only neutralizes the acidity, but also removes the excess discharge, allowing many more sperm to move into the cervix.

Because most of the sperm are in the first three or four drops of semen, the technique of coital withdrawal may be effective when the male has a low sperm count. This is done by a deep penetration of the penis, as the first few drops of semen are released, and then an immediate withdrawal from the vagina in order to leave only the most concentrated semen at the mouth of the cervix.

Sometimes artificial insemination, using the husband's semen, is recommended. The physician places a freshly obtained specimen of the husband's semen at the mouth of the cervix on the expected day of ovulation. Again, the first three or four drops of fresh concentrated semen are used. This process will be repeated two or three times during the fertile period each month. If it is carried out for six consecutive months, conception will occur for approximately 50 percent of the couples with infertility due to a low sperm count.

Here are some simple procedures to follow during intercourse that will greatly increase the chances of becoming pregnant, if no physical abnormalities exist.

1. The wife lies on her back, her legs pulled back against her chest with her hips on two pillows.
2. The husband makes the deepest possible penetration as he begins ejaculation. Then he stops all thrusting until ejaculation is finished, and immediately withdraws the penis. Because 60 to 75 percent of the sperm are in the first three

or four drops of semen, it is desirable to have this semen as undisturbed as possible. Additional thrusting would bring the sperm in contact with the acid vaginal secretions, which are unfavorable for their survival. Sperm usually survive well in the cervical mucus.

3. The wife stays for one hour with hips elevated on the two pillows. She then removes the pillows and remains for one more hour flat on her back.

4. The couple should have intercourse every thirty to thirty-six hours during the three days each month when she may be fertile. (Every twenty-four hours is too often!) There is evidence that the ovum must be fertilized within twenty-four hours of the time of ovulation. (The means of determining the time of ovulation are explained earlier in this chapter in the section on natural family planning.)

5. There should be no intercourse for the three or four days before the calculated fertile period to allow the husband to accumulate the maximum number of sperm.

6. The husband has the maximum number of healthy sperm when he ejaculates regularly, at least every four days. More than four days of abstinence will decrease the number of sperm.

If a doctor finds the wife's uterus is tipped backward (retroverted), a completely different intercourse position should be used for conception. She should get on her hands and knees, then place her chest on the bed. The husband should insert the penis from the male-behind position. He should make the deepest possible penetration as he begins his ejaculation; then, stop all thrusting until ejaculation is finished and immediately withdraw the penis. Though this will be a tiring position to maintain, the wife should remain in her knee-chest position for one hour after the husband's ejaculation. Whether she achieves orgasm has no bearing on the probability of conception.

Even when no specific cause is found for the infertility problem, certain forms of medical therapy can be initiated. There may be repeated tests, observations, and treatment. Much energy, money, and time may be invested by the couple with no guarantee that a solution will be found. In the best fertility clinics, conception in 30 to 40 percent of the patients is considered quite good.

Attitudes about childbearing have changed over the past several years. Many couples are delaying the start of their family so that both partners can pursue a career. When these couples decide to become pregnant, many have reproductive problems. Most of the problems involve "bad eggs" due to the age of the woman. The chances of a woman getting pregnant are considerably lower after age 40, with a significant drop in pregnancy after age 35. The best, most fertile ages are 15 to 24, certainly before age 31. In one study, impaired fecundity is experienced by 4.1 percent of all American women ages 15 to 24, 13.4 percent of those ages 25 to 34, and 24.4 percent of those ages 35 to 44.

When an older woman does get pregnant, that pregnancy is harder to maintain. Women in their forties have a much greater risk of spontaneous abortion, 50 percent greater than women in their twenties. Also, older women have a greater risk of bearing a low-birth weight infant or premature baby.

Couples trying to cope with and overcome their infertility problem are apt to experience many painful emotions in the process—shock, embarrassment, anger, depression, grief, and a continuing frustration. Indeed, infertility has been called one of the major crises of adult life.

In many cases the fact of infertility and the couple's resulting attempts to become pregnant can have a detrimental effect on their sexual relationship and their entire marriage. Here are some of the ways this may happen.

1. One or both of the partners may begin to feel sexually inadequate, because they view conception as the end product of sexual intercourse.
2. One or both may feel inadequate in general—"defective," as one patient described it. They feel "out of phase" with themselves and others, as if a deep unspoken plan they held

for their lives had gone awry. They may temporarily lose their sense of themselves as persons, because the pattern they envisioned for themselves as parents seems denied to them. They may begin to enjoy everything less, including sex, because of their anxiety.

3. One or both may begin to view sexual intercourse only as a means to accomplishing their heartfelt goal of conceiving a child. They may lose their sense of sexual lovemaking as an experience of great worth and enrichment in itself.

4. The requirements of infertility treatment, such as semen analysis and postcoital tests, which the medical staff considers routine, may be embarrassing or distasteful for the couple. The personal intimacy of sex between two lovers seems invaded by these clinical demands.

5. Because they must have sex at certain times on certain days, whether they feel like it or not, they may begin to feel that their sex life is so programmed that it has lost all its romantic spontaneity and genuine passion.

6. They may both become intensely frustrated by the slowness of the process and feel helpless because they have no control over the situation. After all, they cannot improve their own semen or cervical secretions at will. (The physician can help by discussing every phase of the process and keeping them as fully informed as possible.) Anger is often felt but repressed, until it becomes depression, which can seriously affect the level of sexual desire. The wife may have difficulty in reaching orgasm. The husband may experience ejaculatory disturbances. Both may suffer from low libido because they can no longer think of sex as pleasure. It is too closely associated with the emotional pain of infertility.

7. A level of resentment and envy toward other people can sometimes build, until they are robbed of joy in all aspects of their marriage. Sometimes couples change their jobs, their friends, and their lifestyle in response to the internal and external pressures of this time.

8. Women, particularly, say that infertility is an agonizing experience. One patient reported that what bothered her most

was having to take her temperature every morning, so that she began every day with a fresh reminder of her infertility problem and the pain involved. This kind of stress can have a grave effect on the fabric of the marriage relationship.

I have mentioned these unpleasant possibilities because they are very real pitfalls of which a couple need to be aware. If the couple confront them honestly, they can guard against them as much as possible, learning to handle them when they do appear, by using the resources God gives to His own. Every individual must sooner or later cope with disappointment and loss. God knows this and is ready to provide all that is needed to bring His child through the experience in a positive way.

The difficulties pressuring the infertile couple actually have the potential of drawing them closer as they begin to understand each other, reach out to comfort each other, and experience a deepening fellowship together in prayer. They can strengthen each other with the shared assurance of God's perfect plan for their life together and they can develop the patience and faith to wait on Him and to see Him bring it about.

This waiting time is a time to renew their love affair with a great deal of tender, affectionate, nonsexual physical touching. They need to employ all the techniques they know for building intimacy during this period, when pressures threaten to divide them emotionally and sexually. (These techniques are fully described in our book *Love Life for Every Married Couple*.) Above all, they need to be supportive, positive, and totally noncritical toward each other. At this phase of their life, when their sense of self-worth may be at lowest ebb, they need to build each other up by word, attitude, and action.

There are several possible outcomes for the couple who meet the problem in this way—all of them good. They may be among the 40 percent who succeed in having a baby. They may find a gratifying reality in adopting one or more children. Or they may learn to build a satisfying, creative, and productive life together without children, being assured that this is God's perfect plan for their particular marriage.

What counts in any traumatic situation of life is how you choose to respond to it over a period of time. Some couples who have responded to the problem of infertility with faith and the determination to express their love in positive ways, find that there *are* alternatives to being birth parents that bring them great joy as they give of themselves. The love that might have been centered on one child is poured out to many individuals. The book *Childless Is Not Less* by Vicky Love will be a great encouragement.

The Bible expresses this principle with words that have comforted through the centuries:

Sing, O barren, thou that didst not bear; break forth into singing, and cry aloud, thou that didst not travail with child: for more are the children of the desolate than the children of the married wife, saith the LORD.

Isaiah 54:1

12

Sex during Pregnancy

When the baby is on the way, many questions arise and they are of burning importance to the prospective parents: How will this affect our relationship? Will my wife lose her sexual desire during pregnancy? Can I hurt the baby during intercourse? Will intercourse be too uncomfortable for my wife? How long can we have sex safely? What does my wife need from me during this time? How will my husband feel about my changed appearance? What does he need or expect from me? Should we take prepared-childbirth classes? Should we try for natural childbirth? How soon after the baby is delivered can we resume a normal sex life? Are we going to be closer to each other or farther apart when this time is over?

These questions reflect a fact sensed by most husbands and wives as soon as they know a baby is on the way: Pregnancy *is* a delicate time in a marriage and it certainly will have a lasting effect for good or ill on their sexual and emotional adjustment to each other.

Giving specific answers to these questions may be risky, since individuals differ so greatly in their sexual, emotional, and physical response to pregnancy, but I can make some general observations. These are based on medical research and on my own experience as a family doctor who has delivered hundreds of babies, usually to couples I regularly take care of and see for years before and after the pregnancy. In fact many of the girl babies I delivered twenty or so years ago are my obstetrical patients today.

I have observed that pregnancy can be a tremendously rewarding experience for husband and wife, with lasting benefits for their marriage *if* they follow these three simple guidelines:

1. Communicate your feelings.
2. Meet your partner's needs and desires.
3. Share the experience all the way.

Communication

If there was ever a time you needed to talk to each other, it is now. You particularly need to communicate your own feelings about yourself, about the baby, about what's happening, about your marriage, about your fears and joys. Note that I said, talk about your *feelings*. If you're careful to share honest feelings, there's not much room for dispute or argument or taking offense. Since you're saying how you *feel*, not making assertions of fact or accusations, there should be room only for hearing each other and then mutual understanding backed up by mutual support.

Therapists believe that relationship problems are most apt to develop during pregnancy when the husband and wife fail to discuss their emotions. And sexual problems during pregnancy are mainly a symptom of poor communication. For example, it is important for the wife to tell her husband what makes her uncomfortable in intercourse. Suffering in silence only leads to resentment and will cast a negative cloud over the sex relationship. When a sex act is judged as a negative experience, it is more likely to be postponed the next time, or even avoided.

Needs and Desires

Research now indicates that there is somewhat of a progressive decline in sexual interest and sexual drive for most pregnant women. One study, made to determine median weekly frequencies of sexual intercourse during and after pregnancy, yielded these results: first three months, 2.25 times per week; second three months, 2.39 times per week; last three months, 1.08 times per week; after delivery, 2.65 times per week. Other studies bear out the same conclusions. The very slight increase during the fourth, fifth, and sixth months of pregnancy reflects the fact that women are over their early discomfort, have adjusted to the idea of pregnancy, and may have a sense of well-being before an enlarging abdomen becomes a problem.

One commonsense hypothesis has been borne out by research results: Women who have a positive attitude toward their pregnancy maintain a good sexual relationship, while women who have negative feelings about their pregnancy tend to decrease in sexual interest and sexual satisfaction.

Even though the pregnant woman may not need as much intercourse, sexual release should be provided for her, and one thing she clearly does need is loving physical contact. About 92 percent of women tested have expressed a strong desire to be held during lovemaking. Researchers conclude that the need for closeness during pregnancy is a very powerful one for most women.

The wife also needs encouragement and compliments during this period when she may *feel* physically unattractive. Actually, wives who are beloved and honored at this time usually wear a special, beautiful glow. The husband should be even more affectionate and complimentary than usual. Treating her with tenderness and appreciation during pregnancy will pay great dividends in sexual pleasure for both partners and will have lasting benefits.

Here are some words of advice for the wife. Psychologically, your husband needs to feel an emotional bond with you and his baby and he needs to feel like an important part of all that's happening. He also needs to be reassured that he has not permanently exchanged his lover/companion for someone interested only in motherhood.

Remember that although pregnancy may change your sexual desires, your husband is not pregnant. His sexual needs continue at the same level throughout the pregnancy, delivery, and the weeks of abstention afterward. When you are not having intercourse as frequently as you were prior to pregnancy, you should offer manual stimulation to him—*particularly* during the period of abstention. It is usually more stimulating if you use an artificial lubricant, as you squeeze and stroke the penis to bring him to orgasm. Do not ask him if he wants this. Just lovingly initiate this stimulation and give him the opportunity to lovingly refuse, if he chooses. Show your concern for him; let him know that you are longing to give him pleasure, whether or not you feel any desire or need for sexual play. If you then find that you desire to have your husband stimulate you to a climax too (and the doctor has not advised against it), clearly communicate this to him.

Physicians have been in general agreement that intercourse in a pregnancy uncomplicated by bleeding or episodes of premature labor or a history of high-risk pregnancy should be safe enough, at least during the first eight months. If there is no complication, your doctor may tell you to go ahead, as long as you are comfortable. During the last month, there is some reason for concern because of the possibility of infection and premature rupture of the membranes (the water bag). Cases have been reported of membranes ruptured by thrusting of the penis. Reaching an orgasm during manual stimulation may bring on premature labor because of the regular, forceful contractions of the uterus during sexual climax.

Even so, most doctors have believed that a couple can enjoy sexual intercourse until the wife goes into labor, if there is no pain, no bleeding, and no leakage of amniotic fluid. The published results of some research, however, have caused a considerable degree of controversy over this. An analysis of more than twenty-five thousand births indicated that intercourse during the month before delivery does clearly increase the risk and severity of amniotic fluid infections, thus increasing the threat to the baby's life. This is still a rare complication, but you need to be aware of the possibility. You can decrease the risk by thorough bathing by both wife and husband before each intercourse. The husband should use a condom during each intercourse to further decrease the chance for contamination.

Here is some advice on intercourse positions. During the first three months, while the uterus is growing so rapidly, there may be some discomfort. The female-above position will usually enable the wife to position herself for greatest comfort and pleasure.

Enlarging of the abdomen does not begin to interfere with intercourse until about the fifth month. The couple may then want to choose a special position that will afford more comfort for the wife.

Here are some positions particularly useful during pregnancy, but remember that intercourse in these positions must usually be accompanied by manual stimulation of the clitoris for the wife to achieve sexual climax.

1. Husband and wife both lie on their sides, facing each other. Intercourse is begun from the front; or husband and wife both lie on their sides, knees flexed, facing the same direction, with intercourse begun from behind. This is usually very comfortable for both wife and husband and allows manual stimulation of the clitoris during intercourse.

2. The wife lies flat on her back, with her knees slightly flexed or pulled up high enough to rest on her husband's shoulders. He remains in an upright kneeling position, with his knees spread wide apart and her buttocks between his thighs. The penis is then gently inserted in the vagina. This position allows manual stimulation of the clitoris throughout intercourse and does not require any contact with the enlarged abdomen. The wife may be more comfortable with a pillow beneath her buttocks.

3. The husband sits comfortably in an armless chair with his wife sitting on his lap, facing him, with a leg on each side of his body. This leaves his hands completely free for manual stimulation. The head of the penis may be placed just within the vaginal opening, so that penetration is very shallow. This will be sufficient depth for mutual sexual stimulation and can be practiced even during the final weeks of pregnancy when deeper penetration may otherwise be prohibited.

4. In a position similar to that on an obstetrical delivery table, the woman lies on her back with her buttocks on the edge of a low bed, legs separated, and knees flexed over the padded backs of two straight chairs pushed against the bed. The husband kneels on several cushions between the chairs, with his

pelvis at the most convenient level for comfortable insertion of the penis. Obviously, this position requires prior preparation, but it can provide maximum freedom and comfort for both partners at this special time. It offers excellent opportunity for manual stimulation of the wife and provides complete control of the depth of penetration of the penis.

5. The husband lies on his side across the center of the bed. In a cross position, at right angles to him, the wife lies on her back with both knees flexed over his body, as if she were sitting on his lap. The vaginal opening is placed as close as possible to the penis. The penis is inserted from below. The husband *must* use manual clitoral stimulation in this position, to give his wife sexual climax.

In the final three months, with the baby's head well down into the pelvis, there may be a feeling of excessive pressure. For this reason, it is better during this period to avoid the female-above position, which encourages the deepest penetration of the penis.

You must follow your own physician's advice concerning the safety of intercourse and orgasm in your particular case. If you are encouraged to go ahead with lovemaking, and the husband treats the wife with normal, loving care, choosing positions that are comfortable for both, there is no reason for your growing baby to become a barrier to your sexual intimacy and pleasure.

Share the Experience

I encourage the couples who come to me for obstetrical care to participate together in the birth of their child, with the husband accompanying his wife to the labor room and to the delivery room. In preparation for this, at monthly visits to my office, I have the husband actually examine his wife with me and I share with him the information obtained. This allows both husband and wife to better understand the physical changes taking place during pregnancy and to more fully share the experience of bringing their baby into the world. At this time I also give the couple an opportunity to talk over any problems that may have arisen in their sexual adjustment.

About two months before time for delivery, I encourage each couple to attend prepared-childbirth classes. Both husband and wife will benefit from learning together in preparation for delivery, whether or not they choose natural childbirth.

The wife may decide she wants no medication at all, or I may help her choose a method that will diminish her discomfort. There are a number of options, which include regional neurological blocks, inhalation anesthetics, or low dosages of Demerol and tranquilizers. No one should attempt natural childbirth out of a sense of duty. On the other hand, it can be very meaningful for a couple prepared for it. I have seen Christian couples come to the hospital hand in hand, participate together in the birth of their child, and (sometimes!) take the baby home the same day, full of joy at what God has enabled them to accomplish together.

Couples who are totally sharing the childbirth experience attend the classes, spend time on the exercises together, even determine the best foods for wife and baby. The husband gains new experience in sensitivity to his wife and new skill in the art of gentle, caring physical touch. The wife gains a deeper trust in her husband through his cherishing of her. Any husband who is involved in this way will be sure to consider the changes in his wife's body as beautiful, knowing that her body is being transformed to provide nourishment and a comfortable, temporary home for their baby. He may enjoy holding his wife, knowing that their baby is close by.

At the time of delivery, it is the husband's job to massage his wife during the contractions, keep her relaxed, talk to her, and be sensitive to what she is feeling. He may assist her with her learned breathing pattern, but his most important contribution is just the encouragement and reassurance of his presence.

The emotional communication learned during this time is deeply valuable and spills over to bless the marriage for years to come. There have been cases where difficulties that had previously existed in a marriage before the pregnancy were resolved as the two shared in their child's birth!

When the wife comes home from the hospital, she may experience some vaginal discomfort, especially if an episiotomy requiring sutures was performed during the delivery of the baby. Usually a vaginal discharge is present, which changes gradually in color from red to light brown and from a moderate to scant amount. In the first two weeks at home, while the tissues of the uterus and vagina are undergoing a normal healing process, minor discomfort in the genital area may be experienced. By the time the discharge stops, the discomfort should have gone away, and intercourse can be resumed. Generally intercourse may occur within two to four weeks after delivery. Your doctor will advise you.

When intercourse does resume, I suggest that the husband be as careful, loving, and gentle as he was during the first intercourse of the honeymoon. Be sure to have an artificial lubricant on hand. If there is no tenderness of the area near the clitoris, mutual, manual stimulation to sexual climax may be begun at any time after the delivery of the baby. If the couple choose to avoid another pregnancy, even if the wife is breast-feeding the baby and there are no menstrual periods, contraceptive measures should be instituted at least by the time of the six-week checkup.

I trust that the experience of having a baby will be a time of tender concern, communication, emotional closeness, and loving consideration in your marriage, and that you will discover that even in these challenging months, your sexual togetherness is intended for pleasure.

13

Sex after 60...
70... 80...

Sex after sixty can be better than ever! This is not propaganda to encourage the faltering, but a frank statement of fact. Many of my patients have told me that this is true in their experience. In my office a number of couples married forty-plus years have reported wonderful love relationships with more pleasure for both than ever before.

Now if this surprises the reader, it may be that you have been taken in by the myths surrounding oldsters. The myth of the decline and fall of sexuality by age sixty-five hangs on, in spite of all research and information to the contrary. A cartoon published in *Punch* illustrates this false view of sexual incapacity. An old fellow on a park bench is eyeing a gorgeous young thing walking by, while his elderly wife comments to another little old lady: "Albert has a *wonderful* memory, *for his age. . . .*"

Let me assure you who are approaching the sixties or seventies that you will not have to settle for *memories,* if you and your partner remain in reasonably good health and have a loving communication with each other. Attitude is the key factor. For instance, you probably look at life and the inevitability of aging in one of two ways. Some of you may think of life as a series of losses, which must be adapted to. You therefore see sex after sixty as a succession of defeats, with the older person forced to give up more and more territory, as the aging process moves in on the pleasures of lovemaking. Others of you, however, recognize that life is a series of changes but you know that these changes may bring gain as well as loss. You find that as you gracefully adapt to changing conditions, you give up comparatively little, while discovering unexpected treasures along the way. These positive-minded people are the ones who can expect to enjoy sex after sixty, seventy, or eighty.

Here are constructive suggestions for the after-sixty couple that can ensure a continuation or increase in their sexual pleasure.

Know the Truth

Know the truth and it will set you free! I refer to truths concerning your own bodies and the effects of the natural aging process. To know is to understand and to be able to overcome any difficulties that might arise. Here are some facts you should know.

First, if you have experienced good sexual functioning throughout your marriage, you should go into the mature years expecting pleasure to continue. Though some of the timing and frequency of response will change, sexual pleasure is far from over and may improve. Men and women always possess the power to bring creativity into their situation, which will make sex after sixty rich, free, and full of surprises.

You men should understand that it will take more time for you to attain an erection. However, this can work to your advantage because you can maintain the phase of excitement for a longer period. Because your need to ejaculate is less urgent, you will have more time in which to give your wife full satisfaction. You can expect the ejaculation period itself to be shorter and the relaxation phase to end more quickly. More time (sometimes a day or two) will elapse between your climax and the ability to have another erection. Here is a very important thing to realize: *You do not need to ejaculate every time you have intercourse.* Never force an ejaculation when you feel no physical need for it. Forcing an ejaculation could diminish your powers to get and keep an erection. Ejaculate only when you feel like it. At other times, enjoy intercourse without it.

Wives, you should be aware that after fifty, you have less lubrication, and the secretions are produced more slowly. This can be easily remedied by use of an artificial lubricant. The vaginal walls become thinner, less elastic, and more easily irritated by sexual intercourse. You can avoid the problem by taking estrogen or using a vaginal cream containing estrogen, which is absorbed through the vaginal wall. Remember, as I have explained earlier in this book, atrophic vaginitis (thinning of the vaginal walls) is the only physical change of menopause that will interfere with a wife's sexual functioning, if estrogen is not provided. An active sex life can help prevent shrinkage of the vaginal opening.

It should be understood that as long as you have sufficient estrogen to menstruate, you will probably have sufficient estrogen to prevent vaginal atrophy.

Although both men and women experience a shorter orgasm, lasting five or six seconds instead of ten or twelve, it still provides the same physical pleasure. If the wife should experience pain from the contraction of the uterus during orgasm, it is usually a sign that her estrogen levels are below normal. The condition is relieved by taking estrogens by mouth or by regular injections.

Men, the gradual, very slight physiological decline in sex drive with advancing years can be put in proper perspective by realizing that we reach the height of our sexual vigor at about seventeen or eighteen, and the decline begins then! The important thing to remember is that *aging itself will not prevent you from attaining or maintaining an erection.* You may ejaculate less frequently, less forcefully, and with less volume. But because sex is a natural lifetime function, if you have an enthusiastic and willing partner, the gradual physiological decline will have little or no bearing on your sexual relationship.

Wives, you should know that women do not decline physiologically in their sex drive. In many cases women continue to increase in desire from the time of their youth into the seventies and beyond. In this period of your marriage, you may find yourself becoming more and more active sexually, particularly with fear of pregnancy gone. Your enthusiastic participation will provide maximum pleasure for both you and your husband in the years after sixty.

Now I suggest that both of you check your attitude toward aging one more time. Remember, growing older is not synonymous with illness! It does not spell the end of sexual desire and pleasure. Impotence is not a natural development of old age but is almost always a result of the state of mind at any age, affecting the man who worries about the normal changes taking place in his body or who sees himself as "over the hill."

What then, you may ask, about the older couple whose sex life *is* declining? Several factors may be involved. First, not all individuals have a strong sex drive even in their younger years. Some men become discouraged over the years because of continued rejection from their wives. Some, fearing impotence, protect their self-image by transferring sex drive into other channels, such as the drive for financial power. Some men have developed resentments toward their wives, which have diminished their sex drive. Many couples have allowed a set routine to dull the excitement of their time together. All these factors may be responsible for the decline of the sex drive in later life, but the causes are psychological rather than physical in most cases.

Enjoy Yourselves

Understanding your own physiology should be followed up by a decision with your partner to savor together your times of lovemaking and to let nothing interfere with this happy aspect of life. Know that pleasure is possible for you. Your love can be renewed, if necessary, by applying the principles discussed in chapter 3. More skillful sexual techniques, as described in other chapters, can inspire renewed interest. New, creative approaches to lovemaking can eliminate boredom and put the spark back in your relationship. The best "treatment" for a man whose desires are burning low is a warm, receptive wife who offers plenty of loving sexual stimulation. (As one man said, there is a huge difference between being tolerated and being *wanted*.) Enthusiasm on the part of either partner can do wonders for the other one.

Here are some specific ways to find more pleasure in your sex life.

Wife, encourage your husband by letting him know how much he pleases you. Husband, let your wife know how desirable she is to you. After sixty, men may worry about their lack of vigor, and women may fear rejection because of loss of youthful appearance. Loving, mutual appreciation will amazingly enhance your relationship and your total self-concept.

Be aware of what one writer has called the "background music" of the lovemaking experience. I refer to verbal lovemaking, which can richly increase your pleasure, as both of you forget self-consciousness and freely give to each other in word as well as touch.

In touching each other, be sensitive to areas of the body that may not be sexually stimulating, but that may have a powerful and positive psychological effect on your partner. Communicate with one another about this. Be willing to "adventure" in exploring new ways to please each other.

Discover the principle of *reciprocity,* and let it work for you in increasing sexual excitement. Researchers have found that when two people are free of anxieties and inner conflicts, they can learn to thrill to each other's response and respond to the other's pleasure in a gathering momentum of delight, self-forgetfulness, and abandon. On the other hand, rebuff, passive submission, or self-consciousness can have a snowballing negative effect. Agree with your partner to reject these negative influences. Life on this earth is too short to waste time in negative responses that hinder God-intended pleasure. Be on the lookout for them and overcome them with loving communication and mutual understanding. Remember, communication means that you should never make your partner guess at how you are feeling or what you are thinking. Always aim for spontaneity and a relaxed approach to lovemaking . . . because it is fun!

Insist on Privacy

As couples grow older, they sometimes find it difficult to maintain their privacy so that they can enjoy sex in comfortable seclusion. This problem is compounded by the insensitive or ignorant who do not realize that elderly people have sex lives. Your privacy with your mate is a priceless gift which should not be discarded, except in a case of grave necessity. All people—but elderly couples more than any others—need the warmth and touching, the solace and reassurance of physical caring. If you go into some kind of nursing or retirement home, plan on an environment where you can live together with the privacy needed to express your love.

Health Problems

Although people with active sexual interests should not be restricted from living their normal lives, there are times when health problems do interfere and must be handled in a sensible manner so that the physical relationship can be resumed as soon as possible. The following discussion gives some suggestions for the couple after a heart attack, a stroke, or other physical limitation occurs. There also are important facts to be considered when the wife is going through menopause or has had a hysterectomy.

After a Heart Attack or Stroke

The senior years, of course, are the time when a heart attack or a stroke is most apt to occur. Adaptations are needed after such a serious illness, but if the patient has had good sexual functioning prior to the illness, most doctors feel that a return to his usual sexual life will help his total recovery. Often the frustration connected with sexual abstinence will use up more strength than would the sex act itself. The increased pulse rate, blood pressure, and respiratory rate reflect the emotional excitement of lovemaking, but emotional arousal from worry or arguing can have the same effect, without the benefits of physical union between husband and wife who love each other.

Monitoring the heart rates of cardiac patients during sexual activity has shown that the maximum heart rate response averaged 120 beats per minute and was sustained for only ten to fifteen seconds in most subjects. The activity turned out to be less demanding than driving a car through traffic or becoming angry. The energy required for sexual activity has been compared to that of climbing a flight of stairs or briskly walking two city blocks. Significant amounts of body energy are required for digestion after any eating or drinking. Therefore, I strongly recommend that the heart patient avoid having sexual intercourse for at least two hours after a big meal. It is interesting to note also that researchers point out that the sex act performed illicitly becomes a much more demanding function, because this combines the pressure of fear and guilt along with the physical activity.

For the loving married couple who normally come together without stress, manual stimulation to sexual climax can usually be allowed after six weeks, and sexual intercourse may be resumed between the eighth and fourteenth week, when the heart attack has healed without evidence of complications. This should be enjoyed in a leisurely manner, with emphasis on the pleasure of loving and touching each other. Although personal preferences should be considered, there is some slight advantage in using the female-above position if the man has been the patient. In this position the wife may be more protective and at the same time more aggressive in lovemaking during her husband's recuperation.

No specific restrictions are placed on sexual activity in patients with permanent pacemakers, other than limiting physical activity for the first two weeks. The personal physician must make the decision on an individual basis after that time.

Doctors should always deal frankly and wisely with the question of sex after a serious illness, rather than forcing the patient to ask, or simply advising (ominously), "You'd better watch it with sex." Sexual function is never improved by anxious self-watching, and neither is the patient's medical condition.

The aftereffects of a stroke often reduce a patient's confidence and sense of self-esteem. It is a tremendous boost to him to remain sexually desirable to his partner. Almost any physical difficulties can be overcome in loving, constructive, and common-sense ways, if the couple work together with the advice of their physician. Pillows, a handle on the headboard, a higher footboard, varying positions, and orgasm by manual stimulation are just some of the ways problems can be handled. A good sex relationship can be of inestimable value in coping with or preventing a patient's after-stroke depression.

Overcoming Physical Limitations

Strokes and heart attacks are only two of many physical conditions that may impose limitations on a couple to prevent what we would think of as a normal sexual relationship. There are injuries, deformities, and the aftermath of necessary operations to be contended with. One of the most common disfiguring but not disabling operations is the mastectomy (removal of a breast). No couple should allow this operation to diminish their sex life in any way! It is particularly important for the husband to show his wife how much he loves her and how grateful he is that she is living and well. In every situation, two partners who love each other have opportunities to develop imaginative ways to provide full sexual satisfaction for each other, even in what may seem to be the most adverse conditions. Learning these techniques together can become a powerful factor, strengthening their total marriage relationship as husband and wife grow in mutual compassion and understanding. The goal should be for the two to live out their lives together in a wonderful closeness. As this goal is reached for, recovery possibilities are greatly increased. In every case the quality of the lives involved is unquestionably improved.

Occasionally a sudden, dramatic illness is followed by a period of total lack of sexual desire. This can be distressing to both husband and wife, and the reassurance of the physician is required at this point. The patient should be encouraged by the fact that this condition is almost always temporary and disappears when health is improved. It is most important that the couple continue sexual stimulation during the period after an illness because loss of sexual function in the older person often follows long periods of abstinence for any reason.

Many men in the fifty-to-seventy age group develop enlargement of the prostate gland (benign prostatic hypertrophy). When this enlargement produces blockage of the flow of urine, an operation is required for removal of the prostate. After the operation the seminal fluid usually is ejaculated into the bladder rather than out through the penis. The ability to attain and keep an erection is not ordinarily affected by the prostate operation. The man will experience the same sexual drive and the same pleasure during orgasm as he did before the operation, but he should realize that no fluid will be projected from the penis at orgasm. Normal sexual intercourse can be resumed two months after this operation.

After the Menopause

Sex after the menopause can be just the same or better for the wife. Some women have had the notion that they will lose interest and pleasure in sex as they go on past the menopause, but this simply is not true. Changes in the timing of sexual response do not mean that sex is enjoyed less. Many women feel a greater freedom because they have fewer family responsibilities and more opportunity to develop their own identities outside of motherhood.

The woman who is experienced in love, comfortable with herself, and well-adjusted to her husband can accept the physical changes as they come and continue to enjoy a rewarding sex life.

A minority of women may feel their feminine identity threatened by loss of the menstrual process and will make sometimes frantic efforts to regain beauty or sex appeal. A wise, loving husband will bolster his wife's self-esteem, showing appreciation for her in word and action. "Little things mean a lot," as the song goes, and particularly so at this critical time in a woman's life. Her husband may also encourage her to redirect her energies, perhaps into further education or into some Christian ministry. In fact more and more retired couples are now going into missionary enterprises, both at home and overseas, to relieve overworked missionaries on the field.

Some women show definite signs of estrogen deficiency, experiencing hot flushes, nervousness, dizziness, insomnia, irritability, sudden mood swings, depression, and decreased sexual desire. When several of these symptoms are present, most doctors now feel that replacement estrogen should be administered either in oral tablets, by injection, or by patch. In some patients the oral estrogen is apparently not well absorbed, and injections are required. A long-acting estrogen is usually given at monthly intervals. Most of the menopausal symptoms can be readily relieved by carefully regulated dosage of oral or injectable estrogen. Any woman who suffers from these symptoms should seek medical advice for a possible trial on estrogen-replacement therapy. If the estrogens alone do not increase a woman's sexual responsiveness, she may need some low dosage of male hormones (testosterone) injected along with the estrogen. Any vaginal bleeding after regular menstrual periods have ceased should be a signal to see the doctor.

After a Hysterectomy

The hysterectomy operation (the surgical removal of a woman's uterus) should not be a hazard to the couple's sex life. However, difficulties arise from a lack of understanding. Some of the common misconceptions are:

1. A woman will invariably gain weight and lose her figure.
2. Aging will be more rapid.
3. Sexual desire and response will be diminished.
4. A woman will immediately experience all the common post-menopausal symptoms.

Sometimes the husband has the idea that his wife will no longer be interested in sex or, disconcertingly, he treats her as though she were a china plate to be kept on the shelf. I have found it important to talk to the husband and wife ahead of time, dealing with any apprehensions concerning the surgery and aftermath and assuring both that the only change may be an improvement in their sex life, since most women having this operation have undergone discomforts that will now be alleviated.

Preparing for the Golden Years

I advise younger couples reading this chapter to prepare sexually as well as financially for their later years. Retirement will not mean retirement from the pleasures of lovemaking, if you maintain an active sex life now and continue to do so. You should be making emotional investments in your relationship with your partner right now—maintaining open communication lines, living in an atmosphere of empathy and mutual support, practicing love for each other in all that you do and say. Every refusal to allow resentments or hurt feelings to come into your relationship now is an investment in future pleasure and a wonderful closeness, which will continue throughout your life together. As you look forward to your later years, expect to love each other more and more. This has been the experience of many older couples who have overcome anxieties and inhibitions, have put new information into practice, and have learned how to please each other. They say, when asked, that their relationship is enhanced by a mature appreciation of each other and a love of greater depth than they knew as young people.

The maxim that applies best to sex after sixty is simply—*Use it or lose it*. The couple who keep active sexually can continue to enjoy lovemaking after sixty . . . seventy . . . and even eighty.

14

Sexually Transmitted Diseases

> If thou wilt diligently hearken to the voice of the LORD thy God, and wilt do that which is right in his sight, and wilt give ear to his commandments, and keep all his statutes, I will put none of these diseases upon thee, which I have brought upon the Egyptians: for I am the LORD that healeth thee.
>
> Exodus 15:26

While the focus of this book is on sexuality within a Christian marriage, it cannot be ignored that many Christians have made unwise sexual choices at some point in their lives. God's amazing grace offers total spiritual healing, and yet for many, there are physical consequences associated with sexual activity outside of God's design.

Physical consequences are numerous and may even cost a person his or her life. For this reason, single adults are anxious about their own sexual health status or the sexual health status of their potential partner. The questions are numerous. Should I marry someone who has herpes? What about gonorrhea? Genital warts? Will the use of condoms prevent my mate from getting my disease? What is the potential for infection or harm to my unborn children? How can I be sure my partner does not carry HIV—the virus causing AIDS? With all the conflicting information out there, whom can I believe?

My goals for this chapter are to clarify information on specific diseases, give counsel to those who are dealing with these issues, and provide informed and straightforward communication about the risks of promiscuous sexual activity.

In the 1960s the only two venereal diseases of great concern were gonorrhea and syphilis. Each of these diseases could be treated with antibiotics and entirely eliminated from the body. As sexual activity increased during the sexual revolution of the 60s and 70s, numerous new diseases emerged, diseases with more serious lifelong consequences.

In the last ten years the number of people infected with a sexually transmitted disease (STD) has grown at an alarming rate. The World Health Organization now estimates 250 million cases of STDs occur in the world each year. Approximately one out of every four sexually active young adults in the United States is infected with a bacterial and/or viral STD. Sixty-three percent of those newly infected are less than twenty-five years of age.

Most adults do not realize that the STD epidemic is a recent phenomenon. Older adults who engaged in intimate sexual activity outside of a committed relationship as young adults were mostly concerned with issues of pregnancy. They were not likely to contract STDs, much less one that causes premature death. Today's youth are now in a position where they should literally fear death when they consider sexual intimacy.

The impact of these diseases in terms of human suffering, financial costs, and social values is causing us to rethink our sexual behavior. For society, behavioral change is the only effective measure capable of turning the STD epidemic around. The only safe sex today is sex in a monogamous relationship for a lifetime. Abstinence (a word we will define in more detail later in the chapter) must be the choice until marriage.

The term *sexually transmitted diseases* means that organisms causing these diseases are passed from person to person through intimate sexual activity. There are now more than fifty organisms and syndromes we label STDs. The more serious ones include chlamydia, genital warts (HPV), genital herpes (HSV), syphilis, gonorrhea, and most noteworthy, HIV-related diseases. Trichomonal vaginitis and candidiasis are less serious and are not necessarily associated with intimate sexual activity but will also be discussed due to their frequency. We hope to clarify how each of these diseases is transmitted, treated, and prevented. The STDs are grouped by the type of germ that causes the disease: bacteria, viruses, protozoa, and fungi. As you read this chapter, remember three very important points:

1. STDs are often present without signs or symptoms of infection, especially in women.
2. Early detection is critical in order to prevent outcomes such as infertility, cancer, and ectopic pregnancy.
3. Most of these diseases are transmitted by any kind of intimate sexual contact, not exclusively intercourse.

Sexually Transmitted Bacterial Diseases

Gonorrhea

Gonorrhea is caused by the bacterium gonococcus. These bacteria infect mucosal (moist) surfaces of the body: the urethra, cervix, rectum, and throat. Any type of oral, vaginal, or anal sexual activity can transmit this disease.

Urethritis, an inflammation of the urinary tube causing pain during urination, is the most common symptom of gonorrhea in men. Within a week of infection there is usually a puslike discharge from the penis. A small percentage of men (5 percent) never develop any symptoms. Half of women with gonorrhea will show no symptoms either. In women, the gonococcus can cause an infection of the cervix producing a pussy, white discharge. Unlike men, painful urination is less common in women with gonorrhea.

Progression of this infection in men can cause narrowing of the urethra, inflammation of the prostate, and epididymitis (a painful swelling of the epididymis, which lies alongside the testicle). In women there is a risk for infertility associated with pelvic inflammatory disease (PID), a serious infection of the entire pelvic region. PID may cause scarring of the reproductive organs, which may result in infertility or ectopic pregnancy (pregnancy that develops outside of the uterus—sometimes called tubal pregnancy). One episode of gonorrhea causing PID in women is estimated to result in a 12 percent chance of infertility. For men and women, gonococcal infections may spread through the bloodstream to the whole body. This may cause fever, a rash, and arthritis (inflammation of the joints).

Gonorrhea is treated with penicillin or other antibiotics. Until recently, this has worked effectively, but now approximately 20 percent of gonorrhea infections are penicillin resistant. A variety of antibiotics will need to be tried for these resistant infections, and until the effective treatment is determined, the disease will continue to adversely affect the body. This makes treatment much more complicated and expensive and increases the likelihood of long-term consequences.

Chlamydia

The number of chlamydia infections is rising rapidly, especially among teenagers and college-aged young adults. More than five million Americans are infected each year, making chlamydia the most common sexually transmitted disease. This infection in men is usually called NGU, nongonococcal urethritis, meaning urethritis not caused by gonococcus.

Like gonorrhea, chlamydia infects mucosal surfaces. About 30 percent of persons who have a gonococcus infection will also have a chlamydia infection at the same time. Unfortunately you can get both diseases with one sexual act. Chlamydia causes mild discomfort during urination and a watery discharge occurring one to two days following exposure. Women may not have symptoms associated with the infection when it is only in the urethra.

A major complication of chlamydia infection in men is epididymitis. The most alarming outcome of chlamydia infection in women is pelvic inflammatory disease. The rise in infertility rates in the United States are believed to be, at least in part, a direct result of PID associated with chlamydia and/or gonorrhea infections. Babies born to an infected mother may develop eye infections or pneumonia.

Chlamydia is treated with tetracycline-type drugs; it does not respond to penicillin. With STDs both partners must be treated simultaneously so the infection is not passed back and forth.

Syphilis

The rate of syphilis infection was on the decline for many years, but in the last ten years there has been a dramatic rise, especially among minority populations in large cities. Syphilis is caused by a germ named *Treponema palladium,* otherwise known as a spirochete because of its corkscrew shape. This bacteria actually drills or bores itself into the skin wherever it makes contact. An open sore called a chancre (pronounced shanker) is a classic sign of early or primary syphilis, and sores appear on the genitals, in the throat, on the lips, and around the anal area. Syphilis can be transmitted by kissing, intercourse, oral-genital contact, or anal contact.

Syphilis infection is said to occur in distinct stages. Primary syphilis is when a painless chancre appears at the site of infection three weeks following exposure, and the nearby lymph glands (or nodes) may be tender. If untreated, the chancre heals on its own in one to two weeks. The person infected may believe he or she is well, but the infection has not left the body. In another one to three months secondary syphilis develops. Secondary syphilis has symptoms similar to other diseases such as hepatitis, arthritis, and meningitis—fever, rash, muscle aches and pains, large genital warts, and swollen lymph nodes. This stage will also go away but the overall infection is still there. Some patients develop tertiary syphilis, which is the third and most serious stage. This stage damages organs throughout the body and can cause death. Very few individuals today progress to this point because the disease is usually detected through routine blood tests.

Syphilis is treated with penicillin or other antibiotics. It is not difficult to treat, but early detection is very important for successful treatment. Later stages of syphilis must be treated with antibiotics for long periods of time.

Is it safe to marry someone who has had a bacterial STD? Since most cases of gonorrhea, chlamydia, and syphilis are treated with antibiotics and eliminated from the body, there is no risk for infection due to past history of infection. However, the infected partner may carry the long-term complications of unchecked infection such as pelvic inflammatory disease-related infertility.

Sexually Transmitted Viral Diseases

Herpes (Genital Herpes)

Genital and oral herpes are caused by different types of the herpes simplex virus (HSV). On the lips and/or in the mouth, herpes infections are typically called "cold sores" or "fever blisters." The same infection in the genital region is called genital herpes.

Infection in either location develops when the virus comes into direct contact with skin and/or mucosal surfaces. The virus grows and spreads to nerve cells at the base of the spine and can lie dormant there for long periods of time. Essentially, genital herpes could be described as cold sores or fever blisters in the genital region.

In early herpes infection, pain, itching, painful urination, and discharge from the urethra or vagina occur first. These symptoms usually occur within three days to three weeks after infection. Next, small bumps called herpetic vesicles (pustules) develop in the area of the infection. These may itch at first and then turn into small fluid-filled blisters. After ten to twelve days they begin to crust, forming little sores. Tender lymph nodes are also present along with symptoms similar to the flu. The first outbreak is usually the longest, approximately twelve days. Subsequent outbreaks average about five days. The number of outbreaks differs from person to person and is often associated with stress, fatigue, overexposure to cold or the sun, and certain foods. To date, it is believed there are no serious complications for adult herpes infection. Fifty percent of those infected will never have another outbreak.

It is important to note that one can spread the virus to other areas on his or her own body. This is called autoinoculation and occurs when the area of an open sore is touched and then another part of the body is touched spreading the virus to the previously uninfected area. Oral herpes is often spread to children when they are kissed by an adult with an active herpes lesion on his or her lips. It was once believed that herpes was spread only by coming in contact with a herpes sore that would be shedding virus; thus the recommendation was to abstain from any contact during that time. Recent research has proven this incorrect and it is now known that the virus can be transmitted when there is no open sore. It is still very possible to infect someone without visual signs or symptoms.

Newborns who come in contact with the virus during birth may experience infections in the eyes, on the skin, and in the central nervous system and frequently even die. It is very important to make a health care professional aware of potential herpes infection so the proper precautions can be taken during delivery. Pregnant mothers with active herpes sores at delivery will undergo a caesarean delivery. Herpes, as with most viruses, can be treated but not cured. It is considered a lifelong condition.

Since there is no cure for herpes simplex infection, treatment is aimed at reducing symptoms. A drug called acyclovir (Zovirax) can reduce the time of shedding of active viruses, diminish symptoms, and may speed up healing of the pustules. Other recommendations include plenty of rest; a balanced diet; wearing loose fitting clothing, which reduces the warm, moist environment that encourages viral replication; and reducing direct exposure to the sun.

Is it safe to marry someone with a herpes infection? Herpes infection is one of the least serious STDs for adults. Although it is a lifelong infection, most people can manage it without too much difficulty. Marrying someone with herpes will put you at considerable risk for infection.

Human Papilloma Virus (HPV)

Genital warts are caused primarily by the human papilloma virus (HPV). Rates of infection among sexually active youths have been reported as high as 38 to 46 percent, and now HPV infection is one of the most common reasons women visit a gynecologist. Three times as many patients see physicians for genital warts as for genital herpes.

Similar to the other STDs, HPV infection may or may not be symptomatic. Men may form genital warts on the shaft or glans of the penis, or in the area around the anus. Warts in women are found on the cervix, vaginal walls, external genitalia, and around the anus. Warts may be flat or round; as small as a pencil point or as big as one inch in diameter. They may look like cauliflower or little spikes, occur in clusters or alone, and range in color from pink to brown. There is an incubation period between contact and development of the disease that ranges from two months to several years. The act of sexual intercourse moves the virus deeper into the body and spreads it to other surfaces. It is important to know that the virus may be present on the skin even if warts are not visible.

There is great concern among gynecologists over the increasing number of abnormal Pap smears in sexually active adolescents. These precancerous and cancerous conditions of the cervix are thought to be associated with HPV infection. A recent study showed that in 90 percent of all cases of cervical cancer, HPV was present. This does not mean cancer is a direct result of HPV, but there is a strong correlation between the two. Fortunately it appears that early treatment of abnormal cell growth will prevent cancers from developing on the cervix.

Venereal warts are treated in a variety of ways, by medicines placed on the skin that kill the affected area, cryo-surgery (freezing), or laser treatments (burning). Treatment is often painful and at best, inconvenient. In 80 percent of the cases, the warts return and will need to be removed again. Regular gynecological exams are crucial to the management of HPV infection.

Is it safe to marry someone with HPV? There is no way to prevent the transmission of HPV; it is highly contagious and with time, the uninfected partner will become infected. The partner of a person with venereal warts should always be checked and treated. Often an untreated partner will give the disease back to the treated partner.

The greatest danger of HPV infection known today is cervical cancer. This cancer can be avoided with regular checkups and treatment of precancerous conditions by the gynecologist. It is the undetected cases of HPV infection that cause the greatest concern. This infection can manifest itself at any time, so regular visits to the gynecologist are essential.

Acquired Immune Deficiency Syndrome (AIDS)

The most lethal of all STDs is the acquired immune deficiency syndrome (AIDS).

AIDS is caused by the human immunodeficiency virus (HIV), which predictably and progressively destroys the body's ability to fight off diseases. Because there is no standard testing procedure, the exact rate of HIV infection in the United States is unknown. Women, especially those in minority groups, and adolescents are among the fastest growing groups of people infected with HIV. The two primary routes for HIV transmission are virus to blood contact and virus to mucous membranes contact. People are infected by exchange of body fluids through intimate sexual contact, IV drug usage, blood transfusion, or mother to infant before or after birth. Seventy percent of HIV infections in the United States and 90 percent of HIV infections worldwide are now a direct result of sexual activity.

The virus attacks a type of white blood cell called a lymphocyte. Lymphocytes are critical to the body's natural ability to fight infection. Once the body is infected, all body fluids become extremely infectious. Over the next three weeks to six months the body manufactures antibodies to fight off the disease. HIV progressively destroys the immune system and eventually the body becomes susceptible to many types of infections that might otherwise be harmless. HIV-infected persons are most infectious during the first few weeks of infection and toward the very end when HIV has developed into AIDS. However, infection may occur at any point throughout the disease cycle.

Common Questions about HIV/AIDS

How can I be sure my partner is not infected with HIV?
The only way to know is to have a blood test. Both you and your partner need a blood test. Six months after your first test both of you need to be retested. At this point 98 percent of infected individuals will test positive (the other two percent are rare cases and are associated with known immune system dysfunction). It is recommended that partners go through all points of the testing and reporting procedures together. It is very important to note that this procedure will work only when both partners do not put themselves at risk during the six-month waiting period. Ultimately, you can only feel as safe as the degree of trust you have in your partner.

Will condoms prevent HIV infection?

Research by Margaret Fischel, who studied married couples in which only one partner was infected and condoms were used with every encounter, found 17 percent of the previously uninfected partners became HIV positive within 18 months. Those odds are approximately one in six, the same as Russian roulette. The Centers for Disease Control (CDC) has stated that condom effectiveness is as high as 98 percent IF the condoms are used properly and do not break or leak. Many researchers believe this is untrue and misleading. I have never found a health official or medical professional who would be willing to engage in sex, using a condom, with someone he or she knew to be infected.

Will nonoxynol-9 (N9) in condoms provide additional protection?

Nonoxynol-9 is a spermicide and was originally used to prevent pregnancy. Latex condoms with N9 were strongly recommended by public health officials for years. In the laboratory the N9 effectively killed HIV. However, it is now believed N9 actually increases the chance for HIV infection due to N9 irritating the mucous linings. This irritation may open the blood stream or cause a rush of white blood cells to the area, the very cells HIV infects. The CDC has backed off from this recommendation, and in January 1994 the Red Cross actually printed a warning against its use. N9 is a very good spermicide and there is no danger associated with its use unless a partner is HIV infected.

What about French kissing?

Since the virus is present in the oral cavity it is theoretically possible that the virus can be transmitted orally; however, the probability is considered low because of the low numbers of virus present. However, the viral levels in the body change, and thus potential for infection may increase. In the CDC pamphlet "What You Need to Know about AIDS," there is the following statement: "To be safe, experts warn against 'French kissing' with someone who may be infected with the AIDS virus." French kissing is not a safe activity.

What are the chances the virus will be passed to a newborn?

Studies indicate only a 30 percent chance the virus will be passed from infected mother to child. Recent research has shown mothers who are put on the drug AZT during pregnancy can reduce the risk of infection of their newborn to only 10 percent.

Is it safe to marry a person who is infected with HIV?

It is unsafe to marry an infected person. It is medically recommended that, when a partner is HIV infected, the couple refrain from any type of sexual behavior where there is an exchange of body fluids or contact with mucosal linings. Failure to do so will put the partner at risk for HIV infection. Analysis of the medical literature reveals there is a significant chance the noninfected partner will become infected, even with condom usage.

Sexually Transmitted Protozoal Diseases

Protozoa are parasites made up of one cell. Protozoal diseases make up the largest number of STDs worldwide, with trichomonas the most common. Trichomonas may affect males and females and 50 percent of them will have few if any symptoms. Symptoms in women are profuse vaginal discharge and itching of the external genital organs. Men may develop urethritis, prostatitis, or epididymitis. Trichomonas is successfully treated with the antibiotic metronidazole (Flagyl). Both partners must be treated at the same time.

Sexually Transmitted Fungal Diseases

Candida (yeast) is the fungus that infects the genital system most frequently. Candida can exist on the surface of the external genitalia and in the vagina without causing an infection. Occasionally, certain conditions such as diabetes, cancer, or chronic disease may increase a person's susceptibility to develop an infection with candida. Often, when a person is taking antibiotics for another illness, candida will flourish. The candida infection produces a rash, often with a cheesy, foul smelling discharge on infected areas such as the vagina and underneath the foreskin of the penis. Infections are treated with antifungal drugs placed on the infected area or taken by mouth, along with improved personal hygiene.

STD Prevention

There are many misconceptions as to what is "safe," "safer," or "protected" sex. The only way to be safe from an STD is to keep one's body from coming in contact with the infected mucosal surfaces or body fluids of someone else's body.

Abstinence is defined as choosing not to engage in any intimate sexual contact until marriage. Parents need to instruct their children that abstinence means withholding any sexual activity until marriage. There are some Christian adolescents who engage in intimate touching and even oral sex who believe they are being abstinent. STDs do not know one's identity, spiritual status, degree of love, faithfulness, or whether this is a first sexual contact. They are diseases and will be transmitted when given the opportunity. Abstinence is the only means to fight this epidemic and any health communication that advocates anything other than abstinence is shortsighted and doomed to failure.

Gynecological exams for sexually active women are a must. The standard recommendation for beginning annual gynecological examinations is age eighteen or whenever a girl becomes sexually active. If parents have reason to suspect any sexual activity, it is highly recommended that their daughter have regular gynecological checkups. The complications of unchecked chlamydia, gonorrhea, and HPV infection would be greatly reduced if this recommendation were followed.

Despite the many programs designed to educate and inform all at-risk individuals, the only way to prevent STDs is to change the hearts of men and women and help them return to sanity using God's biblical design for sexual behavior: one man and one woman for life in a monogamous marriage relationship. Many of the recommendations on sex given by health professionals today are based on the assumption that people will not change or cannot change their sexual behavior. Condoms do not eliminate risk; it is even debatable whether they reduce risk over the long run. One question then is, if we are reducing risk, how much risk is left? Frankly, no one knows. We do know that God is true and what He says can be depended on in any generation.

Unfortunately little effort is being put into promoting the abstinence message at the current time. Many secularists feel that abstinence is an unrealistic option. We as a nation, however, could see the end of the STD era if we simply followed the abstinence message and God's original design: one man and one woman for life in a monogamous marriage relationship.

Conclusion

Most STDs have the following characteristics:

1. They are transmitted primarily by intimate sexual contact.
2. They can be dormant or exist without symptoms for long periods of time but are still infectious and can be damaging.
3. They can be avoided entirely by following God's plan for sex.

God commands us to reserve sexual intimacy for the husband-wife relationship in marriage. Following this command will always improve relationships and free us from the fear and consequences of sexual sin. If we will hearken to His voice and do right, He will put none of these diseases on us.

For more information on STDs contact:

The Medical Institute for Sexual Health
P.O. Box 4919
Austin, TX 78765
1-800-892-9484

Americans for a Sound AIDS Policy
P.O. Box 17433
Washington, DC 20041
703-471-7350

Focus on the Family
Colorado Springs, CO 80995
719-531-3400

15

Answers to Your Questions

Please explain why God apparently made the facts or techniques of sex so hidden that we have to be instructed in them.

I was asked this question when I was speaking to pastors and marriage counselors at the Continental Congress on the Family held in St. Louis. My immediate reaction was that this is the most important question any Christian could ever ask on the subject. My response both then and now is that God has never hidden anything good from His children. If a couple carefully studies each section of the Bible that relates to sex in marriage, and if the couple shares with each other in open, loving, verbal and physical communication, this husband and wife will in time find the answers all by themselves. They will not need anyone to tell them about the techniques of sex. The Bible is open and frank about sex in marriage, and no man and wife who are free of abnormal inhibitions and who openly communicate with each other need develop any sexual problems. However, people through the years have obscured the facts and principles that God laid out so plainly in the Bible, and as a result many couples need help in correcting faulty techniques and negative attitudes, which may have been long established in their marriage. Newlyweds can benefit from learning the facts and techniques that provide emotional and physical satisfaction at the beginning of their marriage, so that problems are solved before they become stumbling blocks.

238

Why did God make men and women so different in the length of time required for sexual arousal?

If men and women both were satisfied with a short period of arousal, the sex act would become a brief, mechanical experience. If both took a very long time to become aroused, the experience could become boring and monotonous. Some might not even bother. Because men and women are different, the husband is given the opportunity to learn self-control and is encouraged to investigate and employ the imaginative techniques that please a woman. He has the opportunity to develop patience and gentleness in physical communication, while she learns to keep him sexually aroused and intrigued. The differences between men and women provide ground for creative, interesting interaction and enrich the sexual relationship in marriage.

How do I get rid of my inhibitions with my husband?

There should not be any shame in appearing before your husband without clothing or in being nude in bed with him. You should feel totally free to do what pleases both of you in the privacy of your bedroom. Thousands of husbands and wives have benefited from listening together to my cassette tapes *Sex Technique and Sex Problems in Marriage.* Hearing a physician discuss the intimacies of marriage encourages both husband and wife to discuss sexual matters openly with each other. Have your husband read aloud to you the part of this book that deals with the subject of your particular inhibitions and pray with him about these matters. The freedom to communicate your inhibitions to your husband in an open manner is one positive step toward being free of them altogether. Perhaps you and your husband should read together the seventh chapter of Song of Solomon in a modern translation, to realize more fully the freedom that should be expressed in married love.

What advice can you offer to the couple who both work and find that any time they have together is hampered by physical exhaustion?

This couple should be very careful to make special arrangements to retire at an early hour and may need to anticipate and regularly set aside quiet evenings to be alone at home together. I suggest an occasional weekend set aside for a brief and inexpensive vacation for two. The couple can make reservations at a motel in a nearby town for quiet relaxation and enjoyment of each other. If possible, a motel where meals are brought to the room should be chosen. There is little additional expense for this room service and it adds just a little extra sense of luxury, as well as allowing more private time together, which is the real purpose of the trip.

How do you feel about the sexual counseling that encourages self-stimulation while the couple is making love? Is such self-pleasuring antithetical to God's plan for couples to pleasure each other?

I believe that self-stimulation by the wife, in which the husband is also involved, may play a very important part in helping a woman who has had a difficult time reaching a climax. Through this she may learn how to respond, experience orgasm, and establish correct response patterns. However, as soon as she is consistently able to reach a climax, the couple should resume regular sexual intercourse. Otherwise they may fall so into a pattern of manual stimulation that she may be hindered in learning to enjoy orgasm during intercourse. God's plan is for each of the marriage partners to achieve full sexual satisfaction in intercourse. A man's sexual pleasure greatly increases when he knows he is able to satisfy his wife fully by bringing her to orgasm. Thus the wife who *temporarily* stimulates herself as a part of lovemaking between the two (for learning purposes only) is not so much just pleasuring herself as learning to have a response that will also greatly please her husband. Researchers have found that about a third of women almost always require manual stimulation of the clitoris by their husbands to reach a climax, but this is usually done in association with the act of intercourse.

What do people do with the secretions that come out after intercourse?

Keep a small towel handy on the bedside table. A woman who finds that the flow of semen mixed with her own secretions is objectionable may even wish to wear a tampon for a few hours after intercourse.

What is the ideal frequency of intercourse?

Whatever is mutually satisfying to both of you. If you desire to have sexual intercourse every single night and both enjoy this and neither of you feel put upon, then this is all right. Five thousand couples were asked how often they had sex during a week. The average was two or three times per week. You will be able to raise your sexual desire to the level of your mate if you wish to and if you commit this to God in prayer and yield your attitudes to Him. The secret is an enthusiastic involvement in the process of giving and receiving pleasure. Intercourse should not occur so often that it becomes a dull routine.

Would you define normal intercourse?

My favorite definition is one given by Dr. Theodore Van de Velde. He said, "Normal sexual intercourse is that intercourse which takes place between two sexually mature individuals of opposite sexes, which excludes cruelty, excludes the use of artificial means for producing voluptuous sensations, which aims directly or indirectly at the consummation of sexual satisfaction, and which having achieved a certain degree of stimulation, concludes with the emission or ejaculation of the semen into the vagina at the nearly simultaneous culmination of sensation or orgasm of both partners." The only footnote I would add to this is that you should not strive for simultaneous orgasm. It is more important to give yourself in exerting all the skill you have to pleasing your partner, without regard to when either of you will reach an orgasm. In the process you may sometimes experience orgasm at nearly the same time.

Is it all right to use an electric vibrator?

Electric vibrators applied to the genital area can give strong sexual stimulation, but many people have found that when they wish to have normal intercourse, they are then unable to gain satisfaction. This is because there is no kind of sexual activity that can approach the intensity of stimulation produced by a vibrator. Artificial means of producing stimulation should be avoided.

Is there any difference between a vaginal orgasm and a clitoral orgasm?

Medically speaking, the answer is no. There is only one kind of physiological orgasm, whether it is produced with the penis in the vagina, or by manual stimulation of the clitoris. However, women report feeling different sensations from the two orgastic experiences, and more emotional satisfaction is gained by the closeness and intimacy of orgasm during intercourse. So there is a subjective difference observed by many women.

Can a woman have more than one orgasm during intercourse?
A woman's body is designed to be multiorgasmic. If all the factors of love and consideration are present, and if the proper stimulation takes place, she can have as many orgasms as she wants. Hindrances to multiple orgasms would be inhibitions or lack of sufficient stimulation. The multiorgasmic woman almost always desires her husband to continue sexual contact and stimulation all through the time she is experiencing each orgasm. For maximum response, she may occasionally request a brief pause in stimulation. The wife is the one to suggest the timing and intensity of the stimulation.

How long must a man wait after having intercourse to have another orgasm?
He must usually wait from several minutes to several hours before being able to have another ejaculation. The time interval of this recovery period has nothing to do with so-called masculinity. Keener enjoyment will result when the husband waits at least twenty-four hours after orgasm for the body to replenish the supply of seminal fluid. Often a man who is over fifty-five years of age will not be able to have another orgasm for about twenty-four hours.

Do you discuss oral stimulation with couples? Do you find any objection, scriptural or otherwise, to married couples demonstrating love for each other in this manner?
It has come to my attention on many occasions that couples early in their marriage have been unable to achieve sufficient stimulation for the young wife during sexual intercourse. Very often this is because the husband has been unable to sufficiently control the timing of his ejaculation. As a solution they turn to oral-genital sex to bring her to orgasm, and this becomes in a sense a shortcut, avoiding the development of the discipline and skillful control that are demanded in learning how to consistently provide a maximum of

physical pleasure for both through regular intercourse. It is difficult for this couple to imagine that they are now shortchanging themselves because they may both be consistently reaching sexual climax, although without experiencing the unity and oneness that God has designed for their human bodies in basic sexual intercourse. I do not believe that God would have designed so many intricate details of the sexual anatomy to encourage husbands and wives to learn together the skills of bringing each other to fulfillment, if He had not intended these to be used the greater part of the time. Also, oral-genital sex definitely limits the amount of loving verbal communication that husband and wife can have as they make love.

When a couple decide that sterilization is the best answer to their problem of birth control, which one should be sterilized—the husband or the wife?
The vasectomy operation performed on the husband is far simpler, safer, less painful, and less expensive.

What are the most popular contraceptives among married Americans?
Number one is the pill (oral contraceptive). Runner-up is sterilization of husband or wife, according to the National Center for Health Statistics.

At what age may a woman stop using contraceptives without risk of pregnancy?
Menopause usually occurs by age forty-nine, with a normal range of forty to fifty-five. It is estimated that pregnancies between forty-five and forty-nine years occur in one to three instances per one thousand births. After the age of fifty, pregnancies are rare indeed, occurring in an estimated incidence of about one per twenty-five thousand cases. Therefore, contraceptives can be safely stopped at age fifty. When a woman is forty-eight years old or older and has not menstruated in six months, it is considered safe to stop contraceptive measures.

Does the pill have any effect on menopause?
The use of the pill will not delay menopause but it may mask its onset. If the woman's age indicates that she is close to menopause,

a specific way to make the diagnosis is to stop the pill for six weeks and draw blood to measure the plasma FSH and LH. These gonadotropin levels can be determined by any physician by mailing the serum sample to any of several large commercial laboratories. An elevated FSH indicates that the patient is menopausal. If after stopping the pill, she develops menopausal symptoms, especially hot flushes, this gives additional evidence of menopause. If these findings are positive, the doctor can safely recommend that she stop taking the pill.

How does the size of a woman's breast affect her sexual desires and abilities?

Not at all!

The breast continues to be the most exalted symbol of femininity, and the sight or feel of a woman's breasts is a stronger stimulus of male sexual desire than any other part of the body. In our bosom-conscious culture, women attach much significance to this part of their body and they attempt to hide or display this area in accord with their attitudes, desires and goals, modesty, and discretion. Research figures indicate that only about 50 percent of wives gain sexual stimulation from the fondling of their breasts. There is an area surrounding the nipples that gives sexual arousal when very lightly and gently stroked with the hands or with the lips. In a few women, this may even give intense sexual arousal, but other women do not care for it at all. The husband should find out whether or not breast play pleases his wife! Ask her.

Are there any disadvantages connected with having large breasts?

A series of medical symptoms may arise that are directly related to large breasts: fatigue, backache, poor posture, generalized numbness of the arms and especially of the palms of the hands, and painful chronic mastitis, which may produce breast pain and tenderness. A woman with very large breasts must make a deliberate, conscious effort to stand with her back very straight, or she will later develop a typical modified hunchback shape to her upper back.

Why do women sometimes dislike breast stimulation during fore-play?

Some women have the unfounded fear that breast play causes breast cancer. And some women have breast tenderness, especially a few days before their menstrual period. A woman's response may also be inhibited by excessive modesty and lack of pride, even shame, regarding the appearance of her breasts. Sometimes the man gives breast stimulation that is too intense, or too long, or even too light and too brief to be pleasing. The husband must be very sensitive to his own wife's preferences. What is one woman's arousal may be another's boredom—or even aversion. This is what makes the love relationship so private a matter between two people who are discovering how to express their caring in ways that are meaningful and exciting to each other.

What do you think about breast-feeding?

God has a primary plan for the breasts to be used for perfect, trouble-free feeding of your new baby. We know too that the contour, consistency, and size of your breasts is better protected when you nurse your baby. Nursing also hastens the return of the uterus to its original size, usually within a month.

Can you get pregnant while you are nursing a baby?

Yes! While nursing may delay menstruation, it sometimes does not prevent ovulation (release of the egg by the ovary). Therefore, conception can sometimes occur before the first menstrual period after delivery. Women have been known to become pregnant as soon as six weeks after the birth of a baby.

How important is self-examination of the breasts? How often should it be done?

The screening for breast cancer by means of self-examination, as well as physician's examination and mammography, has increased detection of early breast cancer and has saved about one-third more lives of women who were found to have cancer. The self-examination should be carried out at the same time each month, preferably soon after menstruation. Women with a history of breast cancer in their families, and those who have never breast-fed, have a

Breast Self-Examination

This simple 3-step procedure could save your life by finding breast cancer early when it is most curable.

In the shower:

Examine your breasts during bath or shower; hands glide easier over wet skin. Fingers flat, move gently over every part of each breast. Use right hand to examine left breast, left hand for right breast. Check for any lump, hard knot, or thickening.

Before a mirror:

Inspect your breasts with arms at your sides. Next, raise your arms high overhead. Look for any changes in contour of each breast, a swelling, dimpling of skin, or changes in the nipple.

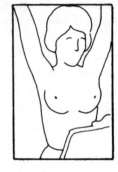

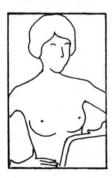

Then, rest palms on hips and press down firmly to flex your chest muscles. Left and right breast will not exactly match—few women's breasts do.

Regular inspection shows what is normal for you and will give you confidence in your examination.

Lying down:

To examine your right breast, put a pillow or folded towel under your right shoulder. Place right hand behind your head—this distributes breast tissue more evenly on the chest. With left hand, fingers flat, press gently in small circular motions around an imaginary clock face. Begin at outermost top of your right breast for 12 o'clock, then move to 1 o'clock, and so on around the circle back to 12. A ridge of firm tissue in the lower curve of each breast is normal. Then move in an inch, toward the nipple, keep circling to examine each part of your breast, including nipple. This requires at least three more circles. Now slowly repeat procedure on your left breast with a pillow under your left shoulder and left hand behind head. Notice how your breast structure feels.

Finally, squeeze the nipple of each breast gently between thumb and index finger. Any discharge, clear or bloody, should be reported to your doctor immediately.

Why You Should Examine Your Breasts Monthly

Most breast cancers are first discovered by women themselves. Since breast cancers found early and treated promptly have excellent chances for cure, learning how to examine your breasts properly can help save your life. Use the simple 3-step breast self-examination (BSE) procedure shown here.

The Best Time to Examine Your Breasts

Follow the same procedure once a month about a week after your period, when breasts are usually not tender or swollen. After menopause, check breasts on the first day of each month. After hysterectomy, check with your doctor or clinic for an appropriate time of the month. Doing BSE will give you monthly peace of mind and seeing your doctor once a year will reassure you there is nothing wrong.

What You Should Do If You Find a Lump or Thickening

If a lump or dimple or discharge is discovered during BSE, it is important to see your doctor as soon as possible. Don't be frightened. Most breast lumps or changes are not cancer, but only your doctor can make the diagnosis.

higher risk of cancer and should carry out the self-examination with great care. The procedure for breast self-examination on the preceding pages was developed by the American Cancer Society and is used by permission.

What causes mood fluctuations just before the menstrual period begins?

The emotional ups and downs that occur during the menstrual cycle, particularly in the four to five days prior to menstruation, are caused by changes in estrogen and progesterone levels. Probably at least half of all women who are having regular menstrual periods suffer from headaches, backaches, cramps, tension, irritability, or depression. However, only about 10 percent of all women suffer difficulties to a degree that their everyday activities have to be interrupted because of the premenstrual changes. Some doctors have found a simple way to explain what effect the hormones have on the woman at this time. They equate *estrogen* (E) with *energy* and *progesterone* (P) with *peace*. In other words, women are more outgoing and active in the first half of the menstrual cycle, when estrogen levels are higher. They gradually become more passive and sometimes depressed in the second half of the cycle, when there is a rise in progesterone. Progesterone often calms the irritable nervousness experienced by women before their period, when their estrogen levels are high.

What treatment is usually given for premenstrual problems?

Usually a mild tranquilizer is given; a diuretic, if water retention poses difficulties; or an analgesic, if there is pain. If these simple approaches are ineffective, hormonal agents may be evaluated. It may be found that an imbalance is present, with not enough progesterone to offset the estrogen in the last two weeks before the period. This can sometimes be prevented by giving progesterone tablets daily for about ten days before each period. See chapter 4.

Is there any risk in taking progesterone?

Yes, there is a very slightly increased probability of venous blood clots, some increase in fluid retention, and the amount and duration of menstrual flow may be altered.

Why do I keep having vaginal discharge?

The three most common types of vaginal infection, which may cause chronic or recurring discharge, are trichomonas vaginitis, candida vaginitis, and nonspecific or bacterial vaginitis. The vaginal discharge that results from any one of these infections may result in painful intercourse, local irritation, swelling, or itching. Untreated, the vaginal infection may continue several months or several years.

Do these infections interfere with sexual intercourse?

Candidiasis (moniliasis), a vaginal fungal infection, is one of the few vaginal problems that may require a patient to avoid both intercourse and any other sexual stimulation for a few days at the beginning of treatment. Candidiasis frequently causes intense itching with redness and swelling of the vulva; often there is also a thick white curdlike discharge, and the extreme irritation of the tissues makes a short period of abstinence advisable. The discharge can usually be cleared up by inserting an antifungal vaginal cream or tablet high in the vagina daily for one week. For relief of pain in case of severe soreness, an ice bag may be applied to the painful area for twenty minutes at a time several times a day. When candidiasis continues in pregnancy, the antifungal medication may be required several times throughout the pregnancy. This same candida fungus causes thrush in the mouth of infants.

How does one get candidiasis?

This fungus infection is commonly seen in a woman who uses unnecessary douching and vaginal deodorants, or in someone with diabetes who is passing more than normal amounts of sugar in the urine. Candida is most apt to appear following a course of antibiotics, or when there are elevated estrogen levels in the system: during pregnancy, just before menstrual periods, or when taking oral contraceptives. Nylon underpants, panty hose, and panty girdles retain extra moisture and warmth, which provide perfect breeding conditions for fungi. Sitting around the pool in a wet bathing suit has the same effect. Cotton underpants are bet-

ter ventilated, and skirts are preferable to slacks when you suffer
from this infection.

Is candidiasis contagious? Can my husband contract it from me?
Yes, he can. It will be seen as a rash on the penis or in the groin,
as an itching reddened area with small round pimplelike places
beyond the redness. Candida thrives in moist, dark places; therefore it is usually limited to the genital area. The man's treatment
requires a bath twice daily to remove perspiration with thorough
drying of the skin involved, then application of a prescription
cream. He should wear cotton underwear and loose-fitting trousers
during the treatment period. If this fungus infection lasts longer
than two weeks after treatment begins, there should be a careful
check for diabetes. The extra sugar in the tissue of the skin causes
the candida to thrive; thus the infection is much more difficult to
eradicate.

Which of the vaginal infections is most likely to become chronic?
The trichomonas infection is the most likely to become chronic.
Symptoms include greenish or yellowish discharge with an objectionable odor, itching and redness, and some pain during intercourse. Because these symptoms are comparatively mild, the infection may be present for several months before treatment is
requested. Trichomonas infection is transmitted from one person
to another by way of toilet seats, bathtubs, towels, or any other
physical means of transfer. This means that both partners should
be treated, because the trichomonas can be harbored under the
husband's foreskin or in his urethra and may not bother him at
all. He may readily reinfect his wife, even though she has been
successfully treated. Therefore, condoms should be used for sexual intercourse during the treatment period.

What causes trichomonas vaginitis?
A tiny parasite, which can be seen only through a microscope,
is the culprit. The trichomonads can be identified in a drop of vaginal secretion. At the present time, treatment consists of metronidazole (Flagyl) tablets given to both husband and wife three

times daily for ten days. If the wife has repeated trichomonas infection, she may need to temporarily discontinue the use of vaginal tampons during menstrual periods. Trichomonas grows best in an alkaline environment, and this environment is provided when vaginal tampons keep the blood (which is alkaline) in the vagina. For this reason whatever treatment is prescribed must be continued, particularly during the menstrual period.

Are antibiotics the answer to these vaginal infections?

Antibiotics are both a part of the problem and a part of the solution. Certainly these infections, when they develop, are treated with antibiotics. On the other hand, vaginal infections can be caused by different antibiotics taken for another problem elsewhere in the body. There are many broad-spectrum antibiotics that will lower the number of normal bacteria within the vagina and allow commensal organisms, such as fungus and trichomonas, to overpopulate and create significant vaginal infections in women. Judicious use of broad-spectrum antibiotics is becoming increasingly apparent, particularly with the advent of resistant strains of common bacteria. There are a handful of antibiotics used for recurrent urinary tract infections that will not encourage the development of yeast infections. It is important to discuss the use of these antibiotics with the prescribing doctor when appropriate. Sometimes treatment in advance for a yeast infection is combined with a course of antibiotics for some other infection. Sexual relations during the time of active infection can lead to a ping-pong effect of urinary tract infections whereby the male may become contaminated and actively infected with an organism that is currently being treated in the female, so it is important that both members be treated simultaneously.

What is the place of erotic pictures and movies in increasing sexual desire?

Many couples do not understand what these erotic movies consist of. They show two or more nude people, performing many different acts of sexual stimulation in extremely varied ways and positions. This would probably be offensive to most Christian couples seeking solutions in their own love relationship. Some psychiatrists who deal with sexual problems have said that they found these movies helpful in opening communication with patients and in sparking communication between husbands and wives who have been unable to talk to each other at all about sexual matters. These movies may lower sexual communication barriers, but viewing sex in this way is likely to produce more problems than it will solve. See 1 Corinthians 6:18.

Why do so many teenage marriages not work out?

First, because teenagers in most cases cannot separate from their parents and become independent. Second, teenagers have changing value systems and they do not yet know what they will want in a mate. Qualities later surface that were not apparent when the young people married. This is because character develops as a response to responsibility or adversity. There is no way of predicting with accuracy how a teenager will respond to the difficulties and demands of married life in the years ahead.

How much should a mother share with her daughter before marriage, using her own marriage as an example?

Much of this will depend on the rapport mother and daughter have in all areas of their relationship. The mother should use judgment in how much detailed information her daughter really needs. No good information should be withheld once the date of marriage has been scheduled. The mother should see that her daughter has access to wholesome sex reference books. If the parents' marriage has been one in which husband and wife have been demonstrating tenderness, fondness, and love for each other, it is a beautiful example for the daughter. If, on the other hand, there have been instances of sexual problems or indiscretions in the mother's own marriage, it would be best not to share these with a daughter, as this may damage the daughter's image of her own father or mother. The most important decisions our children make are in the years following their teens, and an excellent father-daughter relationship is more important at this time than at any other.

Can diabetes cause impotence?

Yes, there are more than three million diabetic men in the United States, and about one-half of them have some degree of impotence from the disease. Diabetes decreases only the ability to achieve or keep an erection. It does not reduce the sexual desire, and in only 2 or 3 percent of diabetics is there any reduction in the ability to ejaculate.

Is there any hope of sexual fulfillment with a husband who is diabetic and having difficulties with impotence?

If the diabetic husband has experienced some problems with impotence, he will already have developed fears of performance. Many diabetic men can continue normal sexual intercourse, if they will follow the procedures described in chapter 8 for overcoming impotence. Because the physical problem often caused by the diabetic condition is inability to have an erection, a loving, interested, and understanding wife can use her hands, preferably with a lubricant, to bring him to orgasm manually. He should use manual stimulation to give her sexual arousal and bring her to orgasm. Sexual fulfillment certainly is possible when the husband and wife care for each other and want to give each other pleasure, even though it is not possible to do this in intercourse.

Please explain the purposes of the premature ejaculation exercises. What are their benefits?

There are three key elements, which, when mastered, will vastly improve the sexual relationship of husband and wife. First, the husband learns to recognize the physical sensations that indicate the point just before ejaculation is inevitable. Second, he learns to break the association between arousal and anxiety in his own reactions. As he finds that his ejaculation is controllable, he no longer becomes anxious about his performance. Third, he learns to prolong the pleasure of arousal for longer periods of time, which gives his wife more opportunity for enjoyment as well.

What about the man suffering from premature ejaculation who blames his wife for not being sexy enough to reach orgasm in the brief time of their intercourse?

A man with this attitude needs more than mechanical training, such as the squeeze-technique exercises. He needs to develop a whole new view of the lovemaking process, which will change his entire approach. The greatest problem stems from the man's belief that once he has ejaculated, the sex act is over. As he becomes aware of his wife's needs for love and tenderness and a good physical climax, and as he learns to meet those needs, the cycle of failure and anxiety and resentment and frustration will be broken—even before ejaculatory control is attained.

What is retarded ejaculation?

This is a condition far less common than premature ejaculation. It is also called inhibited ejaculation. This is medically described as the inability to ejaculate during intercourse at least one-quarter of the time. To contrast with impotence, impotence is the inability to gain an erection when you want it at least half of the time. Inhibited ejaculation is the inability to reach an orgasm.

What causes retarded (or inhibited) ejaculation?

Alcohol can be responsible. So can certain medications such as Valium. Or it can be a psychological factor that inhibits the ejaculatory response just as though the patient anticipated punishment by an electric shock each time he ejaculated or even had an impulse to ejaculate. In some cases there simply is not enough physical stimulation at the glans of the penis in intercourse. Well-lubricated manual stimulation of the glans of the penis by the wife may be necessary. Note that in chapter 13 we said that elderly men do not always need to ejaculate and should not force it. This is different from the inhibited ejaculation suffered by some younger men, who may suffer pain if ejaculation is inhibited.

What can be done about the problem of urine continuing to drain from the penis after a man has finished urinating? It is very inconvenient.

If you are over forty, you may have this problem. The narrowest part of the man's urethra, the tube from the bladder to the outside, is just below the prostate gland and is called the membranous urethra. Just below this part is the section called the bulb of the urethra, which is of larger diameter. The urine remaining in this part of the urethra can be easily forced out by placing the fingers behind and above the scrotum and in front of the anus and then pressing upward and forward very firmly. The man with this problem will need to practice this and experiment to find the exact spot to push to help himself.

Many people seem to think that elderly folk who are still interested in sex are abnormal. What do you think?

I think such an attitude is both erroneous and foolish. It is normal to have a continuing interest in sex throughout one's adult life. People should get rid of their myths about the elderly and let the elderly be themselves—ordinary people with sometimes an extra need for love and affection. The young will eventually learn that they have no exclusive rights to love and marriage. Researchers have shown that normal interest in and capacity for sex continue into the eighties.

How soon do children begin to ask questions about sex?

The earliest questions usually relate to body parts and sexual differences. The question "What's that?" pointing to his or her own or another's genitals is common around two years of age. "Where did I come from?" generally starts at three or four, with specific questions about conception following between five to eight years of age.

It's much harder to explain sex organs to little girls than to little boys, who can see their penis. How do you do it?

The right words should be used without any note of reserve or defensiveness: vagina, uterus, and so forth. It should be explained that her organs are tucked away inside her, that this is God's special plan to provide a very important place where a baby can start growing from a seed. Answer the child's questions without elaborations. If she questions differences between herself and a brother, explain that a little boy cannot have a baby, but that a little girl can someday have a baby and nurse it. All answers to children's questions should be straightforwardly given, communicating that we are God's creation and He has a perfect plan for men and women, as the background of all information on sex. Do not give more information than the child is ready to receive at that time.

What do you do when your child comes home using "dirty words"?
Children get much of their knowledge about sex from other children in the form of "dirty words." This is a signal for the parents to teach the child acceptable words and answer his or her questions about sex, clearing up misinformation he or she may have picked up.

Can you get pregnant just from heavy petting?
Yes! Even though there is no actual entrance of the penis into the vagina, or even contact with the vagina, it is possible for enough semen discharged around the outside of the vagina to get inside and produce a pregnancy. I have been responsible for the obstetrical care of three virgins who became pregnant this way, even though two of them did not know what intercourse was. One was only twelve years old. She was playing with a friend and did not realize she was pregnant until in her sixth month. She would not have known then if her mother had not noticed her increasing size.

Does smoking marijuana have an effect on unborn children?
Yes. Dr. Gabriel Nahas, author of the book *Keep Off the Grass*, reports that the chemicals in marijuana can cross the placenta and reach the unborn child. Laboratory tests with four different kinds of animals show that there is a higher incidence of abortion and other abnormalities when the animals are given a dose of marijuana equivalent to one joint a day.

Marijuana contains at least 421 different chemicals. The effects of all 421 have not been determined, and there are additional ingredients to be isolated. It now seems apparent that daily usage or regular usage will lower the IQ of the user by as much as twenty points over fifteen years of use and is linked to heart and brain tumors.

What is the herpesvirus infection, which is so dangerous when the mother is infected at the time of her baby's birth?
This infection is caused by the herpes simplex virus type 2. In our discussion we will use the popular abbreviation HSV 2, as this

virus is responsible for most of the herpetic venereal infections. Women with this infection also have a higher incidence of cervical carcinoma.

An infection with HSV 2 starts as raised sores or fluid-filled blisters, which develop quickly in one to three days after sexual contact. This initial infection lasts two or three weeks, and may recur over a period of many years. Most common sites are in the genital area. Women may experience very painful sores, fever, aching, and vaginal discomfort. Men usually experience sores on the penis for three to five days with minimal discomfort. Using a condom will help prevent transmission of the virus.

The infection can be spread to other parts of a person's own body, such as fingers and eyes. Treatment with the medicine acyclovir (Zovirax), taken by mouth, is recommended. The infection frequently comes back, even after treatment. These recurrent infections cause patchy groups of blisters. There are few other symptoms and the infection usually lasts about one week. Recurrent herpes infections are often treated with benzoyl peroxide placed on the skin to dry out the area. Individuals with frequent or disabling recurrences may be treated with acyclovir for five days starting when the blisters form. Long-term therapy with acyclovir is sometimes used for severely infected people. In individuals with ulcerations that last despite treatment and in those who are immunosuppressed, intravenous acyclovir treatment may be necessary.

The most serious and frequent complication of HSV 2 is neonatal infection during birth. One-half of all newborns who are infected during passage through the vagina die shortly thereafter. Half of the survivors are mentally retarded.

There is no known cure for HSV 2. At this time the most important fact you need to know is that if you are pregnant and have HSV 2, most infections of the newborn baby can be prevented by having a caesarean section so the baby does not have to pass through the infected vagina.

We do not know why there has been such a great increase recently in HSV 2 infections, but the virus that causes fever blisters of the lips, called HSV 1, can also cause herpes of the genital area, and the great increase in HSV 2 infections has paralleled the increase in frequency of use of oral sex. Unfortunately, there is no cure for HSV 2 infections at this time.

Is it now possible to select the sex of one's child?

There is a good chance of it, due to the research of many years in this field. You may significantly increase your chances of having your choice through careful timing of intercourse in relation to time of ovulation, taking an acid or alkaline douche just before intercourse, determining whether to have minimal or maximal sexual arousal of the wife at the time of the husband's ejaculation, and deciding whether to ejaculate during deep or shallow penetration by the penis.

This is an interesting subject. If you want to pursue it, obtain the authoritative book *Choose Your Baby's Sex,* published by Dodd, Mead & Company, 1977, written by the best known investigator of this subject, Landrum B. Shettles, M.D.

Do you have any suggestions for the pastor who wishes to give helpful instruction to couples who come to him for premarital counseling?

The need is great for more Christian premarriage counseling, which presents both the necessary physical information and the biblical principles of marriage. Many pastors make available a set of the *Sex Technique and Sex Problems in Marriage* and *Before the Wedding Night* teaching tapes to each couple who comes to them for counsel before marriage. The pastors usually encourage the couple to wait until about four weeks before the wedding to listen to these tapes, and then ask that the tapes be taken with them on their honeymoon, to hear again, when each is aware of more specific needs for professional instruction. For further information about these cassettes, write to Scriptural Counsel, Inc., 130 N. Spring St., Springdale, AR 72764. Or call toll free: 1-800-643-3477.

16

All Love, All Liking,
All Delight

A traveler from outer space, able to read current literature on sex in marriage, might easily gain the impression that married love consists of a physical sensation lasting only a few seconds, which everyone is trying for; and this same visitor to our planet might well ask, in his own way, "If that's all there is to the mating process of these creatures, what's all the fuss about?"

Of course there is much, much more—"all love, all liking, all delight," in the words of Robert Herrick. But the secular world has become preoccupied with physical technique; much of the Christian world is debating the implications of the biblical order of relationships in Ephesians 5; and seldom does anyone venture into the area between, where the dynamics of the sexual union in marriage are considered—not physical techniques, not the deep underlying principles, but *how* two people committed in marriage actually interact in love to approach the "one flesh" experience.

After the Bible has dealt with the basic order of husband and wife (sacrificial love and submission), it leaves much to our own understanding concerning these dynamics of the sexual relationship. The Bible's silence does not imply that the last word has already been said, but rather that God in His vast good sense allows each of His creatures to explore the unlimited possibilities inherent in the relationship He Himself thought up. These unlimited possibilities somehow converge into an offering that two people make of themselves to each other, an offering that reflects all that they are separately and all that they will become together.

Without trying to pin down the specifics, which will be as different in every marriage as the individuals involved, we can make these observations about the dynamics of the sexual relationship between man and wife.

First, the sexual relationship is meant to be full of life, rich in emotion, and ever changing within the security of the marriage commitment. When lovemaking takes on a tiresome sameness of routine, both partners may feel a vague sense of dissatisfaction with unnamed longings, even though they do not realize that something precious is missing. That missing something, of course, is the free and active expression of a living love! In such cases, their love needs to be renewed or liberated.

Sometimes a dull routine develops because either husband or wife fears change and tries to keep the act of love static as a security measure. That individual is unwittingly choosing emptiness, not fullness. The choice becomes another form of burying one's goods in the ground, because one is "afraid." The Lord Jesus was not pleased with that approach; nor do we think He is pleased with a lifeless, emotionally barren relationship.

What keeps the relationship vital and moving is a joyous pattern of mutual response, the kind we see pictured in the ever-changing relationship of Solomon and his bride in Song of Solomon. The two lovers had periods of almost indescribable pleasure interspersed with changes of fortune and diversities of feeling. Theirs was not a perfect relationship, because they were human. When he wanted her, at one point, she did not wish to be disturbed. Then after he had turned away, her heart was moved for him, and she sought him until they were reunited. Their reunion became a glorious blending of mutual pleasure, as he poured forth words of intense appreciation: "How fair and how pleasant art thou, O love, for delights!" And she passionately assured him that her delights were all for him.

Those almost perfect moments that sometimes happen between lovers tempt us to become collectors, trying to capture and repeat our favorite experiences. They are pleasant to remember, but a clinging to the past often causes us to miss out on the new delights that are still ahead. The time when our love relationship is admittedly less than perfect will always leave room for movement toward each other. As long as we are committed to each other, we need not fear the constant change within marriage, the ebb and flow of the relationship of two lovers, for it is a sign of life.

C. S. Lewis caught the essence of that continuing change in a few vivid phrases describing his own marriage: "H. and I feasted on love; every mode of it—solemn and merry, romantic and realistic, sometimes as dramatic as a thunderstorm, sometimes as comfortable and unemphatic as putting on your soft slippers. No cranny of heart or body remained unsatisfied" (from *A Grief Observed*).

If the relationship is constantly changing, so are the needs of the two people involved. Therefore, our second observation is that there is no fixed part for each mate to play within the sexual experience. For instance, there can be no "boss" in the mutuality of coming together. While the man is to be tenderly protective, there is no place in love for a rigid dominance on his part. To say that a wife is to be submissive in the overall pattern of the home does not imply that in the sexual relationship she is limited to awaiting his pleasure. She has the equal privilege of initiating the act of love and of offering her own imaginative style of pleasure to the total relationship.

Each can be most truly himself or herself in this particular area of the marriage, with neither person locked into a role that must be played again and again. The husband may be essentially a strong personality, but there are times in the privacy of their love when he will want to be dependent on his wife and free to express this. She may sometimes need the knowledge of his strength and should be free both to be that which he needs and to seek that which she needs. Together each can give the emotional sustenance the other requires. In such a relationship, fantasized sex will be discarded as something outgrown, as much less than the real thing.

Surely part of the delight of the relationship is that opportunity in the privacy of your bedroom to be all that you know you can be, yet may never show the rest of the world. "God be thanked," said Robert Browning. "The meanest of his creatures boasts two soul-sides, one to face the world with, one to show a woman when he loves her!" You can be most totally your true self with your mate.

Perhaps others think of you as stiff, cool, reserved. But with your partner you laugh together; you are free to be passionate or tender as the mood strikes you, protective or dependent, flirtatious or surrendered. There should be room in the sexual relationship for all parts of your personality to be expressed at one time or another. And all the while the expression of your own being meets the need of your mate. "How do I love thee?" wrote Elizabeth Barrett Browning in *Sonnets from the Portuguese,* in one of the world's most famous love poems, "I love thee to the level of everyday's most quiet need, by sun and candlelight."

Our third observation concerns the importance of a lighthearted approach to lovemaking in marriage. Sex with your partner is far more than recreation, of course, but it is that as well: the best, the most relaxing, renewing recreation known to man, and God planned that too. No wonder it is often called "love *play.*" It is fun, not duty; high excitement, not boredom; something to anticipate, not a dreary experience to be avoided if you can. It should be and it can be the highlight of any ordinary day, as two people come together to refresh themselves in each other's love, to find forgetfulness from the cares and insults of life, and to experience the total and wonderful relaxation God designed as the culmination of the lovemaking, with both husband and wife reaching climax. How ironic that couples search for all manner of recreation elsewhere, never having discovered the *fullness* of pleasure available to them in their own bedroom. The Christian couple who have experienced this fullness will praise God together for what He has provided for them!

Fourth, the sexual relationship between husband and wife offers the unique opportunity to care for and be responsible for another human being in the most complete sense possible. Husband and wife are meant to love each other's bodies as if they were their own possessions. Not as mechanisms, which can be used for satisfaction and discarded at will, but as a treasure of great and lasting value. As we realize how infinitely we are appreciated by our mate, we develop the assurance of our own self-worth. C. S. Lewis observed that even his body "had such a different importance" because it was the body his wife loved! This caring and responsibility will extend outward to the homey details of life—paying the rent and keeping the house, buying groceries and cooking good meals, looking after each other all of the time. But it best begins with the sensitive appreciation of the other partner in the love relationship and it continues to be nurtured there.

Inevitably we come to the matter of the mysterious oneness of the sexual relationship. To be two separate individuals, yet merged into one through a physical/spiritual act defies explanation. Yet we have the privilege of living it, of knowing completion through our marriage partner in the act of love.

"The human sexual union . . . leaps the walls of separation and loneliness, fuses our partialities and contrariness into wholeness, joins the fragments of life into a new, unifying identity," wrote George Cornell. That this great completion takes place at a moment in time when we also experience the keenest ecstasy known to human beings makes it a miracle of God's provision to us.

And then it is so uniquely and amazingly personal—our very own experience, which none can match or enter into. No one else can tell us just how to share this life with our mate. The dynamics are for each to explore, experience, and develop into a harmony as near perfection as possible. They will include spontaneity of life, freedom of expression, expectancy of pleasure, sensitivity in caring, and yieldedness leading to completion. But precisely how they will manifest themselves, no one else can say. As you come to know yourself and your lover, you will know best how to love that special one. There will be "intimacy . . . tempered by lightness of touch, . . . partners . . . creating a pattern together, and being invisibly nourished by it," in Anne Morrow Lindbergh's words (from *Gift from the Sea*). Your response of love, liking, and delight in each other will be as a bright thread of joy woven in the ordinary colors of daily life.

"Sex remains indefinable, inexplicable, mysterious," noted Cornell after writing a series of newspaper articles on it. "It's like a piece of Mozart music of which a listener once asked him to explain its meaning. Replied Mozart: 'If I could explain it in words, I wouldn't need music.'" So those who would understand the sexual relationship in marriage must experience it, and experience it the way it was intended to be—spontaneous, free, enjoyable, renewing, and more filled with meaning than words could ever tell.

17

Your Marriage
A Private Little Kingdom

Gaye and I have written *Intended for Pleasure* to help point the way to the sexual fulfillment every married couple can experience. Biblical principles, dynamics and techniques of lovemaking, problem-solving approaches—these all contribute to the total result. The sum of them, then, should be *fulfillment*.

But one thing is still missing. Even if you have appropriated all the other material in this book, you will need this complete picture of God's plan for you and your mate. We speak now of your marriage viewed in a very special way. Look at it with us as a private little kingdom, a kingdom where you and your marriage partner dwell with the King: Jesus Christ, who is none other than the King of kings and Lord of lords!

What do we mean by a *private* little kingdom? That which is private is "removed from public view, secluded, not for common use." This is what marriage was designed to be from the beginning of time—a special world of belonging, apart from the rush and roar of life all about us, where we can always find renewal and refreshment in each other's love.

"Not alone . . . cleaving . . . one flesh . . ." In phrases of rare and sensitive beauty, God's Word sketches the oneness and therefore the privacy of the marriage relationship. *Not for common use, secluded, removed from public view.* Does this describe your mar-

riage right now? God has designed marriage to provide that which you as man and wife need to meet the onslaughts of life. But the Creator's design requires that you carefully maintain the principles of privacy and oneness in the physical, emotional, and spiritual aspects of your marriage.

The private kingdom of your marriage is not to be taken for granted, once established. Attacks on your oneness will come, so be prepared. Look for open *invasion* from the pressures of the outside world—financial pressures, for example. You can think of others; they are easily seen. And yet sometimes they succeed in battering down the walls of your private little kingdom, because you and your partner do not present a solid front to them.

The mode of attack may not be invasion, but *intrusion*. If you leave the gate open, intruders will walk right into your special private world, where no one else belongs but the two of you and your King. Sometimes these intruders are family members, sometimes well-meaning or not so well-meaning friends or neighbors. They barge in. They encourage you to talk. They advise. They criticize. They divide. They cause you to see yourself as separate from your mate, and your kingdom is laid waste. You lose your sense of oneness, and all the blessings that go with it.

The most deadly and subtle of all attacks on your marriage comes in the form of *infiltration*. You must learn to spot and unmask those most vicious enemies of your kingdom: heart attitudes of willfulness, pride, self-pity, resentment, anger, bitterness, and jealousy. They slip in when you least expect them and bring desolation wherever you allow them to operate unchecked.

If all these attacks are successfully resisted and your private little kingdom of marriage flourishes behind God-erected walls, what will characterize that kingdom? What kind of marriage will you have?

First, there will be *security*. You will know a wonderful security in each other's love. This security begins with communication. The sex relationship is a tender yet vibrant form of communication. Sharing, understanding, touching, pleasuring, satisfying the other in the safety of a committed love—this is security! Your hearts will safely trust in each other.

To understand and be understood,
to know, really know, what
another is thinking,
to say what you will and
be sure it is accepted as of value
or sifted through without reproof,
to be you, really *you*,
and know you are loved—
This is near-heaven.
                    Gloria Okes Perkins

Our physical love relationship becomes the walled garden, the inner courtyard of the kingdom, and it is a sacred place. We trust that by now, if not before, you have the biblical perspective of the sacredness of sex in marriage so firmly implanted in your understanding that you and your mate will be able to grow in joy and to increase in pleasure from year to year, as God intended.

Please remember how very important it is to make the act of love a central part of your life. In other words, schedule time for each other. Plan your evenings so that you have nights when you can be alone together to enjoy each other fully, without weariness or interruption. Plan an occasional private weekend trip just for the two of you.

Second, there will be *stability*. You will appreciate a blessed stability in the order of your home if it is established on God-defined lines. You each will know your position, your responsibilities, your rights. You will not be hampered or shaken by fluctuating relationships resulting from continually shifting roles. When you enjoy the stability that order brings, you will find freedom for growth such as you could never know in a fluid situation.

This stability that comes when marriage, home, and family are operated according to God's order can become a powerful safety measure, keeping your kingdom at peace. This means that your marriage will not be a patriarchy where husband rules as a dictator, nor a matriarchy where the wife rules as the awesome power behind the throne. It will not be an anarchy where no one has answered the question "Who's in charge?" (When there are no rules, children usually end up in control, and this is the most destructive government of all.) Instead, your marriage will be a theocracy, where God rules—where the husband is the head of the house, because he is responsible to carry out the will of God; where the wife operates under the covering of her husband's love, wisdom, and protection; where the children obey their parents. "But I would have you know, that the head of every man is Christ; and the head of the woman is the man; and the head of Christ is God" (1 Cor. 11:3).

Third, there will be *serenity*. A private little kingdom operating under the truths of the Word of God surely will have serenity as the very air of the land. Serenity flows from a harmony of beliefs, a oneness of goals, a mutual participation in all that is most important to the man and the wife. Since God is never the author of confusion, serenity will exist wherever God is in control.

Centuries ago, the poet Omar Khayyám wrote:

> Ah, Love! could you and I with Fate conspire
> To grasp this sorry Scheme of Things entire,
> Would not we shatter it to bits—and then
> Re-mould it nearer to the Heart's Desire!

We have counseled with many couples whose hearts said the same thing. They longed to start all over again with each other; their mistakes of the past and their wrong ways of doing things shattered in an instant, so that they could reshape their marriage nearer to the heart's desire.

It *is* possible for you to do this. You can change your world, the world of your marriage, if it is not now the private kingdom of God's design. It *can* be the intimate, precious relationship of total commitment that it was always meant to be.

The resources for this change come from the power of God as made available to you in the Lord Jesus Christ. He can enable you to love and give, to forgive and ask forgiveness, to forget yourself in your caring for your loved one, and, in turn, to receive joyfully from your mate. He can make it possible for you to see when a conflict arises that the real problem is *you*. As you act on the basis of your responsibilities, rather than clinging to your rights, the conflict will resolve itself with an even stronger welding of the two of you into one. He can cause you to be sensitive to each other's needs, always "on the other's team," always seeing that which is admirable in the other, and never focusing on faults and failures. He will make your marriage ever more intimate and harmonious and full of delights.

This truly is a world nearer to the heart's desire, isn't it? But it requires a King for your private little kingdom, a King who can empower you to bring it into being.

That King is the Lord Jesus Christ, who, at a specific moment in history, died on the cross and bore the sins of the whole world. Through that mighty act, He opened the way for all our sins to be forgiven, for the death penalty had already been paid. In Jesus our past is not only pardoned, but our sins forgotten, as if they were put in the bottom of the deepest ocean and remembered no more. After three days in the grave, to demonstrate to all people for all time that He is God, Jesus arose again from the dead with all power and authority and resources for the life of the one who believes on Him. It is written, "But as many as received him, to them gave he power to become the sons of God, even to them that believe on his name" (John 1:12).

If you have not asked Jesus to be your Savior, you can do it now. It can be done as simply as when the man was healed of blindness in John 9:35–38. "Jesus . . . said unto him, Dost thou believe on the Son of God? He answered and said, Who is he, Lord, that I might believe on him? And Jesus said unto him, Thou hast both seen him, and it is he that talketh with thee. And he said, Lord, I believe. And he worshipped him."

Here is a prayer that you may offer to express your faith in Jesus Christ as your Savior:

Dear heavenly Father, I realize I am a sinner and cannot do one thing to save myself. Right now I believe Jesus Christ died on the cross, shedding His blood as full payment for my sins—past, present, and future—and by rising from the dead demonstrated that He is God.

As best I know how, I believe in Him and am putting all my trust in Jesus Christ as my personal Savior, as my only hope for salvation and eternal life.

Right now I am receiving Christ into my life and I thank You for saving me as You promised and I ask You to give me increasing faith and wisdom as I study and believe Your Word.

For I ask this in Christ's name. Amen.

Gaye and I would like to hear from you if you have just now trusted Christ. Our prayer for each reader is that you and your partner will be guided into that oneness that will cause the love in your marriage to reveal to the world the image of the union between Christ and His Church.

> For this cause shall a man leave his father and mother, and shall be joined unto his wife, and they two shall be one flesh. This is a great mystery: but I speak concerning Christ and the church. Nevertheless let every one of you in particular so love his wife even as himself; and the wife see that she reverence her husband.
>
> Ephesians 5:31–33

Suggested Reading

Adams, Jay E. *Christian Living in the Home*. Phillipsburg, N.J.: Presbyterian and Reformed Publishing Company, 1972. A precise and powerful application of scriptural principles to the problems of the home and family.

Allender, Dan B. *Intimate Allies*. Carol Stream, Ill.: Tyndale House, 1995. Rediscovering God's design for marriage and becoming soul mates for life.

Blue, Ron. *Master Your Money*. Nashville: Thomas Nelson, 1986. A step-by-step plan for financial freedom.

Carder, David. *Torn Asunder*. Rev. ed. Chicago: Moody, 1995. Recovering from an extramarital affair.

Conway, Sally and Jim. *When a Mate Wants Out: Secrets for Saving a Marriage*. Grand Rapids: Zondervan, 1992. Proven techniques for saving a marriage from Mid-life Dimensions Counseling Center.

Crabb, Larry. *Men and Women: Enjoying the Difference*. Grand Rapids: Zondervan, 1991. Dr. Crabb explores how we can turn away from ourselves and toward each other, becoming what he calls "other-centered."

Dobson, James. *What Wives Wish Their Husbands Knew about Women*. Wheaton: Tyndale House, 1977. This popular book includes an important section on hormonal problems during menopause.

Elliot, Elisabeth. *The Shaping of a Christian Family*. Nashville: Thomas Nelson, 1992. A valuable resource of ideas and inspiration for parents.

Hendricks, Howard. *Heaven Help the Home!* Wheaton: Victor, 1990. A classic for the Christian home.

LaHaye, Tim and Beverly. *The Act of Marriage: The Beauty of Married Life*. Grand Rapids: Zondervan, 1976. Excellent suggestions for improving the sex relationship.

Love, Vicky. *Childless Is Not Less*. Minneapolis: Bethany, 1984. An encouraging book for childless couples.

271

Mayhall, Jack and Carole. *Marriage Takes More Than Love.* Colorado Springs: NavPress, 1978. Down-to-earth solutions for marital conflicts.

McIlhaney, Joe S., Jr. *1250 Health-Care Questions Women Ask.* 2d ed. Grand Rapids: Baker, 1992. In easy-to-understand language an obstetrician/gynecologist discusses every aspect of a woman's physical development.

Parrot, Leslie III, and Leslie Parrot. *Saving Your Marriage Before It Starts.* Grand Rapids: Zondervan, 1995. A comprehensive marriage preparation program. "Seven questions to ask before (and after) you marry."

Rainey, Dennis. *Staying Close.* Irving, Tex.: Word, 1989. Stopping the drift toward isolation in marriage.

Shettles, Landrum B., M.D. *Choose Your Baby's Sex.* New York: Dodd, Mead, 1977.

Swindoll, Charles R. *Strike the Original Match.* Grand Rapids: Zondervan, 1993. A fresh and detailed look at God's original blueprint for marriage and the home.

Wheat, Ed., M.D. *Love Life for Every Married Couple.* Grand Rapids: Zondervan, 1980. Shows couples of all ages how to add the thrill of romance, the pleasure of friendship, the tranquillity of belonging, the sweetness of intimacy, and the strength of commitment to their marriage. Includes a unique section on "How to Save Your Marriage . . . Alone."

Wheat, Ed. M.D., and Gloria Perkins. *The First Years of Forever.* Grand Rapids: Zondervan, 1988. For engaged and newly married couples.

Wheat, Ed., M.D., and Gloria Perkins. *Secret Choices: How to Settle Little Issues before They Become Big Problems.* Grand Rapids: Zondervan, 1994. Personal decisions that affect your marriage.

Wright, H. Norman. *Communication: Key to Your Marriage.* Rev. ed. Glendale, Calif.: G/L Publications, 1979. Good ideas for the husband and wife who want to enrich their marriage through better communication.

Recommended Audio Tapes

These tapes may be obtained from your local Christian bookstore or ordered from Scriptural Counsel, Inc., 130 N. Spring St., Springdale, AR 72764. Bible Believers Cassettes, Inc., is the world's largest *free-loan* library of Bible study tapes with more than ten thousand different teaching cassettes available. More than one thousand of these are on marriage and the family. Write for further information or send a contribution for a catalog of available tapes.

Wheat, Ed, M.D. *Sex Technique and Sex Problems in Marriage*. To enrich your marriage, three hours of intimate counsel by a Christian family doctor, who is also a certified sex therapist. Revised, 1981. Two-tape set.

Wheat, Ed, M.D. *Love Life*. Listening together to this two-tape set will improve your verbal communication regarding your love relationship. Three hours of positive counsel to enhance your marriage.

Wheat, Ed, M.D. *Before the Wedding Night*. Two-tape set outlining key elements to a successful marriage.

Pursley, Dow, Ed.D. *Planning Your Marriage*. This two-tape set develops a step-by-step approach to planning a marriage for engaged couples and for married couples who have forgotten these important details.

Dr. Pursley is available for counseling at the Wheat Professional Building, 130 N. Spring Street, Springdale, AR 72764, 501-751-5704.

Subject Index

Scripture Index